They Called Them Angels

American Military Nurses
of World War II

Kathi Jackson

UNIVERSITY OF NEBRASKA PRESS   LINCOLN AND LONDON

First Nebraska paperback printing: 2006

Library of Congress Cataloging-in-Publication Data
Jackson, Kathi, 1951–
They called them angels: American military nurses of World War II / Kathi Jackson.
p.   cm.
Originally published: Westport, Conn.: Praeger, 2000.
Includes bibliographical references and index.
ISBN-13: 978-0-8032-7627-7 (pbk.: alk. paper)
ISBN-10: 0-8032-7627-3 (pbk.: alk. paper)
1. World War, 1939–1945—Medical care—United States   2. Nurses—United States—History—20th century.   I. Title.
D807.U5J33   2006
940.54'7573'0922—dc22   2005024228

Copyright Acknowledgments

The author and publisher gratefully acknowledge permission for use of the following material:

"50 Years Ago—World War II and the Navy Nurse," Kathi Jackson, *Navy Medicine*, Bureau of Medicine and Surgery, Department of the Navy, July–August, 1995, pp. 18–22, Courtesy of Jan K. Herman, Editor.

Excerpts from various articles in the *American Journal of Nursing*. Used by permission of Lippincott Williams & Wilkins.

Page Cooper, *Navy Nurse*, (McGraw-Hill, 1946).

Lena Dixon Dietz and Aurelia R. Lehozky, *History and Modern Nursing*, 2nd ed. (Philadelphia: F. A. Davis, 1967).

Josephine A. Dolan, R.N., M.S., *Goodnow's History of Nursing,* 10th and 12th eds. (Philadelphia: W. B. Saunders, 1958, 1968).

Lucy Wilson Jopling, *Warrior in White* (San Antonio: Watercress Press, 1990).

Photographs, Bureau of Medicine and Surgery, Department of the Navy.

Photographs, U.S. Army Center of Military History, U.S. Army.

Photographs, U.S. Army Armed Forces Institute of Pathology, U.S. Army Center of Military History, U.S. Army.

Roberta Love Tayloe, *Combat Nurse: A Journal of World War II* (Santa Barbara: Fithian Press, 1988).

Every reasonable effort has been made to trace the owners of copyright materials in this book, but in some instances this has proven impossible. The author and publisher will be glad to receive information leading to more complete acknowledgments in subsequent printings of the book and in the meantime extend their apologies for any omissions.

To my husband, family, and friends who always had faith in me; to the noble and powerful women for whom this book is written; and to the Good Lord for bringing us all together.

Thank you.

To only a few, among all the world's many gallant women, is reserved the solemn privilege of being a part of the great forces locked in battle, and of being numbered among those elect of earth who, as participants, directly govern the course of history. The nurse, because of her special training and the high calling to which her life is dedicated, brings to the battlefield indispensable attributes which she alone possesses. Voluntarily she comes in response to the utmost need of the men with shattered bodies whose cry is for the compassionate touch of a woman's hand. In responding she nobly pays a double price. She endures all of the ordeal borne by womanhood and in addition she shares with man his bitter lot upon the field of battle.

—L. L. Gardner, Lt. Col., M.C., A.U.S.
Nurses in Action

Contents

Photo essay follows page 98.

Preface

> It took the second world war to bring the American nurse to her national stature. Serving in embattled lands whose names the public had never heard before, in hospital ships on all the seas, and in air ambulances evacuating the wounded by plane, the nurse came into her own as comforter and healer. Femininity in foxholes, with mud-caked khaki coveralls over pink panties, captured the imagination of the public and the fighting men of America. Plasma and penicillin are indispensable when sickness comes, but a pat on the back and the smile of female lips are also needed.
>
> —Victor Robinson, M.D.
> *White Caps: The Story of Nursing*

In every war there are thousands of men and women who perform countless tasks and go unnoticed and I wish a book would be written to honor all of them, but I have chosen the American military nurses of World War II. Why? Because when I hear their stories, I'm astounded and wonder if I could do what they did. Could I live in a jungle, bathe out of a helmet, and clear my tent of snakes and scorpions every night before going to bed? Hardest of all, could I withstand the mental torment of watching men be torn apart and die?

But for years these women have been ignored. As June A. Willenz wrote in the preface of her book *Women Veterans: America's Forgotten Heroines*, "I was amazed at their accomplishment and the corollary lack of recognition by either the public or the government. Their dedication and their willingness to give themselves to their country for defense as volunteers was scarcely noted by anyone. And like the work of many other women in the pages of American history, their participation was unchronicled."[1] But even this comment was made of all women veterans, not just nurses, for nurses are rarely singled out and honored for what they did.

And that's why I wrote this book. I wasn't trying to dig up the dirt that I'm sure I could have found. I wasn't attempting to analyze what happened or why, and I wasn't trying to write a textbook on military nursing. I wrote this book as a dedication to the nurses who served. I want them to read it and say, "I remember that!" "That was my unit," or "How *did* I do it?" I want them to remember what they did and know that their work was appreciated.

This book is also for the family and friends of the nurses—and for the men whose lives were saved. Many of us wouldn't be here today if these women hadn't saved the lives of our fathers or grandfathers.

As for the general public, I think this book will entertain anyone interested in learning what ordinary women accomplished under extraordinary conditions—survival stories that are full of terror, humor, and romance.

While working on this project I was fortunate to encounter the many people I now want to thank. The first of these is my husband, William Jackson. I know it's common to thank spouses last, but there is no doubt in my mind that this project would not have been completed without him. Not only did he provide mental and financial support, he took me on countless trips to libraries and made countless photographs and photocopies. His faith and patience in me is unbelievable, and my love and appreciation for him cannot be measured.

Thanks also go to my always encouraging parents and two handsome sons, and all my family and friends who always believed that this book would be published, even when I did not. I would have given up on myself long ago without their never-failing support.

Innumerable thanks to Dr. Paula Mitchell Marks—friend, professor, and mentor—for being an endless source of information, inspiration, and encouragement. She, along with two other professors and friends—Dr. Anna Skinner and Dr. Tim Green, all three of St. Edward's University—not only encouraged the writing of this book, but let me use it for class assignments and, therefore, gave me their very useful criticism. Two other friends and professors, Pat Perry and the late Dr. Richard Hughes, were also generous with their information and encouragement.

One person at St. Edward's who went above and beyond the call was Allison Carpenter. As the school library's interlibrary loan assistant, Allison helped me immeasurably by locating numerous magazine articles, books, and addresses of other libraries. Other members of the library staff who helped with information and/or encouragement were Bernadine Rettger, Eileen Shocket, Carla Felsted, and Ann Daily.

Several librarians at other schools took the time to track down dates and page numbers for me. They are Dr. Jody Guenther, Baylor University School of Nursing; Norma L. Sellers, Chief Librarian, U.S. Army Academy of Health Sciences Library, Fort Sam Houston; Ruth Kallenberg, California State University Fresno; Mary C. Ryan, National Archives, Washington, D.C.; and the Dean B. Ellis Library, Arkansas State University.

When I began this undertaking, it seemed that I would never find the sources I needed, but doors finally began to open. The first was the U.S. Army Medical Department Museum at Fort Sam Houston in San Antonio. The curator, Thomas O. McMasters, not only allowed me access to his archives, but gave me the names of two local retired nurses who graciously allowed me to interview them.

Fred Berksted, at the Collections Deposit Library of The University of Texas at Austin, took the time and trouble to deliver a box of books to the Center for American History (formerly the Barker History Center) so I could see them on a Saturday afternoon. He also directed me to the University's Southwest Center for Nursing History, School of Nursing, and its director, Dr. Eleanor L. M. Crowder, who generously shared her knowledge and resource materials with me during a very pleasant visit. Another enjoyable visit was with Dr. Crowder's temporary successor, Dr. Quin Bronk, during which I was allowed to choose some WWII-era nursing photos from the school's archives. Somewhere in this process, I learned that the University had back copies of the *American Journal of Nursing*—probably the best single source of information.

Ray Dery, Chief of Public Affairs for Brooke Army Medical Center at Fort Sam Houston, helped immensely when he told me about the position of Army Nurse Corps historian. The five women who held this position during the writing of this book not only sent me great information and fabulous photos, but offered encouragement and answered my many questions promptly and completely. They are Maj. Wynona M. Bice-Stephens, Lt. Col. Patricia B. Wise, Lt. Col. Iris J. West, Maj. Constance Moore, and Lt. Col. Cynthia Brown.

Thanks, too, to Lt. Col. Melanie R. Reeder, Public Affairs Officer, and Joseph W. Hitt, Media Specialist, Fort Lewis, Washington.

The Navy responded in the same friendly fashion. Bureau of Medicine and Surgery Historian Jan Herman and Special Assistant Jennifer Mitchum sent me articles, wonderful photographs, and numerous Navy fact sheets and pamphlets. As with the Army, every time I've requested something, I've been answered generously and promptly.

I met Maj. Phyllis Phipps-Barnes, U.S. Air Force, at the "Quiet Shadows: Women in the Pacific War" seminar presented by the Admiral Nimitz Museum and held on the Southwest Texas State University campus on March 27, 1993. Not only did she answer some questions and give me some leads, she sent me several items published by the 50th Anniversary of World War II Commemoration Committee.

Thanks, too, to Cindy Schneider of *Sally Jessy Raphael* who forwarded my letter to Genevieve Stepanek, one of the nurses on Sally's 50th anniversary of Pearl Harbor show, "I Haven't Seen My Best Friend in 50 Years."

When the time came to seek out more nurses, I sent a notice to several publications, but only two (to my knowledge) published it. These were the newsletter for the Retired Army Nurse Corps Association, Patricia Silvestre, treasurer; and *The Register*, newsletter for the Women in Military Service for America Memorial Foundation, Inc., Peggy Heusinkveld, editor.

I also appreciate the kind words and information I received from Mr. William Nehez, wartime cameraman for the 112th Combat Engineers and 3908 Signal Service.

Special thanks to those family members who helped because their nurse was ill or deceased. Some of the best material came from those who want their loved one remembered.

I also must thank my wonderful agents for seeing the importance of this project and working so hard to get it published. Thank you Jane Dystel, Miriam Gooderich, and Stacey Glick. And to my editors Heather Ruland Staines and Leanne Small, thanks for your help and patience. To my production editor Lisa Webber—you have the patience of a saint and the computer talents of a genius.

Finally, thanks go to "my" nurses—those amazing women (listed in Appendix A) who openly shared their histories with a total stranger. Many of these women sent memoirs, letters, pages of recollections, and newspaper articles. Many even loaned or gave me treasured photos. One woman sent two photo albums so I could choose from a wide variety! I was able to meet two of these women in San Antonio and one in Everett. Two others allowed me to call them at home. No one will ever know how much these women mean to me. As for all the military nurses of this war, there is no way I can put my admiration for them into words. Their dedication and strength overwhelm me.

This project has been a true labor of love, and I only hope I've done a respectable job of accomplishing my goal: to make sure that these women are never forgotten.

NOTES ON DOCUMENTATION AND SOURCES

I've included many quotes because (1) the participants tell the story far better than I ever could, and (2) I'm sadly ill-equipped to translate much of the military or medical jargon and feel it's best not to try. And because of the quotes, there are many tense changes. This is because many of the statements were made during the war and others many years later. Please bear with these changes and inconsistencies.

The many medical descriptions are included not only to show the miracles that nurses helped perform, but to show that these women had to be resourceful and calm in emergencies. Their duty was to heal as many men as they could, and they used their common sense and know-how to do so, even when that meant recycling needles, intravenous tubing, and gauze—something unheard of today.

Although I tried to capture the feel of what it was like to nurse in every theater of the war, I did not find the resources necessary to give each theater the same amount of attention. This is also why there is more information about Army nurses than Navy nurses and so little about African-American and Japanese-American nurses. And if some stories seem repetitious, it's because I wanted to include as many personal accounts as I could.

Please forgive the use of derogatory terms. These were commonly used at the time.

I did not use the women's ranks (except where I felt it unavoidable) because most women received promotions during the war and I didn't want to shortchange anyone. I also hoped that this omission would make the women "equal" and the book, therefore, more personal.

I also tried to use the names the women used during the war (usually maiden names), particularly for those women with whom I corresponded. This was primarily so nurses who read the book will recognize one another. I've included an appendix of these women with their married names.

Finally, I often use "ANC" and "NNC" instead of spelling out "Army Nurse Corps" and "Navy Nurse Corps."

NOTE

1. June A. Willenz, *Women Veterans: America's Forgotten Heroines* (New York: Continuum, 1983), p. xi.

Introduction

There's no glamour about a wounded boy. He is dirty with foxhole grime. He is in pain. His clothes are matted with mud and blood, and he has a week's beard. He is often more dead than alive. And he's tired, so tired.

No, there's no glamour about him. But I've seen his strained, old face relax in peace and go young again at the touch of our hands. . . . His gratitude for a bath and a shave—or clean sheets and a chance to sleep—for our anxiety for our care, is so stupendous that it makes us humble. He is so grateful for so little!

—Quoted in Janet M. Geister, R.N.
"They Need You So!" *Trained Nurse and Hospital Review*,
December 1944

These words by a Navy nurse sum up the feelings of the approximately 77,000 nurses who answered Uncle Sam's call to follow American soldiers and sailors into battle during World War II. By war's end, approximately 230 nurses had lost their lives, 16 of them as a result of enemy action. But despite possible danger in hostile territories, 98 percent of the women who joined the Army Nurse Corps requested overseas service.

By attacking Pearl Harbor on December 7, 1941, the Japanese hoped to weaken both the military strength and morale of the United States; but they greatly underestimated the nation, and American men enlisted by the thousands that very evening. Soon all Americans were hanging blackout curtains; using ration coupons; buying war bonds; and turning in rubber, nylons, grease, etc.—all for the war effort. Even those Americans who had wanted to stay out of another conflict now found themselves key players in a universal one that would eventually involve almost every country in the world.

As the 7,000 or so active-duty Army and Navy nurses tended casualties in those very first days of war, appeals for more nurses were already beginning. At war's end, approximately 52,000 were serving in about 600 Army hospitals overseas and 80 in the United States, 43 Navy hospitals, a dozen Navy hospital ships, and close to 30 Army ships. In addition to caring for American soldiers and sailors, the women treated other allied military personnel, native civilians, and enemy prisoners of war; and they did so in tents and old buildings; aboard ships, trains, and planes; and in traditional hospital buildings. They also trained cadet nurses, corpsmen, WACs, WAVEs, and medical aid men.

Who were these women? Who was the average nurse? One of them, Rosemary Forsythe, ANC, gave this description:

[T]he average Army nurse overseas is not a Florence Nightingale in Crimea, possessed with a fanatical devotion to duty, but a normal girl usually between the ages of twenty-four and twenty-nine with the background of three years of professional training in an accredited nursing school, some civilian and a varied amount of Army experience. She is like the girls back home, with the same capacity for enjoyment and love of duty. She has already formulated a set of values, and quite frequently through her service she develops other admirable qualities heretofore dormant.[1]

But the average military nurse had to be a cut above her civilian counterpart because she took on additional responsibilities due to wartime conditions. The April 1945 issue of *The Army Nurse* states, "As Army nurses are held responsible in the absence of the doctor for anything and everything pertaining to the care of patients, all workers on hospital wards are under the direct control and supervision of Army nurses."[2] Army Nurse Juanita Hamilton put it quite simply: "Nurses are trained to work and adapt to any situation that may arise."[3]

One of the primary differences between Army and Navy nurses is that training corpsmen was "probably the most important single duty" of the Navy nurse, because the corpsmen *were* the nurses on warships. As Col. Julia O. Flikke wrote in her book *Nurses in Action*, "The ability of individuals of the Hospital Corps is largely dependent on the quality of instruction given them by the nurses. . . . The Army nurse instructs wardmen, too, but her teaching is incidental when compared to the fulfilling of her ward duties."[4]

But whether they joined the Army or Navy, most women were blind to what military life, and war, were really like—though they learned all too quickly. Edith Atwell, who joined the Army Nurse Corps because "all my friends were joining," said, "When we reached Pearl Harbor, the impact of the war and devastation really hit me. . . . Although we listened to news on the radio and watched *Movietone News* at the movies, it never compares to actually seeing devastation first hand."[5]

But they adapted and matured as women and as nurses—and as soldiers. When the Red Cross sent out its 1944 questionnaire, they accidentally sent it to some of the nurses already in service. One woman's answers exemplify her growth—and her sense of humor.

Are you employed in nursing at the present time?
Yes. Army nurse for 15 months; overseas 7 months.
Do you believe that you could now meet physical requirements for Military Service?
No.
If you have had additional study since filing your 1943 Red Cross questionnaire, give the type of course and the length of time included:
Opening C ration cans, pitching pup tents, tightening our tents in 90-mile gales, self protection from bombings, building fires, and how to manage bathing and drinking on 500 CC water per 24 hours.[6]

These women, some fresh out of nursing school, went out of their way to make GIs feel safe thousands of miles from home in the most horrific of conditions. They called it "special nursing"—that little bit of extra time the women tried to give the men—and their "greatest agony"[7] was that they could not do more. In her book *American Nursing: History and Interpretation*, Mary Roberts wrote, "A hypodermic for pain could be given quickly, but reassuring a suffering patient and helping him to decide how he would break the news of extensive injury to his family or sweetheart required more time. . . . As they flew from bed to bed, sensitive nurses were keenly aware of their patients' unspoken need for reassurance."[8]

And their efforts were appreciated. From a general: "I've seen them work in Africa, Sicily, and Normandy. I say in all sincerity that no one has done more for the American soldier than the nurses in our hospitals." From a surgeon at a clearing hospital: "The patients make faster progress when a nurse looks after them. She's an American woman who represents home, mother, wife, and sister to the wounded soldier. Just the sound of her voice is sometimes as good as medicine."[9]

Journalist Walter Lippman said that nursing "is one of the very few professions in all the world of doubt and struggle which transcends the conflict and evokes respect and gratitude for all men everywhere."[10] Entertainer Bob Hope put it simply when he called nurses "the world's greatest morale builder-uppers."[11] Even Dwight D. Eisenhower, Supreme Allied Commander, took time to recognize the importance of nurses to the confidence and health of servicemen:

Any words by me would be inadequate to pay proper tribute to the Army nurses and to the work that they are doing here and elsewhere. From Bataan to Normandy, the contributions of American women serving as nurses in our Army have spoken for themselves. One needs only to talk with the wounded or witness our nurses at work in the field and in hospitals to realize that they are taking their places alongside the greatest women in the history of our country. Nothing stops them in their determination to see that our troops receive the best attention humanly possible.[12]

Colonel Flikke, superintendent of the Army Nurse Corps from June 1937 to June 1943, said of these women: "They are filled with patriotism and with an overwhelming desire to be of service. Many of them are giving up important posts and remuneration far in excess of what they will receive in the

Army. But they will have the desire of their hearts, for they will know that they have been of service and shall have their reward—the reward of work well done."[13]

Here is their story.

NOTES

1. Rosemary Forsythe, 1st Lt., ANC, "En Route to the Philippines—January 1945," *The Army Nurse*, June 1945, p. 7.

2. "Increased Responsibilities for Army Nurses," *The Army Nurse,* April 1945, p. 6.

3. Juanita Hamilton Webster Questionnaire.

4. Col. Julia O. Flikke, *Nurses in Action* (New York: Lippincott, 1943), p. 217.

5. Edith Atwell Smith Questionnaire.

6. "Nurse 'Over There' Sends Red Cross Questionnaire," *Trained Nurse and Hospital Review*, October 1944, p. 282.

7. Janet M. Geister, R.N., "They Need You So!" *Trained Nurse and Hospital Review*, December 1944, p. 433.

8. Mary M. Roberts, R.N., *American Nursing: History and Interpretation* (New York: Macmillan, 1955), p. 349.

9. Quoted in Mary Jose, "Night Shift in an Army Hospital," *American Journal of Nursing*, June 1945, p. 430.

10. Quoted in "Your Part in Recruitment," *American Journal of Nursing*, January 1942, p. 5.

11. Quoted in "Did You Know?" *The American Journal of Nursing*, December 1944, p. 1109.

12. "General Eisenhower Pays a Fine Tribute to Nurses," *The Army Nurse*, September 1944, p. 5.

13. Flikke, p. 15.

Chapter 1

Uncle Sam Wants YOU!

This is our hour—the hour toward which everything in our past lives has been leading. Perhaps we have been complacent and indifferent to life's need of us. But now in this time of real danger the future depends on you and me. We cannot deny the fact that the war can be lost. If we and others refuse to believe this and remain careless of our country's danger, the fate of other unprepared peoples can be ours. But now the time of excuses and delays is past. The destruction of the lives and homes of our countrymen has occurred and our liberties are being imperiled.

—Major Julia C. Stimson, ANC
"Our Hour," *American Journal of Nursing*, February 1942

Who were the women who answered Uncle Sam's call and why did they? They were students such as Inez Combites, who joined the Army because she "was just out of nurses training, and the service needed nurses,"[1] and Juanita Hamilton who "decided the Army Nurse Corps was the place to be. It sounded like a chance to travel and be of service too."[2]

For Alice Lofgren there was no question that she would be involved. "Two brothers were in the Army, another brother was doing essential engineering work in Alaska, but I love the ocean, so I chose the Navy."[3]

Roberta Love Tayloe candidly admits that she wasn't anxious to join but "members of the family had been in every war the United States has had, so I guess it was up to me."[4] She joined the Army.

Dora Cline said, "December 7, 1941 angered me, and I wanted to be a part of our defense. It was my Christian duty."[5] She joined the Navy. Marian Tierney said she signed up with the Army because "as a young nurse it was just the thing to do."[6] Mary Barbero joined the Army because "I felt it was my duty as a young nurse."[7] Marion Kern, who also joined the Army, said that everyone was behind the war effort. Dixie Diefenderfer said, "It sounds corny, but when they said there was work to be done over here, I couldn't have tolerated myself if I hadn't signed up."[8] She joined the Army. Madeline Ullom, also Army, also joined out of her sense of dedication.

"[A]ll my friends were joining,"[9] said Ruth Shadewaldt, Army Nurse Corps. "The war was on and nobody was home," said Marian Hooker, ANC. "[I] just wanted to be a part of it and help someone."[10] Elizabeth Harman wanted adventure and naively believed her Army recruiter's promises. "My friends, six of us, were promised we could stay together. Two went to France, four to Persia!"[11] Rachel Gilbert joined the Army because "it sounded adventurous and exciting,"[12] and Agnes Jensen "joined the Army to see the world!"[13] Army Nurse Prudence Burns freely admits that she joined the Army Nurse Corps so she could travel *and* find a husband!

THE RECRUITMENT CAMPAIGN

Nurses were classified and recruited through the joint efforts of the American Red Cross Nursing Service and the National Nursing Council for War Service (NNCWS), an organization made up of six nursing organizations and directed by the Nursing Division Procurement and Assignment Service of the War Manpower Commission. Although women could join the Army or Navy Nurse Corps directly, these organizations worked together to compile an inventory of available nurses, coordinate a recruiting campaign, and contact the women about service.

And though the women were never forced into military service during the war, every patriotic and guilt-evoking ploy was used to encourage them in a recruitment campaign unprecedented in nursing history. In the July 1945, issue of the *American Journal of Nursing*, the editors wrote, "Never before this past winter have nurses and nursing appeared so prominently in the pages of newspapers and magazines. . . . Millions of dollars worth of advertising space and radio time have been placed at the disposal of war nursing campaigns by business and industry."[14]

Even First Lady Eleanor Roosevelt, who had four sons in the service, aided recruiting with a heartrending plea: "I ask for my boys what every mother has a right to ask—that they be given full and adequate nursing care should the time come when they need it. Only you nurses who have not yet volunteered can give it. . . . You must not forget that you have it in your power to bring back some who otherwise surely will not return."[15]

Pamphlets were distributed by the thousands to nursing councils and schools, and military nurses traveled with Army War Shows. Film strips like *Uncle Sam Needs Nurses*, *No Greater Glory*, and *Florence Nightingale and the Founding of Professional Nursing* were donated to film libraries of nursing organizations and shown to high school and college groups; and major women's magazines carried articles on nursing.

The radio advertisements of December 7-14, 1942, generated 10,000 responses, and several radio programs featured well-known personalities to aid in recruitment. Actress Helen Hayes used scripts about real Army nurses in her weekly program and ended each with a personal appeal "to all women who can 'share the care of the sick and wounded'."[16]

Hollywood made two movies about the nurses in the Philippines—*So Proudly We Hail* with Claudette Colbert and *Cry Havoc* with Margaret Sullavan. When a theater showed the Colbert movie, a recruitment booth—complete with Red Cross volunteers, posters, and leaflets—was set up in the lobby.

In the spring of 1943, the NNCWS's Retailers War Campaigns Committee worked with 180,000 major retailers across the country to set up special recruitment displays and information booths manned by nursing students or graduates. In April and May of 1945, the Army Nurse Corps, American Nurses Association, and American Red Cross sponsored an exhibit in New York City called "The Army Nurse in War." The exhibit featured life-size models of surgery under field conditions, an evacuation hospital ward, nurses' tent quarters, and even a section of an air ambulance. The show also featured movies and nursing informational handouts.

But probably the biggest aid for the recruitment of nurses was the Bolton Bill (Public Law 146), which allocated $1,250,000 in 1941, and $3,500,000 in 1942, for nursing education. Proposed by Congresswoman Frances Payne Bolton, the funds financed:

(1) refresher courses for graduate nurses; (2) assistance to schools of nursing so that they might increase their student body (nurses' homes, class rooms, laboratories); (3) post-graduate courses; (4) preparation for instructors and other personnel; and (5) training in midwifery and other specialties.[17]

In her book *History of Nursing*, Josephine A. Dolan called this legislation an "epoch-making action," and wrote, "Never before had the Government recognized nurses as a group; still less had it concerned itself with their advancement. This was an important milestone in the history of American nursing."[18] Another milestone sponsored by Congresswoman Bolton was the bill that created the U.S. Cadet Nurse Corps, a program that provided free tuition; money for books, uniforms, room and board; and a monthly allowance to young women in exchange for a promise to engage in military or civilian nursing for the duration of the war.

The government also encouraged nursing schools to increase their admissions from 15 percent to 30 percent and to "select candidates who were not only physically and mentally fit and fairly mature but able to learn and adjust quickly." Other steps were taken: students adept in the biological, physical, and social sciences were sometimes allowed to graduate sooner than other students; some nursing schools shortened course lengths for those students planning to enter military nursing corps; and more nursing schools were accredited.

REQUIREMENTS

But not just anyone could be a military nurse. In her book *Education of Nurses*, Isabel Maitland Stewart wrote, "Professional qualifications must also be upheld for those who were to carry nursing responsibilities in situations much more complicated and difficult than those confronting nurses in times of peace."[19]

Nurses who applied for military service had to be U.S. citizens (Army nurses could be citizens of any Allied nation), graduates of approved nursing schools, and registered nurses. Navy nurses also had to be members of a nursing organization affiliated with the American Nurses Association.

When the war started, both Army and Navy nurses had to be single, and getting married meant instant discharge. By November 1942, Army nurses, married or not, were recruited for the duration of the war plus six months and forbidden to resign unless found incompetent or mentally or physically incapable. Those who married kept their maiden names on official records unless they requested otherwise. At first, the women were not assigned to the same camps with their husbands, but by early 1943, a woman's marital status had no effect on her assignment.

Women with minor children were, at first, accepted upon acquiring child care outside the camps. Later, women with children under 14 were no longer accepted.

When the war started, Army nurses had to be between the ages of 21 and 40, but the age limit was later raised to 45. The January 1945 issue of *The Army Nurse* gave the reasons for the age limit: "it has been proven that women over 45 years of age cannot stand up to the rigors of overseas duty. Of course, there are exceptions, but the Army must deal in averages and nurse personnel must be regarded as mobile-ready for service anywhere, any time, and under any circumstances that war may demand."[20]

Ruth Claff (who joined the Army Nurse Corps because "I seen my duty and I done it . . . in my new delirium of patriotism") humorously described her attempts to become an Army nurse in her memoirs, *Lady with the Flashlight*. The first attempt was a failure. "They all laughed!" she wrote. "I was turned down—not because I had flat feet or asthma, or because I heard voices when there were none to hear, but because of my approaching senility!" She was too old at 42. When the Army raised their age limit to 45, Claff returned.

Even with my nerve I couldn't face again the snooty young lieutenant who had talked me almost into senile dementia, so a new approach was indicated. I went boldly to the building where the physicals were being done, and just got into a line. When I was asked for my card, I mumbled and fumbled and of course couldn't find it, though I assured the receptionist I had been told to report for my examination that morning, and my card must be around somewhere. Much annoyed and muttering . . . she made out a new card, and sent me on my way with three prospective WAACs and seventy or more soldiers in the rough. I was duly put through my paces, examined for spavins and hoof and mouth disease, and proved sound of wind and limb. . . .

As I inched up to the Wasserman crew I took a ribbing from the boys fore and aft of me, who were exaggeratedly concerned over the possibility of my fainting.   To my sinful glee, the biggest joker of them all passed out cold at sight of his own blood, and I helped lay him gently on a convenient cot.   And for the first time of thousands of times in the army a soldier filling out forms asked loudly "Name?"   "Age?"   "Forty-two," I whispered.   "Did you say thirty-two?" he yelled.   And I yelled in exasperation (I had been having so much fun!)   "No, son, I said forty-two," then glared defiantly at the boys who until then had been treating me as a contemporary.

When she found out that she'd passed her physical, Claff said, "I gloated over bypassing the little snob who had laughed at me in the first place."[21]

Some of the Navy's requirements were more restrictive.   The age limits were 28 to join the regular corps and 40 to join the reserves, and it wasn't until early in 1945 that Navy nurses could marry without being forced to resign, though they still had to be single to join.   Keeping married women out meant that the Navy lost some good nurses—such as Louine Connor.

From a seafaring family that dated back to the Danish Vikings of 1013, Louine Connor joined the Navy Nurse Corps in hopes of working on a hospital ship.   But when she fell in love and got married she was promptly discharged. She attempted to be "the proper stay-at-home sort of wife the Navy expected her to be,"[22] but could do so no longer after Pearl Harbor was bombed and her husband joined the Navy.   Although happy to be accepted by the Army Nurse Corps, Connor was afraid she'd lost her chance to serve on a ship.   And though her dream was fulfilled when she was assigned to the ship *Acadia*, she couldn't help but be a little disappointed that her father hadn't lived to see her continue the family tradition.   One of the last schooner captains, he died only a few months before she received her assignment.   "I wish I could have told him; he would have been so proud,"[23] said Connor.

And so they followed the call.   In the preface of Page Cooper's book *Navy Nurse*, Navy Nurse Captain and Superintendent of the Navy Nurse Corps Sue S. Dauser said,

Womanly compassion has been expressed through the ages by individuals and by religious devotees in the care of the sick and unfortunate.   But modern professional nursing was born in War.   Ever since Florence Nightingale led her courageous little band to the Crimea, nurses have been going to war, sharing the work and sacrifices of the fighting men.*

*Capt. Sue S. Dauser, USN, preface, *Navy Nurse*, Page Cooper (New York: McGraw-Hill, 1946), p. ix.   Used with permission from The McGraw-Hill Companies.

NOTES

1. Inez Combites Hood Questionnaire.

2. Juanita Hamilton Webster, Unpublished memoirs, no date, p. 5.

3. Alice Lofgren Andrus Questionnaire.

4. Roberta Love Tayloe, *Combat Nurse: A Journal of World War II* (Santa Barbara: Fithian Press, 1988), p. 15.

5. Dora Cline Fechtmann Questionnaire.

6. Col. Marian A. Tierney, ANC (Ret.) Questionnaire.

7. Mary Barbero Questionnaire.

8. Quoted in Mary Jose, "Night Shift in an Army Hospital," *American Journal of Nursing,* June 1945, p. 433.

9. Lt. Col. Ruth F. Shadewaldt, ANC (Ret.) Questionnaire.

10. Marian Hooker Stran Questionnaire.

11. Elizabeth Harman Masterson Questionnaire.

12 . Rachel Gilbert Francis Questionnaire.

13. Agnes Jensen Mangerich Questionnaire.

14. "War Advertising Council and OWI in Nursing Campaigns," *American Journal of Nursing,* July 1945, p. 543.

15 . Quoted in "The Time is Now!" *American Journal of Nursing,* August 1942, p. 924.

16. Quoted in "War Advertising Council and OWI in Nursing Campaigns," p. 544.

17. Josephine A. Dolan, M.S., R.N., *Goodnow's History of Nursing,* 10th ed. (Philadelphia: W. B. Saunders, 1958), p. 256.

18. Josephine A. Dolan, M.S., R.N., *History of Nursing, 12th* ed. (Philadelphia: W. B. Saunders, 1968), p. 341.

19. Isabel Maitland Stewart, R.N., A.M., *Education of Nurses* (New York: Macmillan, 1947), pp. 280, 281.

20. "Facts about the Army Nurse Corps," *The Army Nurse,* January 1945, p. 4.

21. Ruth Claff, *Lady with the Flashlight*, Unpublished memoirs, 1947, pp. 1-2.

22. Nan Lincoln, "Captains Courageous," *Bar Harbor Times* "Selects," February 21, 1991, p. B2.

23. Quoted in Lincoln, "Captains Courageous," p. B2.

Chapter 2

From Whites to Fatigues

As we were subject to air raids, we learned to prepare for the safety and comforts of our patients during the raid. All our medical supplies, food, gasoline and oil, and mail were delivered at night under blackout conditions. . . . I certainly profited by the experience while on maneuvers. I wish that all Army nurses could have the same opportunity.
—Dorothy Hicks, R.N., ANC
"On Maneuvers," *American Journal of Nursing*, January 1942

TRAINING

This nurse sounds as if she was well prepared to meet the challenges of wartime nursing, but the U.S. Army Center of Military History quotes one nurse as saying that many women were more likely "to raise their right hands, take the oath, put on their white uniforms and find themselves, in no time flat, on the ward up to their ears in work."[1]

Many nurses were members of affiliated units—groups of graduates and staff members of medical schools and hospitals sent overseas to staff evacuation and general hospitals. Many other nurses were members of auxiliary surgical teams—fully staffed and fully equipped groups that assisted evacuation hospitals in combat zones. Not only did these men and women have to work as one, they had to be in good physical condition to withstand the constant moves and be able to pack up entire hospitals at a moment's notice—all of which meant training as a team.

Whether trained as a team or not, the women had quite varied instruction. Lillian Dunlap, who joined the Army in November 1942, remembers going through gas chambers, crawling under barbed wire, and taking classes in map reading. Rachel Gilbert joined the Army in September 1941, and received training in gas casualty preparation and field operations. Agnes Jensen remembers bivouacs, marching, obstacle courses, survival courses, and special training in tropical medicine and chemical warfare. She joined the Army in 1941. Dora Cline, who joined the Navy in the summer of 1942, remembers close-order drills and gas-mask and lifeboat training. Marian Hooker, ANC, said she received one month of "field training and some nursing"[2] at Camp McCoy and another at Fort Riley.

Juanita Hamilton joined the Army in January, 1942. Of her training, she said, "Of course we had a few Army regulations we had to learn such as salute all ranks, or return salutes from enlisted personnel. They tried to teach us to march in formation, but the sergeant gave up in disgust when he decided we were unteachable. He did not realize we were only going so far in being military all the way."[3]

Louine Connor joined the Army in 1942, and went to Fort Meade, Maryland, where the women drilled in POW issue—thin gray uniforms with black letters on the back—and suffered from the cold until Uncle Sam finally issued topcoats. But they received no military instruction, and Connor said the lack of it was evident at the staging area. "The morale was pretty low, because we had no one to give us instructions, no one to tell us what to do. We knew nothing about the Army regulations or how to live until we stumbled into some incident where we broke one of the rules. Then we were told what to do; we learned that way."[4]

Ruth Shadewaldt, who joined the Army in June 1942, said, "The only special training I had for wartime nursing was listening to the stories that our superintendent of nurses at Brokaw [School of Nursing in Normal, Illinois], Ms. Maud F. Essig, told us about her WWI experiences in France. She encouraged our class to join the American Red Cross, and I did. I did not go to basic training. We went right to work."[5]

Army Nurse Ruth Claff felt that she received more than her share of training, beginning at Camp Edwards in January 1943. "We drilled for the first time that day . . . in 30 below weather, and after two hours of intensive training, we could do a pretty snappy 'about face,' that is, those of us who could still feel their feet enough to move them." There were also uniform and barracks inspections and road marches. Claff said of the experience, "They did their level best to make men of us. I discovered muscles and hidden talents I had never before had occasion to discover. We exercised from morning to night, and then slept between army blankets, with no sheets, no pillows, no dressers, no chairs. We thought we were pretty rugged—we didn't know this was still practically the lap of luxury."

And because the Army wanted personnel to learn to live in extreme climates, Claff also trained in the desert in camps that prepared the women for life in North Africa. According to Claff, "They didn't spare the horses—meaning us!" In 118+ temperatures, they marched "through jungle, over cliffs, killing snakes as we went. We drilled and drilled."

She also recalls "warm, chlorinated drinking water from Lister bags, tent latrines, showers two hours a day, fatigues for nursing, field shoes and helmets.   For neighbors, rattlesnakes, scorpions, black widows and tarantulas." Claff and her tent mates became acquainted with kangaroo rats, which "playfully nibbled at our toes as we napped," and found that a tarantula had "made his home within a foot of my bed." And still they were drilled.

I became a soldier the day we went over the infiltration course. We belly-crawled over 100 yards of naked desert under live machine gun fire, with elbow and knee pads under our fatigues, pistol belt with canteen and first aid kit, helmet and gloves and leggings— in a temperature of 130. . . . One of the nurses just got tired halfway across and stayed where she was until they stopped the guns for the day!   The whole unit went through, from the colonel to me. And we were dirty beyond description—the heat made mud of the sweat, then the sun baked it, and our faces were unrecognizable, even our teeth were coated with mud. [6]

Dorothy Hicks went on maneuvers in Arkansas and Louisiana for eight and a half weeks. In Prescott, Arkansas, their first duty was to turn a high school into a hospital. "This meant setting up medical and surgical wards, diet kitchen, laboratory, and operating rooms. We had to make sure that each bed was canopied with mosquito netting and each ward equipped with supplies for immediate use."[7]   Their kitchen was set up in the home economics room, and other services—communication, post office, radio, medical supply, and receiving and convalescent wards—were set up in surrounding tents. Here the medical personnel practiced receiving patients and assigning them to the proper tents for treatment.

The first mandatory basic training centers for Army nurses (in Fort Devens, Massachusetts; Fort Sam Houston, Texas; and Camp McCoy, Wisconsin) didn't open until July 1943. Although the Surgeon General suggested camp curriculum and most camps followed similar programs, nothing was set in stone. Usually training for four weeks, the women were taught military law and correspondence, how to maintain personnel records, and how to take care of their uniforms and equipment. They also learned how to give immunizations and control communicable diseases.   Bivouac, marching, and calisthenics were usually included. The women also learned military law. This included the rules of military conduct and rights under the Treaty of Geneva (also known as the Red Cross Treaty).

1. The right not to be taken as prisoner of war.

2. The right, if captured, not to be treated as prisoner of war.

3. The right to serve in a professional capacity pending repatriation.

4. The right, if captured, to receive attention equal to that given to the Army medical personnel of the capturing army; this means the same pay, food, and lodging.

5. The right to be armed.

6. When repatriated, medical personnel are entitled to take with them their equipment, materials, and arms.

In order to claim these rights, the nurses had to carry identification cards and wear identification tags and Red Cross brassards—a red cross on a white background worn on the left arm between elbow and shoulder. But they could lose these rights if they committed "acts which would discredit the medical establishment and give an excuse to the enemy for breaking the pact of neutrality that is supposed to protect hospitals." This included anything that could be construed as being "injurious to the enemy"[8] or smuggling correspondence, money, and other forbidden articles through the lines.

The women learned that Uncle Sam, too, held them to high standards. Circular No. 381, issued by the War Department in 1944, gave authority to the military police of each service to "take corrective measures, including arrest if necessary, in the case of any member of the armed forces committing a breach of the peace, disorderly conduct, or any other offense which reflects discredit upon the services. . . . The authority granted herein extends to all female members of the Army, Navy, Coast Guard, and Marine Corps."[9]

Many of the Army nurses sent to England without basic training were put through their paces upon arrival. The course, three weeks of 10-hour days, was comprehensive and strenuous and earned the nickname "Commando Course for Nurses."[10] The women learned evacuation procedures and how to perform blood transfusions in the field. They became acquainted with the latest medicines including penicillin, sulfa drugs, atabrine, and sodium pentothal; and the latest techniques in anesthesiology, neuropsychiatric illnesses, maxillofacial and neurosurgery, rehabilitation and reconditioning; and the proper procedures for using and storing whole blood and blood plasma. The U.S. Army Center of Military History's "History-ANC" includes one nurse's apprehensive description:

Drilled in cold rain and sat in class four hours with wet feet, learning how to cook a chicken (I've seen three since coming over here) . . . yesterday, I learned to climb a tree and cross a river on two ropes strung twenty feet above the water; the trick is to hold on one rope and walk on the other. By putting a stretcher on a pulley a patient was pulled over. I was the patient.

I got three demerits the other day for something my shoes did.[11]

Most Navy nurses learned military procedures and regulations while working in naval hospitals. In her article for the *American Journal of Nursing*, "A Nurse Looks at the Navy," Reba Hartley wrote of feeling lost on her first day at the National Naval Medical Center. In addition to learning new procedures, becoming acquainted with the mounds of paperwork, and learning to "take orders and respect your seniors," she had to learn the "salty lingo"[12] of the Navy since the terms used on a ship are also used in the hospitals.

Assigned to the Oak Knoll Naval Hospital in Oakland, California, Alice Lofgren also learned on the job: "within a day or two I was in uniform, taking care of patients on the burn ward while I also learned the Navy way of doing things." She also received drill instruction and had to pass a swimming test ("easy for me, because I enjoyed swimming").[13]

UNIFORMS

Just as Uncle Sam wasn't quite prepared to train the nurses when war began, he wasn't prepared to dress them either; and women's clothing was designed, tested, and improved throughout the war. An article in the December 1944 issue of *The Army Nurse* reported that the Army had designed two new uniforms. The one for warm climates was khaki twill pants and a long-sleeved shirt. The one for cold climates was actually a liner for the water-repellant pants and field jackets already in use. The outfit (olive drab wool flannel lined with rayon and black felt shoes) could be worn without the outer wear. The catch? These would be available to the overseas nurse "after the first of the year—which usually means July [1945]."[14] The war in Europe was over by then; it would end in the Pacific in a month.

Army Nurse Inez Combites began overseas duty in a blue skirt, white shirt, blue overseas cap, and black tie. She was later issued a navy blue jacket and a navy blue overcoat. Louine Connor also began service in the blue uniform but said it was changed because the Japanese wore blue and the Army feared confusion, especially in the Pacific. The women were then issued olive drab suits (khaki) for winter and light tan shirtwaist dresses for summer. The olive drab, said Connor, "made you look as if you never took a bath."[15] But even the olive drab general service uniform wasn't available to over half the nurses until well into 1944.

Marion Kern began the war wearing a two-toned blue dress uniform and the white starched work uniform, but was later issued a blue seersucker uniform and a partial field outfit—a Mansfield field jacket, men's socks, brown canvas shoes, combat boots, a man's raincoat, and a dark green canvas jeep hat.

In his article for the October 1964 issue of *Surgery*, Dr. John Paul North wrote of his nurses in India: "They left the country about as poorly equipped for duty in a steaming jungle as can be imagined, wearing the old-fashioned blue woolen uniforms and black oxford shoes. No slacks, no field boots, no raingear, although the wise and more affluent had laid in a few elements of a cotton wardrobe at their own expense while in Los Angeles."[16]

In her book *Combat Nurse: A Journal of World War II*, Roberta Love Tayloe wrote, "You would have thought with all the uniforms we had been issued, we would have had something to wear besides our white dresses or blue ones, and white and black dress shoes! The chief nurse finally found us some men's shoes, coveralls, and mess jackets, and later men's long underwear and undershirts."[17]

At first, many nurses were hesitant to give up their traditional white uniforms, but once they arrived overseas, they realized how impractical the whites were, and since Uncle Sam wasn't prepared with alternative work clothes, they adopted men's clothing. After having worn the traditional white uniform when recruiting for the Red Cross, then wearing the GI issue when working in the field, Margaret Kowaleski, a member of an evacuation hospital, told Red Cross correspondent Frederick Clayton, "I've wondered how much influence that spic and span uniform had. Somehow, I'd rather have recruits see me in these working clothes. They are not very photogenic, but we get things done in them!"[18]

But since they weren't designed for women's bodies, the GI issue was also a problem, and author Wyatt Blassingame put it best when he said the clothes came in three sizes: "too small, too big, and—most plentiful of all—too too big."[19]

Constance "Connie" Sansone remembers the problems all too well. "There were two of us that were the same size, both five feet tall . . . and the Army issued uniforms [with a] crotch [that] came down to my knees. . . . I wore a size five-and-a-half shoe, and you couldn't find that in a man's shoe so they had to take me to the boys' department to get my shoes."[20]

Lucy Wilson describes similar problems in her book *Warrior in White*. Her first pair of olive drab coveralls were size 42. "The seat came about to my knees and I weighed under 100 pounds. It was difficult to walk in the sand with nurse's oxfords on, too."[21] Later, the size 42 coveralls were traded for smaller ones and the oxfords traded for Filipino shoes.

Rachel Gilbert said, "The unit tailor was swamped with requests for alterations and finally we received women's fatigues. So much for Unisex clothing!"[22]

Some nurses became so accustomed to wearing men's GI issue that wearing a skirt seemed odd. Another said that after wearing the high-topped men's shoes for so long, "you can expect us to come back with ankles like well-bred fillies."[23] Marian Hooker called the footwear "heavy shoes with Bull Dog toes."[24]

For the most part, Navy nurses served aboard hospital ships or in hospitals and, therefore, were able to wear the traditional white uniforms when on duty. When off duty, they enjoyed the comfort of fatigues and other weather-appropriate clothing.

Although nurses in the South Pacific often relaxed in cotton play suits during the day, everyone covered up before night to protect themselves from mosquitoes. In New Guinea, Ruth Shadewaldt wore tan slacks and a safari jacket with long sleeves. "It was hotter than Hades every day as it rained over 300 inches a year. . . . The uniform was to keep the mosquitoes from biting us. We were issued leggings too, but very few wore them. The slacks were a blessing as we could climb over the obstacles that were in our way. We often had no electricity so could not iron them. We would wash them, hang them up and let [them] dry a little and then put them under the mattress and sleep on them to get some of the wrinkles out."[25]

Nurses in the cold climates wore what was referred to as "foul weather clothing"—parka overcoats with hoods, worksuits of herringbone twill, fur gloves, and field shoes. Author Page Cooper provides a colorful description in her book *Navy Nurse*: "the girls sloshed back and forth in their windproof and rainproof parkas and their four-clasp galoshes. If it wasn't snowing it was raining and the mud was ankle-deep . . . the girls pulled the hoods of their parkas over their caps, stuck down their heads and battled through it."[26]

While in the air, Army flight nurses wore what the men wore: sheepskin-lined leather jackets that zipped up to the neck, lined helmets, sheepskin-lined pants that zipped up to the waist, heavy boots, wool socks, and wool gloves. On the ground they wore a light blue shirt with black tie, navy blue slacks, and brown leather flying jackets. When off duty, they wore the Army Nurse Corps two-toned blue wool uniform and overseas cap. While one nurse, Helen Ilic, said that their uniforms were "catch-as-catch-can,"[27] another, Agnes Jensen, reported that their uniforms were very practical and "looked very nice in all conditions."[28]

That, of course, depended on what year it was. Since Clara Morrey was sent to Africa and the Mediterranean before the flight nurse uniform was ready, she was told to take two pairs of navy slacks and blue regulation shirts. Unfortunately, her other clothing was lost at sea and Morrey found herself in the hot climes for nine months before other clothing arrived. "[Y]ou should have seen our uniforms in that hot African sun. They were bleached to a purple. And when we were on trips, we would put them under the mattress to press them out. Oh, they were terrible!"[29]

In 1942, the Navy nurses' street attire was a dark blue double-breasted jacket and a dark blue skirt worn with a white shirt, blue hat, black tie, and black shoes. At first the women had to wear black hose and gray gloves, but in 1944, these were replaced by beige hose and black gloves. The white dress uniform was a single-breasted jacket and white skirt worn with a white shirt and black tie, white hose, shoes, and cap. There was also a one-piece double-breasted gray dress (with six large, black Navy buttons down the front and a loose belt) that was worn for informal occasions. It was accessorized with gray cap, black shoes, beige hose, gray gloves, and a regulation purse.

The Navy flight nurses wore shirt and slacks of heavy, gray cotton broadcloth in the warm climates and a similar uniform, but of heavier dark olive-green material, in the cold.

By far the most controversial uniform was the seersucker, which came with a cap and jacket and was available in a wraparound dress or pantsuit. Adopted because it was easier to maintain, it was constructed of one piece of material that needed no ironing or starching. Because it wrapped around, it needed no buttons. Even the cap spread out flat to dry. Its striped pattern (brown and white for Army; gray and white for Navy) also provided a little camouflage for the overseas nurse. Before the end of 1943, the seersucker was standard for Army nurses on hospital trains, ships, and overseas duty. By mid-1944, it was standard throughout the continental United States. Toward the end of 1944, Navy nurses outside the continental United States also wore the seersucker.

But many nurses complained about the uniform. Connie Sansone said the seersucker "looked like something you'd use in the kitchen."[30] Helen Pon described the "Mother Hubbard" wraparound seersucker dress as "ugly. . . . I don't know who invented them"[31] and added that her head nurse wouldn't allow the women to wear pants but because the wind blew the dress open, they wore pants *and* a slip underneath.

Rachel Gilbert said the thin material made it impractical for Europe and that the manufacturer mistakenly raised the white stripe instead of the brown, which aggravated the soiling problem. "Add to this the scarcity of laundry facilities and you can guess where the seersuckers ended up."[32]

Some nurses said that it cost the same to clean both uniforms and that the white uniform was a "symbol of their profession." Since so many women seemed to dislike the new outfit, the editors of *The Army Nurse* took a poll. The results, printed in the April 1945 issue, showed that approximately 73 percent of the nurses preferred the seersucker but *just* for the remainder of the war. Many of the women noted that the seersucker was practical and a minor wartime inconvenience. According to one woman, "The color of a uniform is too trivial a thing to affect the morale of an intelligent Army Nurse."[33]

There *was* one government issue that was not only a perfect fit but well liked by everyone, and the January 1945 issue of *The Army Nurse* described its virtues: "The nurses have grown partial to those helmets. It may have no style, no distinctive lines for adding beauty to a feminine face, but it makes up for that lack by its versatility. It's hat, bucket, washtub, bathtub, basket, and chair, and in a pinch serves as a shovel for digging an emergency fox hole."[34] "We had some sinks," said Ruth Shadewaldt, "but those helmets got used for everything. They were the most useful things we had in the world. That and the canteens."[35]

Uniforms may have been ill fitting, ugly, and inconvenient, but a security risk? While in Australia, "Connie" Sansone and a friend were walking down the street when a man took their picture and then asked them their names, the name of their company, and the name of the uniform they were wearing. "We told him everything," she said. The next morning her friend broke the news: "Connie, I'm so mad that they cut me off! They just put your picture in the paper; they didn't put mine!" Sansone's photo was in that morning's *Brisbane Courier*. Vanity may have upset her friend, but it was the breach of security that upset the chief nurse of the South Pacific who called Sansone's chief nurse, who confined Sansone and friend to quarters for a month. "I made history anyway,"[36] said Sansone with a chuckle.

Nurses always tried to find ways to personalize their uniforms, that extra touch that reminded them that they were women, not just soldiers: fancy handkerchiefs worn in pockets of off-duty dresses, shoes with nonregulation heels, hair braided and worn with red ribbons. But it wasn't just the women who wanted to look pretty. Maintaining an attractive appearance was strongly encouraged, even demanded, of the nurses because pretty women made the news and good news helped recruitment.

But there were thousands of other important reasons to look good—the patients. Page Cooper wrote that Navy nurses always wore their white uniforms on the wards because the boys "preferred the white skirts to slacks."[37] In her dissertation "Coping with War," Judith Barger quotes Grace Dunnam, chief flight nurse in Europe, as saying that she wanted her nurses to dress per regulation but was willing to overlook minor infractions, "such as the wearing of red polish, which she felt was good for morale."[38]

Nurses on the Navy hospital ship *Relief* were expected "to appear clean and neatly groomed in [their] crisp white uniform[s]," reports Christine Curto in her article, "Nurse Pioneers and the Hospital Ship *Relief*."[39] In reality, however, many women found it easier to work in fatigue coveralls. Alice Lofgren wrote that the nurses changed into slacks whenever abandon-ship drills were announced ahead of time. "We realized that if we had to climb up or down rope ladders, slacks would be most practical."[40]

Because the first concern of the Army and Navy nurses of World War II was always the patient, the women weren't aware that almost everything they did—from how they were trained to what they wore—was breaking new ground. But by 1943, changes were already evident, and Sgt. Bob Ghio wrote about them in his article for *YANK*, "The Ladies of Assam."

Back in the States an Army nurse was merely a pretty girl on a poster, with a starched and immaculate white uniform, a becoming cape and a sweet and merciful expression on her face. Here in the jungle camps of Eastern India, where the monsoons bring 150 to 300 inches of rainfall annually (and most of that in six months), she has neither the time nor the inclination to pretty herself or to act like Florence Nightingale. She's just another GI.[41]

NOTES

1. Quoted in "History-ANC," File #314.7, U.S. Army Center of Military History, Washington, D.C., no date, p. 9.

2. Marian Hooker Stran Questionnaire.

3. Juanita Hamilton Webster Questionnaire.

4. Louine Lunt Connor Peck, Interviewed by Col. Clara Adams-Ender, A.N., U.S. Army Nurse Corps Oral History Program, Major Wynona Bice-Stephens, A.N., ed., North East Harbor, Maine, August 31, 1986, p. 20.

5. Lt. Col. Ruth Frances Shadewaldt, ANC (Ret.), Taped interview with sister, July 1992.

6. Ruth Claff, *Lady with the Flashlight*, Unpublished memoirs, 1947, pp. 2, 6, 7, 9, 10-11.

7. Dorothy Hicks, R.N., ANC, "On Maneuvers," *American Journal of Nursing*, January 1942, p. 87.

8. Yvonne Hentsch, "The Treaty of Geneva," *American Journal of Nursing*, January 1944, pp. 35.

9. Quoted in "Discipline," *The Army Nurse*, November 1944, p. 12.

10. "Army Nurses' 'Commando Course' in England," *American Journal of Nursing*, September 1943, p. 860.

11. Quoted in "History-ANC," p. 15.

12. Lt. (jg) Reba K. Hartley (NC), USNR, "A Nurse Looks at the Navy," *American Journal of Nursing*, April 1945, p. 294.

13. Alice Lofgren Andrus, "Navy Experiences," Unpublished essay, pp. 1, 3.

14. "New Uniform Trousers Developed for Tropical and Cold Climates," *The Army Nurse*, December 1944, p. 4.

15. Peck oral history, p. 13.

16. John Paul North, M.D., "The 20th General Hospital—I.S. Ravdin, Commanding General," *Surgery*, Vol. 56, No. 4, October 1964, p. 614.

17. Roberta Love Tayloe, *Combat Nurse: A Journal of World War II* (Santa Barbara: Fithian Press, 1988), p. 31.

18. Quoted in Frederick Clayton, "Front-Line Surgical Nurses," *American Journal of Nursing*, March 1944, p. 235.

19. Wyatt Blassingame, *Combat Nurses of World War II* (New York: Landmark Books, 1967), p. 21.

20. Constance Sansone, Telephone Interview with author, July 6, 1992.

21. Lucy Wilson Jopling, *Warrior in White* (San Antonio: Watercress Press, 1990), p. 36.

22. Rachel Gilbert Francis, Letter to author, August 25, 1993.

23. "From New Caledonia," *American Journal of Nursing*, August 1942, p. 946.

24. Marian Hooker Stran Questionnaire.

25. Shadewaldt interview with sister.

26. Page Cooper, *Navy Nurse* (New York: McGraw-Hill, 1946), p. 99.

27. Quoted in Judith Barger, B.S.N., M.S.N., "Coping with War: An Oral History of United States Army Flight Nurses Who Flew with the Army Air Forces in World War II," Dissertation, The University of Texas at Austin, December 1986, p. 107.

28. Agnes Jensen Mangerich Questionnaire.

29. Quoted in Barger, "Coping with War," p. 107.

30. Sansone telephone interview.

31. Col. Helen Pon Onyett, ANC (Ret.), Interview with author, December 19, 1991.

32. Francis letter to author.

33. "Results of Informal Survey Show Seersucker Preferred," *The Army Nurse*, April 1945, p. 8.

34. "Helmets Have Many Uses for Army Nurses in France," *The Army Nurse*, January 1945, p. 12.

35. Lt. Col. Ruth Frances Shadewaldt, ANC (Ret.), Questionnaire.

36. Sansone telephone interview.

37. Cooper, p. 106.

38. Quoted in Barger, "Coping with War," p. 108.

39. LCDR Christine Curto, NC, USN, "Nurse Pioneers and the Hospital Ship Relief," *Navy Medicine*, May-June 1992, p. 25.

40. Alice Lofgren Andrus Questionnaire.

41. Sgt. Bob Ghio, "The Ladies of Assam," *YANK*, September 13, 1943, no p. #.

Chapter 3

Following the Troops

Earnest determination is written on their faces—they have a
duty to perform for their country. Fighting men all over the
globe have priority on the most skillful service their heads,
hands, and hearts can render.

—Capt. Marion E. Thuma, R.N.
"Task Forces, ANC," *American Journal of Nursing,*
January 1944

And, thus, the adventure began. After training to be a nurse, making the
decision to join the Army or Navy, and being drilled in military procedures
and new medical techniques, thousands of women left home and its comforts
to face the unknown. Many wondered if they would come back or, even
worse, if they would do a good job. But they did a fantastic job and their
efforts made a brighter future for many soldiers, sailors, and marines.

Task Force nurses (those going overseas) were sometimes given only 48
hours to report to their point of embarkation. Those who traveled from their
homes were told to take their oath of office before leaving so their pay could
begin and they could be reimbursed for their first-class travel expenses.

More often than not, the age-old military slogan of "hurry up and wait"
applied as the women were sent from camp to camp only to wait—from hours
to weeks—in a staging area for a final boarding call. Dora Cline spent a
month in San Francisco waiting to go to New Caledonia. Helen Pon went
from Fort Devins, Massachusetts, to Charleston, South Carolina, before going
to Camp Kilmer, New Jersey, to board the USS *Monticello* to go to North
Africa. Louine Connor went from Fort Meade, Maryland, to Fort Story,
Virginia, where she was given orders for sea duty and put in charge of getting
10 nurses to New York's Staten Island. Eugenie Rutkowski traveled by train

from Louisville, Kentucky, to Fort Dix, New Jersey, and left the next day for New York and embarkation.

Mary Brady Zurney, part of the 56th Evacuation Unit, traveled via troop train from Fort Sam Houston, Texas, to Camp Shanks, New York. "Other than being crowded and not being able to get off the train at stops, we had a fairly nice trip and saw some beautiful country," she said. "Our train arrived at Camp Shanks at 11:30 P.M. to one of the coldest places I had ever seen. The camp was being constructed while we were there and the heating system refused to heat and the plumbing, well it just didn't work. There, for the first time, I slept between two army blankets and strangely enough, I didn't mind."[1] The 56th was at Camp Shanks almost a month before boarding the *Mariposa*.

Juanita Hamilton was sent first to Fort Belvoir, Virginia, then to New York. "What a life!" she said. "In a hotel—on per diem, in uniform—waiting to go to some unknown exciting land, and men all around! It was enough to blow the mind of this ole country girl. We almost wore the subway out going to [the] Brooklyn Naval Yard for per diem and shots—then clubbing all night—Copacabana, the Stork Club—and a lot in between." But the partying ended when the women were sent to Fort Dix, New Jersey, where they weren't allowed to leave the base and were kept on a 24-hour alert. Although New Jersey was "the coldest place I have ever been," Hamilton said they spent their off-duty hours in the Officers' Club and a nearby restaurant. "With the help of about 200 officers, we survived that period."[2] Their next stop was back to New York for a physical, then to the Brooklyn Naval Yard to board ship.

Upon arrival at the city of embarkation, nurses were met by the chief nurse of the port city and given instructions and housing in barracks or hotels. It was at this time that they sent their civilian clothing back home and put everything except what they needed for the trip in their foot lockers. Family members were sent cards—complete with an APO address—to let them know that their nurse had arrived safely.

It was also at this time that official paperwork was processed; immunizations and physicals given; blood typed; identification tags issued; insurance and pay allotment papers signed; uniforms issued, altered, and marked; and field gear distributed (one bedding roll, two mattress covers, four blankets, and one tent with poles and tent pins). Other gear included a helmet, gas mask, and pistol belt with canteen. The canvas field bag held a few personal articles and mess gear (an aluminum dish with a cover that served as a divided dish; knife, fork, and spoon).

In her book *Nurses In Action*, Col. Julia O. Flikke quotes a nurse describing her preboarding preparations.

On our arrival at our Port of Embarkation there were pictures to be taken, fingerprints and our identification cards had to be handed in and replaced by another type. There were many trips to the Signal Corps, the Port Surgeon's Office, the Chief Nurse's office . . . to a warehouse for clothing, to someplace else for "helmets, steel, troops" . . . Finally, about twenty-four hours before we were due to sail we were told that we were "moving out to an Unknown Destination." Then we made no phone calls, we wrote no letters, we visited no friends. We did not want it on our consciences that we had let out any information of our impending departure.[3]

Using every inch of space possible, the women put what they could inside the bedding roll. Ruth Shadewaldt said, "[W]e had these bedrolls that were supposed to be flat. You'd put something in each end [and] then roll them up like a tight sausage."[4] Some of the items added were extra sanitary napkins and diapers to use when the pads ran out. (Although the women were issued one box of pads a month, they menstruated more frequently because of the rigorous life-style and cold weather.) Army Nurse Helen Pon once ended up with pink sanitary pads because she'd added a tube of toothpaste to her bedroll! Louine Connor was surprised at how meagerly she was able to live, though she said she did miss pretty undergarments.

Packing for a trip with Uncle Sam wasn't easy because the women didn't know where he was sending them and, therefore, didn't know what to take, and even advice in nursing journals was contradictory. In the December 1942 article, "On Going into the Army: What to Take Along and What to Expect in the Way of Equipment," the editors of the *American Journal of Nursing* recommended taking a foot locker and suitcase, both marked with name, rank, and serial number. Since only essential clothing and personal items should be taken, the editors published a list of what the government would provide and then suggested these additions: two pairs of dark blue slacks (one wool, one washable), two dark blue pullover sweaters, lots of hose (white, beige, wool, silk, cotton, rayon, nylon), lots of underwear (same materials as hose), warm underclothing, pajamas (instead of gowns), several girdles, one flannel robe, and one cotton housecoat. (Note: Everything issued by the government remained property of the government and had to be turned in when the nurse was sent to a different climate.)

The different types of material were recommended because there were countries whose abundant cricket and ant population enjoyed making meals of rayon, silk, and nylon, and since the nurse didn't know where she was going, it was best to take a variety.

Additional suggested personal items were a waterproof money belt, washcloths, bath towels, small clothesline and clothespins, soap, laundry soap, face cream for 60 days, several toothbrushes (some not nylon), cleansing tissues, as many sanitary pads as can be carried, sewing kit (rustproof pins and needles with thread and material to match stockings and uniforms), combs, brushes, and hairpins (also rustproof), clothesbrush and dry-cleaning fluid, bandage scissors, wristwatch, stationery, two fountain pens and ink (in a rubber container), pencils, a couple of flashlights with extra batteries, jackknife, small hammer, can opener, cigarette lighter with plenty of fluid and flints, and air-mail stamps.

By August 1943, the same publication carried an article that told nurses to "Travel Light if You're Going Overseas." This time they reminded the women that most medical units had their own PX that carried paper, pens, cigarettes, sanitary supplies, and toilet items. They did recommend, however, that the women bring some hard-to-find items such as cleansing tissues, stockings, and plenty of warm clothing. And though soap was plentiful in some areas, it was rare in Africa and could be traded for almost anything, so some women took a two-year's supply (180 bars).

But some of the nurses who listened to the "travel light" advice regretted it. In the March 1944 issue of the same journal, Army Nurse Bessie Lawrence told nurses to take items that she and fellow nurses had found that they missed: a camera, radio, extra watch and extra pen, long underwear, a sleeping bag, and "unless your commanding officer forbids it," a formal for those occasions "when you will want to be out of uniform for a little while."[5]

When Alice Lofgren finally got her orders to report to Norfolk, Virginia, she said the days became "full of shopping for items on a list of things we were required to have on the ship with us, including a pair of navy slacks, extra stockings and personal supplies to last for months at sea. Along with our regular ward duties, we managed to pack, making sure our travel orders didn't get misplaced, giving away things we couldn't take with us, and saying good-by to friends."[6]

But when she was told to buy a trunk, she hadn't been told what type. "So, being very naive and not having any better sense, I went into San Francisco and bought a big wardrobe trunk. When I arrived at the ship, they said we couldn't store our things in a trunk like that but that they'd provide sea chests, which they did."[7] Lofgren sent the trunk to her sister, who didn't want it. To this day, she doesn't know what happened to it.

Finally, after all the traveling from one place to another, shopping, packing, and processing, it was time to board.

Quietly, outside their quarters, they line up in passenger list order, wearing strictly GI uniforms: helmets, olive drab blouses and skirts, khaki shirts and ties, russet gloves, bags, and shoes. Precious gas masks are tucked under left arms; bulging field bags, overcoats folded over them, are slung from carrying straps. Securely hooked to web belts encircling their waists are scrupulously clean canteens filled with fresh water (not to be used until ordered) and first aid pouches containing unopened first aid packets (for personal use only in an emergency).[8]

Red Cross workers handed the women goodie bags and the Gideon Society gave them small copies of the New Testament with hymns in the front and the Florence Nightingale pledge in the back.

Mary Brady Zurney said, "The nurses and officers went up one gangplank while the enlisted men went up another. After carrying a full pack on my back for one afternoon . . . I only wanted to hit my sack."[9]

Juanita Hamilton was a little apprehensive.

My first panic hit me when I started up the gang plank. It looked like a huge monster to me—hundreds of feet high and thousands of feet long, and the gang plank almost straight up. I said to myself, "What have I done now?" But there was no where to run. There were no bands playing, and no porters to carry my luggage. A couple of sailors laughingly watched me lug my barracks bag up the gangplank and pointed in the general direction of midships when I asked for the nurses' quarters. That was a good example of the saying: "The Army does the work, the Navy gets the pay and the Marines get the glory."[10]

Eugenie Rutkowski, however, had a different experience.

There we were greeted by a military band blasting away marching music. Providing the music was very wise. The music and the rhythm supplied the necessary edge we needed to carry our heavy bags up an incline into the ship. During all this activity the Red Cross ladies hand-fed us bites of donuts and sips of coffee. At departure, watching the Statue of Liberty was a tear-jerker. I remembered my mother and dad telling me of their reaction to seeing the Statue of Liberty on arrival to the U.S. in 1907. I stayed on deck until the only thing in sight was water.[11]

Ruth Claff was "thrilled speechless" when she first saw her ship. "We filed from one boat to the other, getting the usual Red Cross doughnuts and coffee in transit. The band and the spectators, the high excitement as we crossed the gangplank! I had heard stories about gangplank fever," she said, "how could anyone get scared at the last minute? It's the thrill of a lifetime!"[12]

NOTES

1. Mary Brady Zurney, "Jeannie of the Medicine Show," Unpublished essay, no date, p. 1.
2. Juanita Hamilton Webster, Unpublished memoirs, no date, p. 6.
3. Quoted in Col. Julia O. Flikke, *Nurses in Action* (New York: Lippincott, 1943), p. 149.
4. Lt. Col. Ruth Frances Shadewaldt, ANC (Ret.) Taped Interview with sister, July 1992.
5. 2nd Lt. Bessie Lawrence, ANC, "What to Take Overseas," *American Journal of Nursing*, March 1944, p. 289.
6. Alice Lofgren Andrus, "Navy Experiences," Unpublished essay, November 1993, p. 4.
7. Alice Lofgren Andrus, Interview with author, November 20, 1993.
8. Capt. Marion E. Thuma, R.N., "Task Forces, ANC," *American Journal of Nursing*, January 1944, p. 18.
9. Zurney, "Jeannie of the Medicine Show," p. 1.
10. Juanita Hamilton Webster, Unpublished memoirs, no date, p. 7.
11. Eugenie Rutkowski Wilkinson, Letter to daughter, no date.
12. Ruth Claff, *Lady with the Flashlight*, Unpublished memoirs, 1947, p. 16.

Chapter 4

The Pacific Theater

Thus when Japan struck, the nurses who were stationed in the Pacific carried on their work to the last sterile dressing and their last ounce of strength. When supplies gave out they improvised; when plasma ran short they gave their own blood; when the bombs dropped they cut away the caked garments of the survivors, and from some unguessed sources of fortitude they conjured up a smile.

—Page Cooper
Navy Nurse

The war in the Pacific—and the United States' entry into World War II—started with the bombing of Pearl Harbor on December 7, 1941, and it was in those early-morning hours that Army and Navy nurses began exhibiting the calm determination and bravery that would get them through the dark days ahead.

And days looked dark indeed. Within hours of bombing Pearl Harbor, the Japanese attacked Guam and destroyed most of the aircraft at Clark Field in the Philippines. The next day the Japanese attacked the Navy yard at Cavite, near Manila, home of the U.S. Asiatic Fleet. On December 11, they took command of Guam. On Wake Island Marines began fighting the Japanese on December 8, actually turned them back on December 11, but lost the island on December 23. According to Lt. Col. Clayton R. Newell, "With the fall of the Philippines on 6 May, the Japanese seriously threatened to achieve their goal of dominating the Pacific basin."[1]

As the war continued, Americans became familiar with names like Guadalcanal, the Solomons, Tarawa, Kwajalein, Saipan, Tinian, and Guam. Small islands such as these took their toll on American lives—3,110 casualties on Tarawa, 16,500 casualties on Saipan, 7,800 casualties on Guam—lives that needed the medical expertise and concern of American nurses.

HAWAII

Nurses stationed at Pearl Harbor hospitals weren't expecting war on that sunny December morning, but when it came, they went to work setting up beds and preparing blood, drugs, and bandages. These were women such as Gertrude Arnest, chief nurse at Pearl Harbor Naval Hospital, who "resolutely adjusted her peaked white cap banded with the two gold stripes that mark her rank, walked calmly across the shell-furrowed lawn to the hospital . . . a hail of anti-aircraft shells was falling around her, shrapnel whistled close by. Having entered the hospital, she stayed there ten days with her nurses who worked till they dropped."[2]

Lenore Terrell Rickert was on rounds at the naval hospital when she heard the sound of airplanes flying overhead. "I'm ashamed to say the rising sun on its wings meant nothing to me at all. It could have been Chinese," she said. Incoming wounded soon arrived "strapped onto Jeeps, in the back of bread trucks, on small boats, in ambulances."[3]

Another nurse remembered "peacefully eating breakfast" in the dining room when an officer rushed in announcing the attack. "Of course," she said, "no one believed him." When she returned to her room, she turned on her radio to hear the announcement, then ran into the street. "Formation after formation of planes passed overhead at a high altitude; then we noticed the spurts of anti-aircraft fire and the sound of the bombs dropping."[4] The radio announcer repeated his previous message and followed it with orders for all service personnel to report to their posts, and for all doctors and nurses to report to the Army hospital.

Helen Entrikin, also at the naval hospital, began seeing patients around nine that morning—many of whom had been burned in flash fires on the ships or hit by shrapnel—and said that the only breaks taken by doctors and nurses were two-hour naps.

Another nurse at the naval hospital was Genevieve Van de Drink (known as "Van"). She said that they worked solidly for 24 hours then worked shifts of 4 hours on and 4 hours off "until help arrived" and that one of her worst nursing experiences was "accepting the destruction of so many, many young men." Her story continues:

From sun down to sun up with black out giving nursing care to critical patients by the light of a flashlight covered with blue cellophane.

The overwhelming smell of burned flesh and skin will never be forgotten. On one occasion as I was on my way to get more supplies I heard my name called out from a gurney. It was called out by a former hospital corpsman with internal injuries, and one arm and two legs missing. I have never forgotten the fear in his eyes as I held his good hand and tried to comfort him. He died within minutes, but not without prayers of peace.[5]

While Helen Entrikin was working at Pearl Harbor Naval Hospital, her twin sister, Sara, was nursing with the Army Air Corps at Hickam, where she saw, amid the smoke, "steel girders from the ships flying up in the air." The number of wounded soon overflowed the 50-bed hospital. "We got casualties, so many casualties, and they just kept coming."[6] Six months of medical supplies were used on that one day.

Mary Louise Laager Geisler was taking temperatures at Tripler General Hospital when the attack began. As some of the men were looking to the skies and saying, "What is the Navy doing in bombing practice on Sunday morning?," Geisler looked up, "and I saw those planes."[7] When her chief nurse told her to prepare for casualties, she said, "I didn't even know what a casualty was."[8] Later, she said, "As far as I could see there were litters with patients dying, some already dead, and it was up to me to bring in as many as we could." And then there was the 17-year-old sailor who asked her to remove his graduation ring and send it to his parents. That moment, said Geisler, was "the only time that day I cried."[9]

Dorothy Young, an operating room nurse at Tripler, spoke of the futility. "We gave them morphine. Put the mark on their foreheads M for morphine. They were coming to us in trucks—not ambulances. Trucks. The trucks kept backing up and delivering them. Bodies, most of them. Bodies."[10]

Heroism became the norm that day in Hawaii, and stories of exceptional acts of bravery abound. One nurse, Rosalie Swenson, was a patient, yet she "reported in uniform and worked constantly in the ward for battle casualties until she was ordered back to bed."[11] Countless numbers of men left their sick beds to join the fight—one man cut off his own cast. A doctor recovering from an appendectomy reported for duty.

Yet life was so very different on December 6. "Van" was attending a formal dance "on the highly decorated festive top deck"[12] of the *Arizona*. Mary Geisler was "dancing at the Royal Hawaiian Hotel. . . . I got back to the nurses' quarters about four a.m. and went on duty at seven."[13]

But the next morning brought war, and Page Cooper poignantly described the dramatic change to America's life-style in her book *Navy Nurse*: "there was no return to the remote and fragrant days before the raid . . . [the nurses] folded away their pretty summer dresses . . . and lived in the only uniforms they had, the white ones they wore on duty on the wards. In these they dined in Honolulu and danced at the army and navy officers' clubs with gas masks over their shoulders and helmets on their arms."[14]

GUAM

Just hours after they attacked Pearl Harbor, the Japanese attacked Guam, Midway, Wake, Manila, and Singapore. Most of these areas were defenseless because one-quarter of the U.S. Pacific Fleet had been sent to the Atlantic. Though the Allies tried to stop the Japanese at the Malay Barrier, they were unsuccessful. The fall of Singapore and the bombing of Darwin, Australia, broke this Barrier and left Australia and New Zealand "virtually undefended."[15]

Even as Guam was being attacked, Chief Nurse Marion Olds and four other Navy nurses—Lorraine Christiansen, Virginia Fogarty, Leona Jackson, and Doris Yetter—remained calm and went about their duties. There wasn't time to huddle in a ditch, said one, even when the hospital was being machine-gunned. On the third day they watched their country's flag come down the flagpole for the last time and knew they were prisoners.

For a month the nurses were allowed to remain in their quarters and continue their duties as if being a prisoner were an everyday occurrence. But Japanese officers ate their food and Japanese soldiers "wandered at will through the hospital and nurses quarters, picking up whatever struck their fancy: odds and ends, scissors, pictures and cigarettes."

In early January, the nurses were transported to a prison camp in Shoku, Japan, where inmates included 396 male prisoners and one mother and child. Housed in an old army barracks, the nurses slept on straw mats on the floor and endured the "freezing cold with nothing but an inadequate stove for heating." Their daily food ration was a small loaf of bread, rice, and "rather unpalatable soup. Once a week there was a hunk of meat in the soup and sometimes as a rare treat there was fish."[16] To keep up their spirits the women talked, played bridge, and attended language classes given by another inmate.

Life improved when the women were taken to Kobe and housed in an old hotel, although they hated being separated from their patients and corpsmen. They now had hot water several hours a day, cold water in their rooms, real beds, better food, a supply of books, and the company of American missionaries, an American teacher, and some businessmen. The nurses even enjoyed tea parties in spite of the fact that the amount of tea needed for one good cup had to be shared among 20 to 30 people. News of their internment reached the United States via a Japanese broadcast that said the women were being sent to Kobe for "light confinement."[17]

Although the Japanese tried to persuade the women that there was no longer a U.S. military, the women didn't believe them and weren't discouraged, especially when they saw an American plane heading toward Tokyo. "The sight of that plane," said Olds, "made us want to get out more than ever, to get back to our own Navy where we could do some good."

Since the Japanese had no women in their military, they didn't know what to do with the Navy nurses, so in June 1942, they traded them. When asked about her plans, Olds said she wanted to "go to a hairdresser!" But when asked about her long-range plans, she said she was "going right back to duty. We are urgently needed."[18]

THE PHILIPPINES

Although the Japanese began landing small forces on southeastern and northern Luzon on December 8, 1941, they didn't land their major forces until December 22. Maj. Gen. Jonathan M. Wainwright was put in charge of holding back the Japanese in the north while Brig. Gen. George M. Parker, Jr., in charge of the southern Luzon forces, moved his men to the Bataan Peninsula. Gen. Douglas MacArthur moved his forces to the island of Corregidor (known as "The Rock") and declared Manila an open city. It was in Japanese hands by January 2. Though MacArthur was becoming a legend back in the States, he was known as "Dugout Doug"[19] to the starving troops on Bataan who knew that their leader had visited the Bataan front only once and seemed to prefer the safety of Corregidor where they knew he was "eating well."[20] His departure to Australia, even though at the command of President Roosevelt, "did little to endear him to his men,"[21] who, by that time, had heard a radio broadcast in which Roosevelt made it clear that those on Bataan would not be receiving any reinforcements. It was at about that time that they began calling themselves the "Battling Bastards of Bataan" and even composed a poem:

> We're the battling bastards of Bataan,
> No momma, no poppa, no Uncle Sam,
> No pills, no planes, no artillery pieces.
> And nobody gives a damn.[22]

They also put these words to the tune of "Camptown Races":

> Dig those foxholes deeper dug,
> Dig down, dig down,
> Dig those foxholes deeper dug,
> Dig them all the way.
> Bombs going to fall all night;
> Bombs going to fall all day;
> Dig those foxholes deeper dug,
> The Nips are on their way.

Wainwright was put in charge of the U.S. forces in the Philippines and sent to Corregidor to take over MacArthur's command. Maj. Gen. Edward King, Jr., took charge of the 76,000 troops in Bataan.

At the time of the U.S. entry into war, nurses were stationed in many places on the island: Sternberg General Hospital in Manila, the Station Hospital at Stotsenberg near Clark Field, the Station Hospital at Fort McKinley in the south of Manila, and the Station Hospital at Fort Mills on Corregidor. By the end of December, all nurses were sent to Bataan where they opened two hospitals: General Hospital No. 1 and General Hospital No. 2.

Part of Hospital No. 1, in Limay, was an old barracks where most of the wards were nothing more than beds under bamboo trees. Hospital No. 2 was in an area of cleared jungle near Mariveles Mountain. Hospital beds were made from bamboo poles and palm fronds and were three decks high and six beds across.

Patients could be brought in only at night because of constant bombing and artillery fire during the day. Water could be boiled only during the day because the fire showed up too well at night. Nurses used flashlights covered with blue paper on their nightly rounds.

Because MacArthur's prewar plans had been to defend the entire chain of the Philippines, most of the food, ammunition, weapons, and medical supplies had been stored in various locations throughout the islands. The unexpected retreat to Bataan and Corregidor meant leaving these items behind, and soon there wasn't enough food on Bataan to feed the American and Filipino troops and Filipino civilians for even a month.

Medical supplies were also dangerously low. One surgical ward with 292 patients had only 6 medicine glasses, 15 thermometers, and a single teaspoon. Oddly enough, some of the shortages produced good results. When the sulfa drugs used to combat infection ran out, wounds were allowed to heal by exposing them to fresh air and sunshine, and according to Col. Julia Flikke in her book *Nurses in Action*, "Fatalities from gas gangrene became a rarity and infections grew fewer."[23] Unfortunately, the shortage of mosquito nets exposed many to the nighttime malaria-carrying mosquitoes (daytime mosquitoes carried dengue fever).

Navy Nurse Ann Bernatitus said that they found hospital gowns wrapped in newspapers dated 1917, and "abominable"[24] medical equipment. They had to sterilize instruments in kerosene-operated pressure cookers or in Lysol-filled foot tubs. "How quickly you needed the instrument determined how purely things were sterilized,"[25] she said.

She worked in the bamboo hospital at Limay until the end of January, when most personnel were evacuated farther south to the Little Baguio hospital. The doctors and nurses were about to leave when a truckload of wounded arrived. "With the stretchers set on a couple of wooden sawhorses, by the light of a lantern hung on a bamboo pole, the surgeons went to work, using what instruments they could find in the one surgical kit among them." A second attempt to leave was interrupted by shouts from stretcher bearers that they had a man who needed an amputation. Again the doctors and nurses stopped to operate.

After surgery the patients went to No. 2, five miles farther into the jungle on roads that were "dusty, the mosquitoes attacked in squadrons; [and] there were very few drugs with which to check malaria and dysentery."[26] For three months, Bernatitus moved from one improvised hospital to another, worked almost 24-hour-long days (in one 8-hour shift she saw 285 patients), and treated both American servicemen and Japanese prisoners. One bombing episode demolished the hospital. Another blasted the men out of their beds and into trees.

Bernatitus told of men who might have been saved had there been enough supplies and medicine. And she told tales of courage—men who knew that they were signing their death warrants by begging to be removed from an operating table so "one of those fellows that has a fighting chance" might be treated. She also recalls the false sense of security everyone felt by putting "huge red crosses 50 feet in size" around the hospital compound. "The Japs could not have missed the crosses," said Bernatitus. "They used red crosses, symbols of mercy, as targets, and our boys lay there in the sun and waited for death from the sky."[27] Author Page Cooper said that the Japanese apologized for hitting the hospital, yet they did it again nine days later and killed 70 patients.

Nurses barely missed being killed in some of the attacks and, like their patients, were exhausted and sick from disease and lack of food and sleep. Many times one nurse would be in charge of 250 patients, and though they were assisted by Filipino nurses and corpsmen, there were never enough of them to care for the 2,000 patients at Hospital No. 1 and the 7,000 at Hospital No. 2. By the time she left Bataan, Bernatitus "was becoming so thin that her eyes seemed twice their size, and her slacks had a deep pleat at the waist, but everyone was punching a new hole in his belt."[28]

In her autobiography *Warrior in White*, Army Nurse Lucy Wilson described the worsening conditions.

Not only was there a shortage of food, clothing, and mosquito netting, but most troops got no cigarettes or coffee. They were exhausted and many needed shoes, raincoats, blankets, and shelter halves; uniforms that were ragged and threadbare were little protection against the cold nights, thorny jungle, and insects. So they drank unboiled water, ate roots, lizards, snakes, snails, and any other thing they could find; and due to unknown things being poisonous, some died with food poisoning before reaching hospitals.

And medicine was running out. "I'll never forget the awful suffering those with cerebral malaria went through, and the frothing at the mouth before they died, for lack of quinine," said Wilson. Other maladies included hookworm, dengue fever, scurvy, beriberi, amebic dysentery, common diarrhea, dysentery, and injuries. Jungle conditions, fatigue, stress from constant air and artillery bombardment, and malnutrition were additional problems.

And then came the phosphorus bombs. The swelling and smell of the resulting wounds were terrible, said Wilson. All the women could do was cut away the dead or contaminated tissue, cut gashes in the wound, and let the air heal it. If this treatment didn't cure the gangrene, "the only alternative was amputation."

Then there was the awful sight of "feeding men with their jaw or half their face missing and just a tongue sticking out—it was so difficult for them to swallow."[29] The nurses couldn't feed the men intravenously because they had neither the necessary equipment nor a way to filter the water.

As the Americans blew up their ammunition dump, and with "shells whistling over their heads,"[30] the nurses made their way to Corregidor—followed by a Japanese bomber. According to Helen Summers, ANC, "The ship pulled away and began zigzagging and that bomber kept circling us in the most malicious fashion."[31]

Although Corregidor provided more protection with its maze of concrete-reinforced underground tunnels beneath several hundred feet of rock, the

Americans still endured constant gunfire and hunger—and a constant bombing and shelling that interfered with the power plant and ventilation systems. In her article for *The Army Nurse*, Alice R. Clarke wrote,

Everything was done which possibly could be done to improve the sanitation but the stench of human bodies, of septic wounds, of gas gangrene, was overwhelming. In the hospital laterals there were blowers which helped a little to purify the air, but during the bombings, dust, dirt, and rocks were blown in through them. The food was almost gone; a very small stock being hoarded to make it last for how long no one knew. The medical supplies were dwindling rapidly; the death rate was increasing alarmingly.[32]

Bombing continued and soon POW arm bands were issued. Then came word that some nurses were to be evacuated. According to Helen Summers, "When we left Bataan the doctors knowing they would be prisoners simply shook hands with us—some of them kissed us—and walked away. There was no ceremony about our departure from Corregidor. Our goodbyes were simple but hard; words didn't count. My name was called as one to go out—that of my best friend wasn't. . . . We could only say to each other 'Till we meet again'."[33]

Ann Bernatitus recalled her departure. "It was an eerie, moonless night and sounds of shelling from the attacking Japanese were closing in. Silently we crept into small boats and after maneuvering them beyond the touchy mine fields, we saw it—the submarine USS *Spearfish*, our means to freedom, cast a low, dark, yet inviting shadow upon the water."[34]

Bernatitus, Wilson, and Summers were among the nurses who left the island that night, May 3, 1942, on the *Spearfish*. At first, the sailors didn't realize that their guests were female because the women wore pants and helmets, but Summers said that when they did, "we heard a whistle and then a startled voice, 'Oh, boy—women!'" She added, "We weren't too tired to laugh."[35] The sailors soon remembered, however, that women were supposed to be bad luck on a submarine—and here were 13 women! But the trip was uneventful, and the women even received the proper initiation upon crossing the equator.

Other nurses attempted escape on two PBY flying boats on April 29, 1942. Both planes landed at Lake Lanao, Mindanao, for gas but the next morning only one was able to leave; the other failed to gain altitude and crashed into a coral reef. Expecting another plane to come after them, the passengers (including 10 nurses) stayed by the Del Monte airfield at Danzalan, and moved inland only when Japanese landed nearby. This continued for a couple of weeks until the Americans saw that all airstrips were demolished and there was no hope of rescue. They reported to the Philippine General Force Hospital where they helped care for patients until May 10, when Mindanao surrendered.

Prisoners of War—Army Nurses

Although constantly watched by their captors, the 10 nurses were still allowed to treat their patients until they were moved, on July 2, to Santa

Catalina in Manila. With all they had gone through, this was the worst moment for the nurses: "the sight of seeing our beaten soldiers taken away was almost unendurable for these nurses who had gone through so much already,"[36] wrote Alice Clarke.

On August 17, the women were taken to Davao Prisoner of War Camp. Part of the trip was on board a Japanese freighter where the nurses lived in the hold with no sanitary facilities. Some suffered from recurring malaria, some were suffering from fatigue, and one was still wearing bandages put on in Bataan. The one bright spot on the trip was when the freighter stopped in Zamboanga and the nurses were allowed to bathe in a freshwater stream.

Conditions were better in Davao. The nurses enjoyed fresh fruit again and were able to borrow money for extra food from the Filipinos and wealthy internees. All 10 of them slept in a small room on the floor without blankets. After one week they were put on another ship and taken to the harbor at Manila where they were supposed to meet still another ship and be repatriated.

But no ship came.

Americans remaining on Corregidor became prisoners of the Japanese on May 6. To some, surrender brought "great relief that the month of continual bombing was over," and most, like Hattie Brantley, were tired of eating 1918 cornmeal and hoped that now they might get some real food. They soon realized, however, that that wasn't going to happen and gratefully took what was rationed by the Japanese: rice, canned meat, salmon, and tomatoes. (They could have all the canned tomatoes they wanted because the Japanese didn't like them.) They did get bread made daily by their own baker, and some of the mess staff made secret trips back to the tunnel for hidden items like corned beef hash.

The nurses were "interrogated . . . in minute detail about their personal histories,"[37] but they weren't mistreated. Brantley said it may have been because they "looked old and bedraggled by now!"[38]

Brantley and the others, joined on August 24 by the nurses who had tried to escape by PBY, now began their new lives in Manila at the Santo Tomas Prison Camp. There they lived in a dormitory where 400 women shared four showers and four toilets. There were two bathtubs—one for children and one for the women to use to wash their hair. According to Clarke, "The sanitary facilities, which were adequate in the beginning, soon became insufficient, especially when the water supply did not work fifty percent of the time."

Each woman was allowed a space 40 inches by 6 feet, including the aisles. (Brantley said that if a woman told a guard she wanted privacy, she was told to close her eyes!) Their beds—bamboo cots with grass mats and beach towels—came with complimentary bedbugs until the women discovered that throwing out the mats and rinsing the bamboo cots with boiling water kept them vermin-free.

As soon as they arrived, the nurses established a hospital in the school's educational building and had, by war's end, established three more. Under Japanese supervision, a camp-chosen committee ran a central kitchen and a

Holy Ghost Home for children and, at first, members of the committee were allowed to purchase food from local Filipino vendors who were allowed inside the camp. Money for purchases was from a central fund to which many interness contributed.

All prisoners were allowed two hours of exercise in the yard after lunch and dinner and many used the opportunity to grow gardens. Everyone was expected to work at least two hours a day. The usual routine was for the men to do the cleaning while the women prepared the food.

Although they weren't molested, the nurses "hated the ceremony they were put through . . . the polite bowing which had to be done whenever a Jap soldier appeared, whether he be a private or a general."[39] And until a governing committee was formed for protection, the Japanese entered the women's quarters at night for roll call, "approaching them with bayonets and peering into their faces."[40] There were also tales of being slapped for slight offenses and reports of Red Cross relief supplies being stolen and ruined by their Japanese captors.

They were allowed to send one postcard a month and an occasional cablegram, but they rarely received any mail. Most of what they did get didn't arrive until March 1944. Brantley said that she received only two Red Cross packages in three years and learned of her father's death in a card received several months after he died.

At first the Japanese prison commander, Commandant Koruda, was polite to the prisoners and gave them reasonably good treatment because "when victorious, we can afford to be magnanimous." But his attitude and treatment changed when the Allies began winning the war in 1944, and he declared "slow hunger"[41] on the prisoners. Brantley said that rations were cut every time the American forces were successful in battle.

As food rations declined to the equivalent of one-half cup of rice per person per day, the Japanese quit allowing vendors to enter the camp, and soon the supply of stored food was exhausted. By the last six months of captivity, people were dying from malnutrition and starvation.

When rescue became imminent, the Japanese discontinued all forms of social life, including classes. They confiscated all monies and photographed internees with numbers on their chests. With the first Allied air raids, they began storing arms, ammunition, and gasoline next to the hospital walls.

Prisoners of War—Navy Nurses

Eleven Navy nurses were also prisoners of war in the Philippines.

Canaçao Naval Hospital—"right in the target zone"—filled with patients after an hour-long raid on December 10, 1941, during which the Navy Yard was wiped out. "It was really a shocking scene," said Dorothy Still. With no power and too many patients, triage was impossible, but the nurses did what they could to get the most severely wounded to surgery.

When both Canaçao and Sternberg (in Manila) were full, joint Army-Navy medical units were set up throughout Manila. By the time the Japanese entered Manila in January, the nurses were at another hospital, Santa Scholastica, which the enemy ignored unless they needed hospital supplies. "They also began to slap around and beat up the men," said Still. "But they ignored us—the nurses."[42]

Soon, all Allied civilians and nurses were sent to Santo Tomas, but when conditions became too crowded in May 1943, the Navy nurses were sent to Los Banos. Once the agricultural college of the University of the Philippines, the compound was now a prison camp that housed 800 American and British men, both military and civilian. Upon arrival the nurses were forced to pose for propaganda pictures on the lawn holding glasses of water and talking to other internees, thus appearing to have a tea party.

As the Japanese took over more and more space in the camp for their own wounded, the American nurses were moved to barracks built of bamboo matting walls with thatched roofs and enclosed by a double barbed-wire fence, each built to house up to 96 people. At first the women were allowed to build privacy walls but that was stopped. While it lasted, they had a good plumbing system: a wooden trough connecting two huts that was flushed every 15 minutes.

People did what they could to personalize their huts. Each front lawn contained a cook shack with a charcoal stove, a table, and homemade chairs made out of woven ropes or bamboo. According to Cooper's *Navy Nurse:*

Here in a charcoal stove made of clay they re-cooked their prison food, cockroaches and all, and added what little tidbits they had managed to acquire. Here they sat in the evening, entertained their friends and smoked their cigarettes of corn silks, papaya leaves, dried mango, rolled in whatever paper they could find. A host was magnificent indeed if his cigarettes were rolled in toilet paper.

American ingenuity really saved the day when everything broke, wore out, or disappeared. Most of hospital equipment and all of the cooking utensils were made by pounding out the creases in corrugated tin. When soap ran out, more was made out of wood ashes and coconut oil. Adhesive tape was made from the sap of rubber trees boiled down to hard white chunks and softened with gasoline, but "even good adhesive tape didn't stick well on damp skins."[43] Worn-out sheets and pillowcases were used for bandages and stramonium leaves were dried and made into cigarettes for patients with asthma.

Prisoners were fed two meals a day of vegetable soup, corn and rice, tea, and occasionally fruit. In early 1943, food was still ample because internees were still able to supplement the rations with items purchased with their own money from local vendors. But things began to change later in the year when the Japanese civilian administrators were replaced by Japanese military personnel. The two daily servings of rice turned into a watery, pasty lugao, and eventually the total diet consisted of 250 to 300 grams of unhusked rice (polai) that was dried and rolled out between rocks. One report said that there were about two deaths a day, most due to starvation. Laura Cobb said, "We got so we didn't especially mind the weevils, but the cockroaches and worms made eating tough going much of the time."[44]

But freedom was getting closer. According to Dorothy Still, a special rescue operation was put into place in early 1945 after MacArthur learned that the Japanese were going to execute the inmates at Los Banos.

AUSTRALIA AND NEW ZEALAND

The first nurses in the Southwest Pacific arrived in Australia in April 1942, and treated casualties from the Middle East campaign. When one of them saw her first Australian soldiers, she realized that, "we had come to the War and IT had come home to us. . . . War is now to us an Awful Actuality and not something we hear about on the radio. Our friends are being killed—these gay young lads we danced with last week; these fine young men who told us their plans for the future. . . . We don't discuss their deaths; we pat each other on the shoulder and say, "Well, he's had it'."[45]

Most of the nurses, such as Army Nurse Esther Paine, loved their new assignment. "Australia is really beautiful with flowers growing all year round; the climate is ideal—cold mornings and nights and warm during the day. I am feeling fine and would not want to trade places with any nurse back in the States."[46]

Juanita Hamilton, ANC, said that Southport, Australia, was:

a beautiful resort community with miles of white sandy beaches and the blue Pacific Ocean lapping softly at its shores. Lots of beach houses, a hotel and some pubs, several small restaurants and a movie house with double features every time it opened. I saw more movies than I ever had seen before or since. We had been given another school to make a hospital of, so we had good living quarters again, a nice tennis court, and best of all, indoor plumbing. We were back in civilization.[47]

The Red Cross turned several homes and buildings into clubs and rest homes so the nurses had somewhere to relax and enjoy themselves. The three sites in Australia were in Townsville, Brisbane, and Sydney; the site in New Zealand was in Auckland. Little things formerly taken for granted, such as linen napkins and fresh orange juice, were sometimes the details that made these places special to these women so far from home.

The nurses received a lot of attention everywhere they went and were showered with invitations to dinners and teas and often given bottles of wine by restaurant patrons. Army Nurse Ann Deeds said, "It was nothing to be stopped on the street and told, 'I've been wanting to talk to an American nurse for a long time,' or, 'Good morning, sister, how do you like Australia?'" The nurses were invited to speak at public assemblies ("anything about America"),[48] be judges of baby pageants, and participate in parades.

And the nurses tried to pay back the kindness whenever they could. Army Nurse Ruth Kinzeler told how they raised money for a kindergarten by dressing as gypsies and telling fortunes, holding raffles, and collecting donations for food items. For Christmas they made small felt animals, and bought paper hats, toy balloons, and ice cream. The nurses felt that they had "contributed in a small way to the happiness of the community in which we have lived and worked for these many months."[49]

The nurses also appreciated the kindness shown them in Auckland, New Zealand, where private families opened their homes to them. To repay such hospitality, the nurses pooled the amount they would have spent on rent and presented it to the mayoress for charitable purposes.

But with all the hospitality, the women missed American coffee. As one nurse said, "Australians, like the English, make good tea, but they don't seem to be interested in coffee. It is almost impossible to buy on the market here."[50]

NEW CALEDONIA

Because of its mild and malaria-free climate, New Caledonia was home to seven station and two general hospitals where the nurses treated patients from nearby island chains.

In an article she wrote for the *American Journal of Nursing,* Dorothy Hufcut described the life-style. The women "lived four in a tent, washed themselves and their clothes in a nearby stream, and lined up with their mess kits before open fires. They used candles for light, [and] slept under mosquito nets." Their unit moved three times, and the women lived in constant rain from April through June. One woman told Hufcut that she sometimes "wondered if the tent could possibly take any more water without springing a leak."[51] The women wore pants, high rubber boots, raincoats, and pith helmets.

One nurse wrote with pride of the tents or native huts that made up their hospital. "What fun and work we had organizing the place, and don't think that we aren't proud of it now." Of her work, she said she felt like Florence Nightingale making nightly rounds with her flashlight. "At home, I would never think of being out alone in the dark but now, making rounds from one ward to the other, seems quite natural."[52] But "while the work was arduous and living conditions difficult, all agreed that it was well worth their efforts. The patients were truly grateful for all that was done for them and delighted to have American nurses caring for them."[53]

Recreation included watching movies, eating steak dinners, collecting seashells, visiting an old Catholic mission, walking, mountain climbing, horseback riding, meeting the locals, and making fudge for the patients. Watching movies was fun, said one nurse, because, "The stage setting is perfect. The screen is placed against a background of coconut trees and overhead shine the stars and the Southern Cross."[54]

NEW GUINEA

When General MacArthur put troops in the major port of Port Moresby in April 1942, New Guinea became the center of the Pacific War and remained such until the end of 1944. What was called the Papua Campaign began when the Japanese landed on the northeast coast of New Guinea on July 22, 1942, and attempted to reach Port Moresby by land. They came within 30 miles before they were stopped. Although the Papua Campaign officially ended on January 23, 1943, there were other Allied and Japanese confrontations around New Guinea until May 1945, and there were some Japanese forces that did not surrender until September 13, 1945. According to author Charles R. Anderson in his government pamphlet *Papua*, the Allies suffered high casualties (8,546) because the campaign was the Army's first in a world-war tropical theater and, therefore, a learning experience for its leaders.

The first nurses in New Guinea landed in Port Moresby in October 1942. One of them, Juanita Hamilton, said, "There were many cheers and stares as we rode the 17 miles in open trucks to our field hospital," then "[we] received a huge welcome from our outfit."[55] They set up a tent hospital and saw it filled to capacity in less than a week.

But the weather left a lot to be desired. Army Nurse Ruth Claff said it rained so much that they "dug a ditch down the middle of our home to carry off the surplus water."[56] Abbie Ratledge said that the dampness made mold grow on "nearly everything we owned." Their envelopes became self-sealing and had to be torn open to be used and then glued back together. "We soon learned to bury them between newspapers six inches under the sand. The papers kept them clean, and the moisture in the ground kept the envelopes unglued,"[57] said Ratledge.

The rain also brought the dreaded malaria for which personnel were to take the preventive Atabrine tablets. Too often, however, the pills caused their own problems. Golda Johnson's skin turned yellow. Edith Vowell's hair turned an odd shade of yellow and her skin turned light green. When Juanita Hamilton took the pills, her stomach cramped and her ears rang, so she decided she'd take her chances with malaria. The result? "I was never sick a day in New Guinea."[58]

The women's arrival brought the domestic touches of irons and ironing boards, mirrors, and even a beauty parlor. The women even named their tents—Juanita Hamilton's was "The Coconut Grove"; Ruth Claff's was "Westinghouse"—and decorated them with homemade quilts, planted palms, and starfish. They had vegetable gardens for fresh produce and a nearby river for swimming.

According to a 1942 article in the *New Orleans Times-Picayune*, the nurses "live in tents under a blazing tropical sun. Sometimes they have to run for the trenches when Jap bombers come over. There is little in the way of recreation. But they are happy."[59] And though one nurse said she missed soft drinks and ice cream, another, Irene Gabryolek, said, "Everyone of us is content because we're doing the job we signed up to do."[60]

Happy and content they may have been, but living in the islands took extreme dedication and a strong survival instinct—and enormous doses of creativity and humor. To survive the horrific temperatures, Army Nurse Connie Sansone said that they sometimes "wore" only wet towels at night. With a helmet full of water nearby, the minute the towel dried, "you'd wake up and dip it again in the helmet . . . so that you could go back and sleep another 30 minutes. It was very bad."[61]

Ruth Claff said that they wore only bra and panties when inside the tent, and that male visitors were supposed to yell, "Man in the area," when approaching. Not surprisingly, the warning was usually yelled too late. "The men saw to that!"[62] said Claff.

Besides the heat, humidity, and mosquitoes, there were numerous other insects and vermin. A rat ran over Connie Sansone's feet as she sat writing a letter. Another time she heard something running up and down on top of her mosquito net and soon realized that there were rats "all over the place. . . . I jumped out of bed and said, 'What the hell's going on?' real loud so everybody would have to wake up." Then she saw that "someone had eaten cheese in a can and had left the can on top of my mosquito net."[63]

Ruth Shadewaldt, ANC, shared a shower with chameleons. "We had one that was pea green and he used to live on the rope of our shower. You'd be taking a shower and see him running around up there and hope he stayed up there."[64]

Ruth Claff shared her Hollandia quarters with ants ("in well organized armies"), locusts, centipedes, spiders, and butterflies ("as large as crows"). Also on the island was a bat with a three-foot wingspan and "lizards in abundance, in profusion in our tents, in our mosquito bars—almost, and occasionally literally, in our hair."[65]

When Edith Vowell dove into a trench to escape a Japanese attack, she found herself face to face with a giant, hairy-legged spider. After making a quick escape, Vowell said, "That spider looked a lot bigger and more deadly than any Japanese airplane."[66] From then on, she carried a shovel during air raids.

As for the food, Ruth Shadewaldt said that the "potatoes were dehydrated, the carrots were dehydrated, the beets were dehydrated, everything was dehydrated. We got meat from Australia and because of the lack of refrigeration, it was salted and our cooks didn't know enough to soak it first to get the salt out of it, so it was so salty that you could hardly eat the stuff. . . . Once in a while we'd get some fresh meat." Candy bars melted and the flour contained boll weevils. Even the water was awful. "In the hospital in each hallway there was a Lister bag full of that awful water with chlorine in it. It killed whatever . . . but that water tasted just awful, you could hardly drink the stuff, but you had to have something to drink. And they made lemonade out of this powdered stuff. We called it battery acid."[67]

Abbie Ratledge said that their hospital's hot cakes "were the biggest garbage pail filler. They must have cooked them at five in the morning. By the time they cooked thousands of them, and carted them about the wards in the little food carts, some wards a good two blocks from the mess hall, the poor patients took one look at them and turned their heads. Some brave soldiers got away with a few of them, but it was an effort."[68]

Ruth Claff said that they received cigarettes once a month ("usually moldy") but no fresh food, cold drinks, ice cream, or butter ("well, there was a canned substitute that was full of paraffin so that it wouldn't melt"). Meals "were atrocious. The smell of the greasy canned mutton and pork that was served shredded and horrible for almost every meal but breakfast (which was usually flour and water pancakes with a so-called syrup made of sweetened water) turned most of us away from the mess hall when we were within fifty yards of it, in that muggy heat. We worked it this way. One of us would brave the smell, go to the mess hall and make several sandwiches of fairly moldy bread and peanut butter . . . and jam . . . I've heard that K rations were better balanced."

Despite the food, nurses always found ways to enjoy themselves—sometimes just by savoring the natural beauty of the islands. Ruth Claff wrote fondly of one hospital's location. "The hospital and nurses area were located in a dreamy spot in a valley, with a clear, lovely running brook, with rapids and pools and a most delicious gurgle! It was about fifteen feet wide, full of big rocks on which we rested our helmets full of clothes, while we did our weekly wash standing knee-deep in the cool current, winding up by washing us, our hair, and rinsing the works by lying in the shallow water and letting the beautiful water run over us, washing all our suds and troubles downstream." It was enough, said Claff, to make one wonder why everyone doesn't "go primitive."

And of Milne Bay, she said, "the sunsets were incomparable. I thought I had seen sunsets on the desert and on the ocean, but here the stars came out newly washed and polished . . . and the colors in the sky cast a glow on the very air, like colored spotlights. Breathtaking stuff. There were mud and mosquitoes and heat and humidity, but I was so busy trying to absorb the prodigal beauty that I forgot the discomforts."

Abbie Ratledge said that they played cards and cribbage, read, and listened to music. Ruth Shadewaldt said that she saw some USO shows (one with Jack Benny), wore hibiscus flowers in her hair at dances, and played endless bridge games. Juanita Hamilton said she spent a lot of time playing her guitar. Ruth Claff said they shared everything. "Magazines months old, small town newspapers that meant nothing to us personally, were read and reread until they were like tissue paper, but handled with such care that they were still intact."[69]

Playful rivalry between the states followed the nurses into war. Prompted by the sight of a Texas flag hanging in the 35th General Hospital's recreation hut, Carrie Coleman requested an Arkansas flag from her state's governor. "[W]e nurses of Arkansas can't let the Texas nurses get ahead of us," she said. The governor sent a flag with a note: "There isn't a thing in Texas that we don't have in Arkansas."[70]

Although Ruth Shadewaldt arrived in New Guinea when the fighting was over and treated few battle casualties, she still had plenty of patients. One poor man had been burned by electrical wires. "I took care of him and knew he was dying," she said. "We talked and talked and I [wrote] to his mother.

That was really sad because he was in so much pain. He was burned all over—his head, face, hair."[71]

Abbie Ratledge's patients included men with malaria, schistosomiasis, hepatitis, pneumonia, diphtheria, gonorrhea, syphilis, and galloping tuberculosis, but the saddest were the patients who never left their ward—"the men with no faces."

Some had their nose blown off; some had no jaw; some were sans chin, nose and jaw; and a few had only a forehead left. I went through this ward and stood in amazement and perfect wonder how these valiant nurses dealt with the problem of feeding these cases. Most of them were tube fed, and hours were spent getting nourishment into them. Some were so horribly disfigured they were in a private area from the others. I gnashed my teeth at war. These are the living dead, who will spend the rest of their lives in a closed section of some Stateside hospital. The fatal bullet was more merciful.[72]

Ruth Claff worked with psychiatric patients. "[T]he patients were so young and sheltered and pathetic. It made my blood run cold to see them when a sudden noise would startle them—ducking under the cots, trying to dig into the floor, shaking with terror." She continued:

The crickets alone were a threat to our sanity. They sounded like a boiler factory at the rush hour. . . . I had one patient who was recovering from malaria, apparently doing well, who couldn't stand them. He started with crying spells that he couldn't control, and we just had to do our best to snap him out of the beginnings of a pretty neurosis. He had good insight and a sense of humor, and would cooperate with us. He was ashamed of his crying but there it was, and only evacuation would help some of them.

And medical personnel weren't immune to the jungle's effects. When one nurse became infected with jungle rot, "she was covered from head to foot, and looked like something out of Mars." The condition almost drove the woman crazy before she was evacuated to the States. Another nurse died from the infection, and still another survived but was left with scars. Evacuation seemed to be the only cure, said Claff. "They learned at long last that there was no sense in treating it on the field. . . . Some were ten and twelve time repeaters."

On the "picturesque" island of Hollandia, Claff saw her "first close view of the results of real starvation." Among the Japanese prisoners were Formosans "pathetically thin and weak—and young—not over sixteen most of them. At mealtime these scrawny children sat erect in their cots, fastening their eyes on the kettles of food, and there wasn't a sound until it was all distributed and eaten and cleared away. And then a lot of them tried to slide out the side of the wards to raid the garbage cans."[73]

Juanita Hamilton saw Japanese and Chinese patients when touring an Australian Hospital and said, "I was prepared to hate the Japs on sight, but found I had given most of the candy and cigarettes to them before we got to the Chinese."

Some of Hamilton's patients were men from the 32nd Infantry Division who'd been fighting in the Owen-Stanley Mountains, many of whom suffered from jungle rot. "These boys had marched and fought long hours and days in the fetid jungles, without a change of shoes and socks, and in the swamps and rivers of the area. They had skin lesions like we had never seen before. The Army Medical Corps had no drugs to combat it and no diagnosis for it, so 'Jungle Rot' became the name."[74]

Lillian Dunlap said that her year with the 363d at Dobodura—a station hospital with 10 wards of 100 patients each—opened her eyes to the true effects of war injuries. "It was quite an experience. Me, a fairly young nurse right out of nurses training, to see all these things you'd never seen during the three years of training." Working 12-hour shifts, one nurse and one corpsman were in charge of 25 patients during the day and 100 patients at night. "There were times when I'd cover two wards so I'd have a corpsman on each of the two wards, then I'd cover the 200 patients back and forth."

A nearby airstrip meant accident victims, many with burns and broken legs. Burn victims were wrapped with Vaseline gauze, mechanics waste, and pressure bandages, then placed under mosquito nets because of the insects they attracted and because they started to smell. When the 11th Airborne Division was stationed nearby, Dunlap said, "Each time we'd see them go up [to train], we'd turn the beds down knowing we were going to get some fractured ankles, legs, or backs or something." One young paratrooper had lost a leg yet continued to polish his boots "just as if he was going to wear them again."

According to Dunlap, "The evacuation system in the Pacific was not like it was in Europe. We had patients—burn patients, paraplegics—in our hospitals for months. Lying there in our jungle hospital because they didn't have the ships or planes to evacuate them back down to Australia, so many of our patients would be there for a long time where over in the European Theater, they were able to evacuate them and get them back to a general hospital in England or back in the States."[75]

ELSEWHERE IN THE SOUTH PACIFIC

The first major offensive in World War II was the Battle of Guadalcanal (August 7, 1942 through February 9, 1943), which gave the American troops their first experience with the "fanatical resistance"[76] of the Japanese who would rather starve to death than surrender. Reflecting on the battle, General Alexander A. Vandegrift, USMC, said that it "will never be forgotten by those [U.S. troops] who fought there. . . . For them it will always have a special significance. They came through four difficult months that were hell-laden with heat, sweat, dirt, loneliness, disease and death. But they did far more than that. They destroyed the myth of Japanese invincibility in that laboratory of jungle warfare and set the pattern and the spirit for the victory to come. Our nation could have asked little more of any men."[77] The battle also resulted in the loss of 25,000 Japanese troops. The Americans had relatively few losses and received a huge morale boost.

Although the nurses saw many casualties with horrible burns from bombed or torpedoed ships, they never showed shock or revulsion. They knew that in addition to physical pain, the men suffered mentally—worried about how those back home would react to their condition. To help with their recovery, the nurses used various methods of diverting the men's attention. A common way was to ask one patient to help another. When Navy Nurse Theresa Hayes had trouble cheering up a patient who'd lost a leg, she asked another patient for help—an older man who'd lost both hands and whose jaw was wired in place after being shattered by a bomb. The older man sat down on the younger man's bed and asked for a cigarette. As the younger man reached for one, the older one said, "You'll have to light it—and hold it for me." The experience made the young man realize that there were many men much worse off than him, and "from that time on he became more cheerful and began to recover."[78]

For fun, the nurses shared magazines, newspapers, records, and radios with the patients and each other; made fudge; watched movies; saw tours by Bob Hope, Jack Benny, and the Royal New Zealand Air Force Band; and enjoyed gardening, picnics, swimming, fishing, and boating at a nearby plantation house. They collected pets—a bird named Delores and a dog named Stinky. One nurse, Jeanne Anne Elder, was chosen "Miss Guadalcanal" by the Marines.

The Battle of the Philippine Sea (June 19-20, 1944) occurred when the Japanese tried to block the landing of American forces on Saipan in the Marianas. According to Admiral Raymond A. Spruance, by winning this battle the Americans, "broke the Japanese effort to reinforce Saipan . . . gave us control of the eastern portion of the Philippine Sea and ensured that our later landings on Guam and Tinian could go through without further Japanese naval opposition."[79]

Sarah O'Toole was one of the Navy nurses who arrived on Tinian Island ("very beautiful . . . small and picturesque") in the Marianas in early 1945, and she was pleasantly surprised at the nurses' quarters: five large Quonset huts partitioned into rooms for two plus a reception area. The bathing facilities—complete with showers, laundry tubs, hot water, and flush toilets—were in a separate hut. The huts sat on a hill overlooking the ocean and were surrounded by a camouflaged fence. O'Toole was quick to acknowledge that they were lucky. "We are the only people so fortunate on the entire island. No other organization has such conveniences. It makes us very happy that we are Navy nurses, because we are cared for so well." Most of the patients ("sad casualties from the various campaigns")[80] arrived via hospital ships after each engagement and stayed from 60 to 90 days before being evacuated or sent back to duty.

ALASKA AND THE ALEUTIANS

Although they, too, were in the Pacific, nurses who served in Alaska and the Aleutian Islands lived a totally different life-style than those serving elsewhere in the vast ocean. Instead of fighting snakes and scorpions, these nurses fought blinding snow and subzero temperatures. Instead of treating patients who had tropical diseases and life-threatening battle wounds, they treated patients with stateside-type ailments: the common cold, appendicitis, work-related accidents, and so forth. In his article "Where Blows the Williwaw," Corp. W. J. Granberg described the islands as gray and dismal and said that there was always loneliness and "the feeling of living on the edge of nowhere at the forgotten end of the world."[81]

But they were anything but forgotten between August 1942 and July 1943, when American forces battled the Japanese over the tiny islands of Kiska and Attu, which the Japanese had occupied primarily as a diversionary tactic for their attack on Midway. Although American casualties were few, their horror stories were astounding. The Japanese, they said, blew themselves up with hand grenades. So sickening was the sight of dismembered body parts that the GIs became ill.

Neither were the nurses immune from danger. On a flight to a nearby island, the plane carrying Chief Nurse Lucile Hendricks and two other nurses went down and was never found. In Hendricks's honor, a plaque was placed above the door of her pet project—a new recreation hut.

Early in the war, Navy nurses were sent to the two Navy bases on Kodiak and Dutch Harbor. On Kodiak, they staffed a dispensary that served not only the sailors, marines, and Seabees, but also many of their wives and babies. Some of their patients were airmen with frozen feet, pneumonia, and broken bones.

Nurses on Dutch Harbor saw very few cases of cold and flu, and the only epidemic was the mumps brought in by 35 merchant marines from the States. The women also treated casualties from Russian freighters and the nearby Soviet refueling base.

By fall of 1943, Attu was back in American hands, and Chief Nurse Judy Wilson and nine other Navy nurses landed on the island to staff the dispensary. The women were met with more than the usual number of stares and whistles because the men hadn't seen a woman in three years. According to *Navy Nurse* author Page Cooper, "The boys at the army camp five miles away came by in trucks and stopped to whistle . . . or sometimes just sat and looked." The attention made the women especially pleased because for once they had arrived before the Army nurses.

"They were pioneers," said Cooper. "[A]t first they had no butter and no fruit, but soon the ships began to bring supplies—when a ship came in with fresh lettuce, the whole post held a celebration. The water was yellow, they picked strands of tundra grass out of the holes of the shower sprinkler before they could take a bath, the williwaws blew, but the Seabees requisitioned a couple of bicycles for them, and the supply officer gave them a dog which they named Shemya (girl)."[82]

Early in the war, there was no modern plumbing, and the women bathed and washed their clothes in helmets. Although conditions improved within 10 months, Evelyn Durward said that five of them shared a Quonset hut equipped with Army cots and furniture made from boxes, crates, and foot lockers. "It's funny," she said, "but anywhere you hang your hat, even for a short time, becomes home."[83] The hospital was a Quonset hut too, with a center main ward and wards on each side. There was also a bathroom, shower, and running water.

Weather dominated life in the islands, especially the williwaws, described by Cooper as "that fantastic wind which seems to blow from every direction at once. . . . Day and night the wind blew, the rain poured, snow and sleet cut the face. . . . Sometimes it was almost impossible to climb the fifty wooden steps that led from the quarters to the road below." The nurses were told not to walk to the dispensary without a corpsman when the williwaws blew, but many took the chance and "were compelled to fall on their faces and clutch the boardwalk until a Seabee came along in a jeep and rescued them."[84]

Corporal Granberg wrote that the weather in the Aleutians could change in five minutes. One minute their huts were buried in snow, the next they were blanketed in fog. Rain made the ground turn to mud and summer brought mosquitoes. Because they spent so much time indoors, the nurses enjoyed dances, songfests, and plays, and shared letters and newspapers.

During the spells of good weather, the women toured Dutch Harbor on Unalaska where they visited a restaurant, bakery, shops, an old Russian church and cemetery, and even the hotel in which Jack London once lived. They climbed mountains, had picnics, and attended dances and movies. One group of nurses was even invited aboard a Russian freighter. Evelyn Durward loved life in the Aleutians. "The country is very beautiful so we enjoy hiking and long walks, taking pictures and sometimes visiting ships. During this particular season, skiing, snowshoeing, and skating are very popular."[85]

And the natural beauty was astounding, especially the flowers: "blue, white, yellow; wild iris, violets, lady's slippers as big as the orchids in the florists' shops, lupines so full on the stalk that one branch made a bouquet."[86] Bernice Gorski collected 25 varieties of flowers during her stay.

Granberg believed that the nurses in the Aleutians deserved a lot of credit. "As unhazardous and uncolorful as the nursing job may be, it tells only half the story, for it takes a real woman, a woman with wide horizons within her own mind to stand life in the Aleutians, to bear the monotony and loneliness."[87] Some of the women even missed their life on "the bleak rock" and wanted to return "because life was more vivid there and what they were doing seemed to have more value."[88]

TOWARD JAPAN

In preparation for invading Japan, the Allies bombed Japan, raided its shipping and coastal areas, and captured more islands for stopover points between Guam and Japan. One of these islands, Iwo Jima, was 760 miles south of Tokyo—close enough that planes could carry bombs in place of the extra fuel needed for long flights. But the only place to land on Iwo Jima was where the Japanese were entrenched with 21,000 men, hundreds of cannon, thousands of machine guns, and hidden pillboxes with walls five feet thick. And each Japanese soldier was told to fight to the death and take at least 10 American lives with him. It was this mindset that greeted the Americans as they prepared to take the island, and it was this resolve that resulted in the loss of 600 Marines on the first day.

By the time the island was taken, 6,821 Marines had died—"the heaviest toll in Corps history"[89]—and more than 13,000 others had been wounded. The Battle of Iwo Jima (February-March, 1945) was "the greatest concentration of troops for the area involved in the history of modern warfare and the largest force of Marines ever to be committed in a single battle [60,000]. In the words of Fleet Admiral Nimitz, Iwo Jima was the battle 'where uncommon valor was a common virtue.'"[90]

Okinawa was chosen as the next island needed as a base for landings in China or Japan, and was invaded April 1, 1945. Although it was the last major land battle of the war, its capture cost 49,000 Allied casualties and 109,000 Japanese deaths.

Navy Nurses Olivine St. Peter and Alice Goudreau were among those on Guam who treated casualties from these invasions—amputations, appendectomies, tracheotomies, dysentery, gastroenteritis, and malaria, head and abdominal injuries, and partial or full paralysis cases. Pressure sores were especially prevalent among men who had spent several days waiting to be evacuated because the sores were caused by waiting on beaches in canvas cots and litters under rough, wet field blankets. Most of those with gunshot wounds and neck and spinal injuries didn't make it.

Burn wards created an odor so bad that one Red Cross worker—"a true angel of mercy"—sprinkled cologne on sheets and pillows to erase the smell long enough for the men to eat.

Oxygen was usually administered through nasal catheters instead of face masks because "the patients were highly apprehensive, frequently irrational, and would often tear them off." Oxygen tents weren't practical either because the rubberized material deteriorated in the humid climate. Said Goudreau, "A casual observer entering the ward housing our patients with chest wounds would have been positive we held them together with rubber tubes!"

And then there were the neuropsychiatric patients, many of whom were ambulatory.

The large number of men with war neuroses was almost unbelievable. They arrived by the hundreds. These were the traditionally tough marines, experienced campaigners, who with outstanding gallantry had established beach head after beach head in the islands of the Pacific. Most of them, some little more than boys, were in such a severe state of shock that they had to be led by the hand from the planes and ambulances.[91]

RECLAIMING THE ISLANDS—AND FREEDOM

After spending the war in captivity, nurses in the Philippines knew that freedom was finally near when American planes dropped flyers that read,

"Cheer up, Christmas is coming, today or tomorrow!"[92]   Dorothy Still remembers hearing the rumbling of tanks and machine-gun fire and smelling U.S. gasoline and then seeing amtracs crash through the compound and men jump out. "Oh, we never saw anything so handsome in our lives,"[93] she said.

But with all the excitement, one of the nurses said, "We didn't have much time for celebrating, for the casualties among the internees and soldiers started to mount. We went back to the hospital immediately to care for the patients." The hospital took some direct hits and people were killed. "To see the torn bodies of people who had waited for this day for so long, only to die or be maimed when their freedom was so close, was almost unbearable." The prisoners were taken to a beach and convoyed away in amphibious tanks.

And it wasn't over yet. During the fighting for liberation of the camp, 65 Japanese officials barricaded themselves inside one of the buildings and used some of the male internees as hostages until the Americans allowed them to leave the camp. The Japanese then targeted the camp and, when all was lost, retaliated by executing 1,500 Los Banos civilians. Of the approximately 4,000 prisoners at Santo Tomas, 315 had died, but all of the American nurses had survived.

By November 1944, American nurses were returning to the islands, many of whom had left there during the dark days of 1942. When they arrived at the camps in February 1945, and tried to relieve the overworked and tired medical personnel, the newly freed nurses said, "There was enough work there for many, many more; so we stayed on duty with these girls although they objected to it."[94]

Ruth Shadewaldt returned to Manila and found the place "a mess. . . . Sunken ships all over the harbor . . . debris and junk everywhere and the people living in hovels." Visiting Corregidor "was an experience to remember. It sure gives you a tug at the heart strings to think of all those men trying to defend that small place."[95]

It was in Cebu, in the Philippines, that Lillian Dunlap saw what horrors the Japanese had inflicted on civilians:

On one Sunday afternoon, we received word that we were going to get a bunch of Filipinos in from the island of Negros that the Japanese had infiltrated. They were old men, old women, and children. The Japanese had butchered them—cut off a little girl's earlobes, stuck bamboo shoots under their fingernails, cut off a pregnant woman's breasts and stabbed her in the abdomen—all kinds of that type of injury. Those patients couldn't understand us. We'd come after them with intravenouses, and they thought we were going to torture them, even when we tried to put them on a bedpan, until we had our Filipinos who could interpret for them what we were doing. Once they knew what we were doing for them, it was different, but they were frightened.

When two little boys who'd lost some fingers and had belly wounds from picking up hand grenades and other war debris were ready to be evacuated to the Filipino Hospital, the nurses weren't ready for them to leave, "because we wanted to take care of them." So every time there was an inspection, the nurses wrapped the little boys' hands up in bandages so it looked as if they weren't well enough to be moved.

Dunlap's unit also cared for about 150 Japanese prisoners. Although they were never hostile to the American nurses, the nurses weren't allowed to be alone with them. "They were in sad, sad shape,"[96] she said, not having received the same care as American soldiers.

All of the women who spent time in the Philippines became heroines and were honored with awards and receptions. During a reception for those who escaped in 1942, one speaker said that the women "represent[ed] at the front all womankind in this war." Another speaker, Lt. Col. Carlos P. Romulo, the last man to leave Bataan, said that the nurses "did not falter and they gave of themselves without stint."[97]

New York Sun columnist Dave Boone said of the nurses, "The American nurse at her best is one of the grandest human beings on earth. She was at her best out there in Bataan and Corregidor. . . . I guess no matter how brave and self sacrificing any man or woman may feel today these girls make 'em feel small time."[98]

The Navy nurses at Los Banos were honored by fellow prisoners, the Wightmans of Evansville, Indiana, who said, "We who were in camp will never be able to forget or repay them for the many favors that they did for one and all there. We are absolutely certain that had it not been for these nurses many of us who are alive and well would have died. Their unselfish care and human understanding in the most trying circumstances will always be in our hearts."[99]

What next? How did the women react to freedom after so many months in captivity? For many, their first thoughts were of food. Navy Nurse Laura Cobb savored the K-rations, chocolate bars, and cigarettes from the rescuing GIs. Dorothy Still enjoyed a steak dinner in Leyte with the commander of the 7th Fleet and Southwest Pacific Force.

Many of the women suffered from malnutrition and fatigue and were hospitalized. The others rested in a beachfront convalescent hospital where they were fed, photographed, interviewed, and pampered. Some had lost weight and all were tired and malnourished. Page Cooper said that this was typical. "[I]ndeed freedom wasn't a reality until they saw in the mirrors of Honolulu how thin and gaunt they were and how much a few luxuries and a beauty parlor could do toward wiping out the evidence of prison years."[100] When looking in a store window, one of the nurses said, "You know, we have missed four Christmases."[101]

And while they were happy to be home, many requested further overseas duty. Leona Jackson returned to Guam. "Every night sees several emergencies and many very ill patients. . . . This is nursing!"[102] Helen Summers felt the same way. "I came out fine! I'm ready, any time they call me, for overseas duty."[103]

"It made me a stronger person,"[104] said Earlyn Black Harding about her 1942-to-1945 internment. Madeline Ullom said that being freed by the 1st Cavalry was one of her best wartime experiences.

Hattie Brantley said that the prisoners got through their ordeal because they supported each other and had faith in the United States and in God. Their motto in camp was "Help is on the way." Defeat, said Brantley, was being a POW. "Victory is being a survivor."[105]

NOTES

1. Lt. Col. Clayton R. Newell, *Central Pacific*, Series: The US Army Campaigns of World War II (Washington, D.C.: U.S. Army Center of Military History, 1992), p. 6.

2. Mary M. Roberts, R.N., *American Nursing History and Interpretation* (New York: Macmillan, 1955), p. 343.

3. Quoted in Terry Box, "They Also Served," *Dallas Morning News*, December 5, 1991, p. A:28.

4. "Honolulu, December 7, 1941," *American Journal of Nursing*, March 1942, p. 317.

5. Genevieve Van de Drink Stepanek Questionnaire.

6. Quoted in Box, "They Also Served," p. A:28.

7. Quoted in Susan Bolotin, ed., *Pearl Harbor: December 7, 1941-December 7, 1991*, Life Collector's Edition, p. 36.

8. Quoted in Scott W. Wright, "Nurse Remembers Attack's Deadly Effect," *Austin American-Statesman*, December 5, 1991, p. A:13.

9. Quoted in Joe Treen, Don Sider, Joseph Harmes, Kent Demaret, Janice Fuhrman, "Bloody Sunday," *People Weekly*, December 9, 1991, p. 45.

10. Quoted in Thomas B. Allen, "Pearl Harbor: A Return to the Day of Infamy," *National Geographic*, December 1991, p. 75.

11. Quoted in "More Army Nurses Win Honors," *American Journal of Nursing*, August 1943, p. 774.

12. Stepanek Questionnaire.

13. Quoted in Bolotin, p. 36.

14. Page Cooper, *Navy Nurse* (New York: McGraw-Hill, 1946), p. 12.

15. Col. Robert S. Anderson, M.C., USA, editor-in-chief, *Army Medical Specialist Corps* (Washington, D.C.: Office of the Surgeon General, U.S. Army, 1968), p. 3.

16. Jane Maggard Speck, "Captured on Guam," *Trained Nurse and Hospital Review*, December 1942, pp. 414, 415.

17. "American Nurses Prisoners in Japan," *American Journal of Nursing*, April 1942, p. 448.

18. Quoted in Speck, pp. 415, 416.

19. Arthur Zich, *Rising Sun*, Series: World War II (Alexandria: Time-Life Books, 1977), p. 95.

20. Associated Press, *World War II: A 50th Anniversary* (New York: Henry Holt and Co., 1989), p. 78.

21. Zich, p. 95.

22. Quoted in Lucy Wilson Jopling, R.N., *Warrior in White* (San Antonio: Watercress Press, 1990), p. 38.

23. Col. Julia O. Flikke, *Nurses in Action* (New York: Lippincott, 1943), pp. 173, 176.

24. Melissa A. Rosenbaum, "A Navy Nurse Remembers," *U.S. Navy Medicine*, Vol. 72, June 1981, p. 22.

25. Quoted in Rosenbaum, p. 22.

26. Cooper, p. 30.

27. Quoted in Rosenbaum, pp. 24, 25.

28. Cooper, p. 31.

29. Jopling, pp. 39, 41.

30. Flikke, p. 183.

31. Quoted in Janet M. Gesiter, R.N., "She Came Back from Bataan," *Trained Nurse and Hospital Review*, October 1942, p. 253.

32. Lt. Alice R. Clarke, ANC, "'Thirty-Seven Months as Prisoners of War' as Told by Liberated Army Nurses to Lieutenant Alice R. Clarke, Army Nurse Corps," *The Army Nurse*, March 1945, p. 10.

33. Quoted in Geister, p. 254.

34. Quoted in Jennifer Mitchum, "Navy Medicine May-June 1942," *Navy Medicine*, May-June 1992, p. 32.

35. Quoted in Geister, p. 254.

36. Clarke, "'Thirty-Seven Months . . .'," *The Army Nurse*, p. 11.

37. Anderson, *Army Medical Specialist Corps*, p. 231.

38. Lt. Col. (Ret.) Hattie R. Brantley, Lecture, *Quiet Shadows: Women in the Pacific War—A Symposium*, Southwest Texas State University, San Marcos, Texas, March 27, 1993.

39. Clarke, "'Thirty-Seven Months . . .'," *The Army Nurse*, p. 11.

40. Cooper, p. 194.

41. Quoted in Clarke, "'Thirty-Seven Months . . .'," *The Army Nurse*, p. 11.

42. Dorothy Still Danner, "Reminiscences of a Nurse POW," *Navy Medicine*, May-June 1992, pp. 36, 37.

43. Cooper, pp. 197, 199.

44. Quoted in Jessie Fant Evans, "Release from Los Banos," *American Journal of Nursing*, June 1945, p. 463.

45. Quoted in Flikke, pp. 151, 154.

46. Lt. Esther W. Paine, ANC, "From Australia," *American Journal of Nursing*, October 1944, p. 989.

47. Juanita Hamilton Webster, Unpublished memoirs, no date, p. 20.

48. 1st Lt. Ann C. Deeds, ANC, "There Goes an American Nurse," *American Journal of Nursing*, September 1944, pp. 847, 848.

49. 1st Lt. Ruth Kinzeler, ANC, "An Overseas Venture in Kindergarten Aid," *American Journal of Nursing*, December 1944, p. 1139.

50. Quoted in Flikke, p. 155.

51. 1st Lt. Dorothy L. Hufcut, ANC, "Pioneers in New Caledonia," *American Journal of Nursing*, June 1943, p. 591.

52. "Army Nurses in Ireland and India, New Caledonia, and Africa," *American Journal of Nursing*, February 1943, p. 212.

53. Hufcut, p. 591.

54. Quoted in Flikke, pp. 156-157.

55. Webster, Unpublished memoirs, p. 17.

56. Ruth Claff, *Lady with the Flashlight* Unpublished memoirs, 1947, p. 17.

57. Abbie C. Ratledge, *Angels in Khaki* (San Antonio: Naylor Co., 1975), p. 31.

58. Webster, Unpublished memoirs, p. 18.

59. "American Nurses at Guinea Bases Happiest of All," *New Orleans Times-Picayune*, November 24, 1942, no p. #.

60. Quoted in "American Nurses at Guinea Bases Happiest of All," no p. #.

61. Constance Sansone, Telephone interview with author, July 6, 1992.

62. Claff, p. 27.

63. Sansone telephone interview with author.

64. Lt. Col. (Ret.) Ruth Frances Shadewaldt, ANC, Taped interview with sister, July 1992.

65. Claff, pp. 19, 28.

66. Quoted in Wyatt Blassingame, *Combat Nurses of World War II* (New York: Landmark Books, 1967), p. 104.

67. Shadewaldt taped interview.

68. Ratledge, p. 70.

69. Claff, pp. 18, 24, 29.

70 . Quoted in "Army and Navy Nurses Tell Us," *American Journal of Nursing*, May 1945, p. 408.

71. Shadewaldt taped interview.

72. Ratledge, p. 71.

73. Claff, pp. 22, 27, 30-31.

74. Webster, Unpublished memoirs, pp. 18, 19.

75. Brig. Gen. (Ret.) Lillian Dunlap, ANC, Interview with author, December 20, 1991.

76. Elizabeth-Anne Wheal, Stephen Pope, James Taylor, *Encyclopedia of the Second World War* (Secaucus, NJ: Castle Books, 1989), p. 199.

77. General Alexander A. Vandegrift, USMC, "Victory at Guadalcanal," *Battle Stations! Your Navy in Action* (New York: Wm. H. Wise, 1946), p. 138.

78. Quoted in Blassingame, p. 108.

79. Admiral Raymond A. Spruance, USN, "The Battle of the Philippine Sea," *Battle Stations! Your Navy in Action* (New York: Wm. H. Wise, 1946), p. 272.

80. Lt. Sarah O'Toole, R.N., USNR, "In the Southwest Pacific: They Pioneered on Tinian," *American Journal of Nursing*, December 1945, pp. 1013, 1014, 1015.

81. Corp. W. J. Granberg, "Where Blows the Williwaw," *American Journal of Nursing*, July 1945, p. 535.

82. Cooper, p. 107.

83. Lt. Evelyn Durward, ANC, "'Home' in the Aleutians," *American Journal of Nursing*, April 1944, p. 398.

84. Cooper, pp. 99, 106, 99.

85. Durward, p. 398.

86. Cooper, p. 104.

87. Granberg, p. 535.

88. Cooper, p. 106.

89. Associated Press, p. 275.

90. Lt. General Harry Schmidt, USMC, "The Battle for Iwo Jima," *Battle Stations! Your Navy in Action* (New York: Wm. H. Wise, 1946), p. 322.

91. Lt. Alice Aurora Goudreau, R.N., USN, "Nursing at an Advance Naval Base Hospital," *American Journal of Nursing*, November 1945, pp. 885, 886.

92. Alice R. Clarke, R.N., "Thirty-Seven Months as Prisoners of War," *American Journal of Nursing*, May 1945, p. 344.

93. Danner, p. 40.

94. Quoted in Clarke, "Thirty-Seven Months as Prisoners of War," *American Journal of Nursing*, p. 345.

95. Lt. Col. (Ret.) Ruth Frances Shadewaldt, ANC, Letter to Agnes Summers, August 25, 1945.

96. Dunlap interview with author.

97. Quoted in "The Heroic Nurses of Bataan and Corregidor," *American Journal of Nursing*, August 1942, p. 897.

98. Quoted in "The Time Is Now!" *American Journal of Nursing*, August 1942, p. 924.

99. Quoted in "Former Internees Pay Tribute to Navy Nurse Internees," *American Journal of Nursing*, October 1945, p. 856.

100. Cooper, p. 201.

101. Quoted in Cooper, p. 201.

102. Quoted in "Army and Navy Nurses Return to the Philippines and Guam," *American Journal of Nursing*, April 1945, p. 317.

103. Quoted in Geister, p. 252.

104. Quoted in Scott W. Wright, "Women's War 'Whited Out' of History Books," *Austin American-Statesman*, December 5, 1991, p. A:12.

105. Brantley lecture.

Chapter 5

The Mediterranean Theater

When they reached land, they rolled up their slacks and waded ashore.

They spent that first night on the beach, eating canned rations and drinking water from their canteens. Eventually, some were taken by jeep to a three-story building that had been turned into a hospital. There were wounded men everywhere, some French, some American, some Arab. One American tugged at the hem of Nurse Ruth Haskell's slacks and asked for a drink of water. As she lifted his head to let him drink from her canteen, she asked, "Where are you hurt?" The man gasped. "An American woman! Where did you come from?"

—Shaaron Cosner
War Nurses

This interchange probably happened hundreds of times throughout the war, and one can only imagine the comfort and appreciation GIs felt when seeing an American nurse. Ruth Haskell, whose unit served in North Africa during the first days of Operation TORCH (the invasion of North Africa, November 8, 1942), wrote, "There has never been a time in my life that I was so proud to be a nurse, to be able to help."[1] And she was just the tonic the men needed. Known as one of the cheeriest nurses on duty, Haskell shouted her patients awake each morning saying, "Wake up, you great, big, beautiful things." Instead of asking to take a pulse, she'd say, "Let me hold your hand."[2]

The Allied invasions of North Africa, Sicily, and Italy opened the door to Europe and captured bases on Casablanca, Oran, and Port Lyautey that provided protection for Allied shipping. When Allied forces moved successfully to Algeria and Tunisia, they once again had access to the Suez Canal and British oil resources in the Middle East.

For medical personnel, these campaigns would be the testing grounds for organizational skills and medical techniques that would became the norm for coming invasions. The countries certainly provided a hotbed of medical problems: respiratory ailments; heatstroke, heat exhaustion, and prickly heat; chronic vitamin deficiency; an exotic disease called leishmaniasis (the Baghdad sore); gastrointestinal disorders such as diarrhea, bacillary and amebic dysentery, and bacterial food poisoning; and typhoid-paratyphoid infections. Other diseases were malaria, yellow fever, smallpox, and venereal disease.

Partly to blame were the personal habits of newly arrived soldiers who'd not been properly trained in hygiene and sanitation. Other causes were contaminated water supplies, lack of sewage disposal systems, and general unsanitary conditions that promoted extensive fly breeding. In his book *Medical Service in the Mediterranean and Minor Theaters,* Charles Wiltse wrote, "Flies were so thick in parts of Tunisia that it was risky business to open one's mouth to speak."[3]

NORTH AFRICA

On November 8, 1942, nurses watched the Allied fleet bombard the North African shore then disembarked as the men did, climbing down off the ships into small assault boats, five to a boat, along with three medical officers and 20 enlisted men. In her pamphlet about the Army Nurse Corps, Judith A. Bellafaire described the event: "The nurses wore helmets and carried full packs containing musette bags, gas masks, and canteen belts. Only their Red Cross arm bands and lack of weapons distinguished them from fighting troops. They waded ashore near the coastal town of Arzew on D-day of Operation TORCH with the rest of the assault troops and huddled behind a sand dune while enemy snipers took potshots at anything that moved."[4]

They slept in shell-damaged houses, ate canned rations, drank water from canteens, and slept on the floor under their overcoats. Surgery was performed in the barest of conditions—a single dim light bulb, a dripping faucet, equipment sterilized over the flame of one burner. No gloves or gowns to cover hands and filthy clothing. Patients arrived nonstop.

Mobile hospitals were located so far to the rear that the clearing stations took on more patients than they'd planned or expected, and the surgeons could perform only emergency care—administering plasma to prevent shock, controlling hemorrhage, and closing sucking chest wounds. Amputations were performed only when necessary to stop hemorrhage. There weren't enough beds or personnel, no intravenous fluids, no special diets, and no way to check the whole blood for malaria or syphilis. "As a result," wrote Charles Wiltse, "patients were evacuated as rapidly as possible, the majority in six to eight hours after surgery and some while still under anesthesia."[5]

Theresa Archard described the frustration of trying to treat too many patients near the front lines in her book *G.I. Nightingale: The Story of an Army Nurse.*

Patients were coming in. Badly wounded boys—the worst yet—serious belly wounds from mine explosions, head and chest wounds. The head wounds were really bad, brains oozing from some of them. The sucking chest wounds gave up frothy, bright red blood with each expiration.

This time it was not a question of receiving ten or twenty patients at a time. Sometimes as many as twenty ambulances pulled up every few hours, which usually meant eighty patients. . . . The admitting officer decided what was to be done to each patient. If he needed an operation he went to the preoperative tent and waited his turn. In the meantime, he was fluroscoped and the site of the shell fragment marked, so that no time would be lost in the operating room.

Those operating rooms! Ten tables going night and day, no sleep for the doctors—they worked the clock around.[6]

According to author Bellafaire, all units soon "became expert at meeting the challenges of combat while caring for incoming patients."[7]

They also became experts at moving. The 77th Evacuation Hospital packed, moved 150 patients a distance of 60 miles, unpacked, and began treating an additional 500 patients 12 hours later. In one 45-day period, the unit treated 4,577 men.

In her book *Combat Nurse: A Journal of World War II*, Roberta Love Tayloe wrote that her unit, the 9th Evacuation Hospital, landed at Oran nine days after the first Yank assault troops waded ashore. From there, they went to the Tunisian front and treated 1,698 patients without one death.

But there was time to enjoy the surroundings, and Tayloe wrote of Oran Harbor: "The sunset lighting up the bare mountains was spectacular with its orange-red hues. Oh, to be an artist! When you are surrounded by such beauty, it is hard to believe that you are in a war and may be strafed by some plane or shot at any moment!" But the city of Oran, which "looked a bit exotic from the harbor," wasn't very appealing up close. "The streets were filthy and [the] buildings all needed paint, long before the war, I think."[8] During their time off, the nurses would often go out to eat and tour with the doctors.

Helen Pon described Oran as having "lovely Mediterranean days and cold, frigid nights."[9] Their tents weren't winterized and were very cold even with the wooden floors. Some of her fellow nurses developed pneumonia. Pon came down with pleurisy.

Navy nurses had better accommodations: huts with hot and cold water, closets, and bedside lamps. They hung signal flags for curtains and painted cans for ashtrays and wastebaskets.

And while the Navy nurses made tea balls from tea leaves tied in gauze and discovered that canned milk made "delicious chocolate milk and eggnogs . . . when topped by a scoop of hand-frozen ice cream,"[10] Pon said that Army nurses ate a lot of powdered eggs and potatoes, and meat about twice a month. Their menus depended on what the mess officer could get at the depot or what nurses could get on their own.

As always, the Red Cross provided clubs for the nurses. The one in Oran had a reception room, dining room, snack bar, bedrooms, lounges, powder rooms, showers, and even maid service.

Always on the move, the 9th Evacuation Hospital soon found itself high in the Atlas Mountains. Tayloe wrote:

Arrived in a torrent of rain; found where our tents were, the ground covered with water. We had to find stones, etc. to put our belongings on, to keep them out of the water after our tents were pitched. It was much colder up here, and we really did not have the clothes for it. (Later, we wore men's long underwear). The engineers were unloading crushed rock for roads in this sea of mud and water. . . . We used anything we could find—cardboard, etc.—for floors for our tents. The hospital equipment arrived, and for the first time we were set up for real business.

Next they moved by truck and train toward Tebessa near the Kasserine Pass.

We were six to a compartment, no heat and no light. . . . We slept, one on each seat, and the other four either on the floor on the seat cushions, or in the baggage racks. Our mess was set up in railroad stations enroute, or "C" rations. Most of us did very well, for at every stop there were urchins selling oranges, fresh eggs, and lemons, and we bought small kerosene stoves through the window, where most of the bartering was done. The most depressing news was that it had taken us twelve hours to go fifty miles.[11]

For her work during the fight for Kasserine Pass, Mary Ann Sullivan—who had already been commended for her work aboard the *Maasdam* when it was torpedoed en route to England—became the first nurse in the North African Theater to receive the Legion of Merit.

During the entire period, while enemy planes soared overhead, bombing Thelepte Air Field one-half mile away, and later with enemy planes overhead at Gafsa, Lieutenant Sullivan showed no personal concern, and her action was in keeping with the highest traditions of the Army Nurse Corps. When the Nazis took the pass, so hurried was the American retreat that the "Commando Truck" [mobile hospital] carrying wounded and its staff raced to safety with only an armored rear guard between it and the enemy.[12]

Near the town of Constantine, Roberta Love Tayloe said they slept in their bedrolls under "a canopy of a dark blue velvety sky, studded with the most enormous twinkling stars." The next day they toured the city and enjoyed two days of hotel food and the last bath in a bathtub for a long time. In a few days, they were back on the road to Tebessa.

Through hills and tiresome deserty plains . . . where much strafing was going on . . . we were ordered to wear helmets at all times. . . . We had our canteens of water and "C" rations for the day. No "comfort" stations and no trees—males on one side of the road, females on the other.[13]

On May 9, 1943, the 9th set up shop in a group of old school buildings near Mateur and treated German victims of auto accidents, booby traps, gunshot wounds, malaria, hepatitis, and dysentery. Some of the nurses came down with dysentery and several were sent home.

Charlotte Webber, of the 38th Evacuation Hospital, described her life in Africa:

We live in tents somewhere in Northwest Africa and love it. Only we don't take baths, wash our hair, shave, or wash clothes—just one big, dirty, happy family. It's cold at night. I sleep on an Army cot in my sleeping bag with my wool robe on and four Army blankets over me.

We've named all our little streets in the field—my ward tent is on the corner of Kentucky Ave. and Second St. Our mess tent's called "New York Hotel" and my tent is named "My Old Kentucky Home."

I certainly have a time trying to talk French with these French people. Those two years I had in French in Cynthiana High do come in handy. When I was in town I went to a shop to buy some pins; the French shopkeepers kept jabbering to us and we couldn't understand a thing they said. Finally, I gathered they wanted us to go with them for a drink of wine. Well, they left their shop wide open and took us down to their house, sat us down, and brought out three bottles, and finally FDR's picture, and we all drank a toast to Roosevelt.[14]

Theresa Archard described the meagerness of the nurses' quarters at her base:

Those tents were something to see—a double row of beds or cots in each tent, sixteen beds or twenty to twenty-five cots. There were no tables, chairs, or miscellaneous furniture. A packing case served as cupboard, desk, and catch-all. Our chlorinated water supply stood there in five gallon cans. One little potbellied stove was in the middle of the tent, and on this we heated water for baths and hot water bottles.[15]

Frances Wells said, "Although I have been homesick at times, I have never been as happy as I am now in North Africa. This seems to be what I have really wanted to do." She tells of her stay there:

A GI tour varies from very comfortable accommodations to sleeping in a luggage rack in a flea-infested train, but I have heard much less complaining here, in fact not a thousandth of what I heard in comfortable civilian hospitals. There are girls here who never washed their own clothes when they were in the States and who now take a bath in a helmet full of water and then wash their clothes in it. We will be pretty rugged when we get back.[16]

Another nurse wrote of her time in North Africa:

I didn't know that Africa has so very many hills. The afternoons are warm, but the nights are as cold as the autumn nights at home. There is not much in the way of entertainment, but our days are so full that I'd rather write letters and then go to bed. The soldiers are wonderful to take care of, for they are so glad to see an American nurse and so grateful for the least little thing a person does. I wouldn't miss all of this though it has its drawbacks. Don't worry about me, for I've never felt better.[17]

During her first trip home after service in Africa, Bernice Wilbur, ANC, told a reporter that frontline nurses "are used to digging and diving into slit trenches; they can bathe in a helmet full of water; they stay awake and on duty as many hours as necessary; and in a matter of a few hours they can take down a tent city housing hundreds of men." And Wilbur should know. One of her hospitals moved twice in 24 hours.

She also described the frugality of army life. "Not even the metal bands around crates are wasted. Oil which is no longer useful for lubrication is spread on ponds to control mosquitoes. Lumber is salvaged to make bedside tables, coat racks, tent floors, and desks. Not a drop of water is wasted. Every ounce of medical supplies is used for the purpose intended. . . . All food is consumed without waste or leftovers and the only exception to the strict rationing is that wounded men receive 50 percent more food than others." According to Wilbur, "I doubt that even a whiff of anesthetic is allowed to evaporate."

Although happy to be home, Wilbur was quick to tell the reporter that she was going back. "It's hard, tough work with little chance to play, but I know of no other which gives greater solid satisfaction. . . . I'm going back. There is a tremendous amount of work to be done and I made them promise me a round-trip ticket before I left."[18]

SICILY

Sicily was at once a proving ground for the lessons learned in Africa and a dress rehearsal for Italy. . . . The most important development was the use of field hospital platoons, with attached surgical teams, for treatment of nontransportable casualties in the division area.

The Allied invasion of Sicily—Operation HUSKY—took place on July 10, 1943. In addition to being a second open door to the continent, the occupation of Sicily would "relieve some of the pressure on the Russian front, help knock Italy out of the war, and open the Mediterranean to Allied shipping." Author Charles Wiltse said that "hospitalization in the Sicily campaign showed marked improvement over practices in Tunisia, even though preinvasion plans were not always carried out to the letter."[19]

Wiltse also wrote that Sicily was another hotbed of disease with its flies, fleas, lice, bedbugs, mosquitoes, contaminated water, and horrendous sanitary conditions. Even though the men had been immunized against smallpox, typhoid, paratyphoid, typhus, and tetanus; were given atabrine or quinine four times a week; and had been instructed on sanitary procedures, they suffered from dysentery, sandfly fever, and malaria.

And the invasion brought casualties.

"The ambulances came day and night," wrote Army Nurse Mary Ann Harman. "The Army nurses worked twelve hours, fifteen, eighteen, but the wounded were bathed, fed, and given expert nursing care. There was a preponderance of shrapnel wounds and burns requiring skilled and sympathetic treatment."[20]

Col. Raymond Scott wrote about the 60 nurses, 4 officers, and 88 enlisted men of the 11th Evacuation Hospital for the October 1943, issue of the *American Journal of Nursing*. Although they were supposed to follow the infantry, they almost beat them and called themselves "Commandos." Their equipment didn't arrive for 24 hours, so the first day's meals consisted of one B- and one C-ration. And even though they dug foxholes while bombs dropped around them, the nurses, wrote Scott, "were a happy group of girls." By the afternoon of the next day, the 11th was taking patients and saw 900 in three days. They moved to Agrigento and began treating patients by five that afternoon.

A lot of time was spent in foxholes as the Germans made their attacks, but most often the women continued to work. "Everyone was frightened at first," said Scott, "but later paid no attention to it. . . . During the bombing there was comradeship; everyone joked and laughed."[21]

ITALY

Their truck driver told them to jump out and hit the dirt. Doyle [a nurse with the 95th Evacuation Hospital] saw GIs crawling towards them and asked if they were coming to fetch the nurses.

"Sweetheart, we're all on the front line and you're ahead of us," answered one of the soldiers.[22]

The Allied invasion of Italy—Operation AVALANCHE—began when 70,000 men of the Fifth Army (including the famous Darby's Rangers) landed in Salerno on September 9, 1943. But it was a costly win—3,500 American and 5,500 British casualties. At one point the men fought "on frozen mountaintops where it was too cold even to dig fox holes or slit trenches. Over trails impassable for horses and mules, the men of the [45th] division carried on their shoulders equipment and supplies to the front lines."[23]

Winning the beachhold of Salerno meant that the Allies now controlled the Mediterranean, but as they continued their march through Italy, they faced even harsher conditions and heavier opposition. December 1943, saw "one of the most stubborn and grueling fights in the history of modern warfare. It was winter campaign at its worst. Mud was everywhere: knee-deep, wheeldeep; foxhole engulfing mud. There was a lack of sufficient winter clothes and equipment; rain and snow, cold and sleet; guns and trucks bogged down in soupy ground; machine gun barrels froze, shoes wore thin in a single day on sharp rocks jutting through ice and snow."[24]

And the casualties mounted.

By the end of 1943, the Fifth Army had nearly 40,000 casualties and 50,000 sick, and the trend continued the next year. In an attempt to cross the Rapido River in January 1944, the 36th Division lost 2,900 men in 20 hours. Even the successful landing at Anzio turned into a trap that took the battle of Cassino—at a cost of 42,000 casualties—to free those at Anzio and enable the Allies to reach Rome on June 4.

When the nurses attempted to land in Salerno on September 10, 1943, their ship, the *Newfoundland*, was bombed even though it was clearly marked as a hospital ship. While only 3 of the 103 American nurses suffered minor injuries (though all lost their belongings), 6 British nurses were killed. After returning to Africa on rescue ships, the American nurses finally made it to Italy on September 25.

September 1943 saw an overcrowding of hospital beds because some units were slow setting up due to lost or delayed equipment and because of the heavy troop buildup. According to Lt. Col. Paul K. Sauer, the commander of the 95th Evacuation Hospital, the overcrowded conditions meant that many patients slept on litters and others on the ground.

By October, field hospital platoons were set up next to division clearing stations. Clearing-station personnel performed triage and sent patients who could withstand an ambulance trip to the evacuation hospitals. Others were taken by litter to field hospitals where they remained until strong enough to be moved. If units had to move before these men were well enough, members of the unit stayed behind with them.

Typical medical problems of the Italian campaign were malaria, sandfly fever, dysentery, respiratory diseases, infectious hepatitis, typhus, trench foot, and venereal disease. One enemy attack at Bari Harbor on December 2, 1943 destroyed a ship carrying mustard gas, the release of which led to 628 casualties including 69 deaths. Trench foot became a major problem in areas where the men were forced to remain in wet areas for long periods of time. In some places, such as Anzio, men were forced to remain in cramped positions in water-soaked foxholes for 10 to 12 hours at a time. Nothing could be done for the men at Anzio, but studies of their situation helped with the ordering of winter clothing for later campaigns.

A Red Cross correspondent, Frederick Clayton, wrote about some of the field hospital nurses he met in Italy—Cordelia Cook (who became the first American woman to be twice decorated in WWII), Ruby Duff, Lillian Reiners, Helen Kein, and Margaret Kowaleski—nurses who worked "in the very thick of the battle atmosphere"[25] where you could hear constant explosions and shelling. But the women, said Clayton, joked about bathing and washing out of helmets, eating rations, and living in muddy conditions. And they were quick to tell Clayton that they wouldn't trade their jobs for any nursing job anywhere else. "Give us field hospital work every time. We feel we are indispensable!"[26]

"Hell's Half Acre." "Purple Heart Drive." "The Front without a Back." These are just some of the names given to the narrow strip of land about 15 miles long and 7 miles deep, a space so small that the four evacuation hospitals—no more than tents—were often recipients of enemy shells. Even today, Anzio is synonymous for an area so hellish that one wounded man asked to be sent to the front because "we are better off there than here."[27] A bombardier said of men leaving the area, "Even minus an arm or leg, they are still happy to be leaving Anzio."[28] Anzio was so hellish that medics joked that "replacement tents were sent to Anzio daily with rations."[29]

The Allies thought that a surprise landing behind German lines at Anzio would hasten the Allied northward advance through Italy. What they didn't expect was the strong German resistance. And because of the German air raids and long-range shelling, Charles Wiltse wrote, "There was, in fact, no safe area on the beachhead, since every foot of the ground held by Allied troops could be observed by the enemy and reached by his guns."[30]

And because the evacuation hospitals were as close to the front as the clearing stations, all surgery was forward surgery. As author Harry Noyes put it, "Medical facilities that usually stood miles apart were next door to each other at Anzio. And all were constantly subject to enemy fire in a way and for a length of time never endured elsewhere in World War II."[31] (Note: It wasn't that the Germans were eager to ignore the Geneva Convention by attacking the hospitals, it was that the hospitals were surrounded by legitimate targets—ships, fuel and ammunition dumps, and trucks—and their large red crosses just made the Germans' job easier.)

It was at Anzio, perhaps more than anywhere else, that medical personnel earned the awe and respect of the fighting men. "The battlefront work of the nurses inspired the troops with an 'if-the-nurses-can-take-it-so-can-we' attitude."[32]

And it was at Anzio that the Army's medical units suffered the most casualties: 92 killed, 387 wounded, 19 captured, and 60 reported missing in action. Four nurses—Mary Roberts, Elaine Roe, Ellen Ainsworth, and Virginia Rourke—were the first women in the U.S. Army to receive the Silver Star. Six nurses gave their lives. One nurse, Anna Spillman, recalled:

I've been overseas twenty months in Bizerte, Sicily, Salerno, Cassino, Anzio, and southern France. Although I experienced my first bombing in Bizerte and my first real hardship at Cassino, Anzio was undoubtedly the worst place I have been in. We were under continuous shell-fire there and had to work from eighteen to twenty hours a day. The cases we got were the worst imaginable—blown-off arms and legs, sucking wounds of the chest, injuries which demanded continuous nursing care—but even the nurses were being hurt, and there was a grievous shortage of them.[33]

Nurses of the 95th Evacuation Hospital seemed to attract disaster. In addition to being on the *Newfoundland* when it sank, they were at Anzio on February 7, when, in an effort to lighten his load to escape a British Spitfire, a German pilot released his load of bombs right over their hospital's surgical section. Three nurses—Blanche Sigman, Carrie Sheetz, and Marjorie Morrow—were among the 26 killed. According to one account, "Morrow was giving plasma in a ward tent when Sigman and Sheetz stopped to help her. They continued working through the raid and were killed instantly by a bomb."[34]

Helen Talboy, a nurse with the 95th, was a veteran of the Tunisian, Sicilian, and Italian campaigns; a member of a convoy attacked by submarines; and aboard the *Newfoundland* when it was bombed, yet she volunteered to go to Anzio. It's no wonder that when reporter Kenneth Dixon first saw her he wrote, "The tension was beginning to tell. Helen was one of the most jittery," he said. "She has been through too much. She is about to go to pieces." But his opinion of Helen Talboy soon changed.

When German bombs hit the hospital . . . Helen was on duty in the surgical section, which was punctured by hundreds of shrapnel holes.

Without a moment's hesitation, she took charge. She collected the surviving nurses, gave them bandages and first aid equipment, and started them caring for the wounded, lying crumpled and moaning over the bloody hospital area.

She supervised the first aid and saw to it that the dead were covered as quickly as possible, bringing some merciful semblance of order to the whole nightmarish scene.

The same nurses who seemed so near breaking a week ago were busy everywhere. Late last night they were still working. Nurses from other units came up and volunteered to help, but these tired veterans insisted on caring for their own.

Nearby I saw some men weeping, standing in small, shaken groups. Some of the nurses were crying, too, but soundlessly—the tears on their cheeks in the pale moonlight were the only sign.

It is easy to sit in a comfortable, warm house and speculate on how brave we would all be under conditions such as those under which these nurses are working. It is even easy to speculate on our bravery if we are in actual combat theaters far enough behind the battle lines to be comparatively safe, but it is quite another thing to be in the midst of it for a prolonged period AND STILL BE ABLE TO TAKE IT.[35]

Two nurses—Glenda Spelhaug and La Verne Farquhar—were off duty on February 10. Spelhaug was preparing dinner in her tent and Farquhar had stopped by to borrow a book when a shell exploded outside the tent and killed both women. As Sidney Hyman wrote in his account, "The Medical Story of Anzio," "It is difficult for the mind to conceive how a pot cooking on a stove or how the desire to secure a book constituted a strategic target for enemy fire. Yet . . . the most prosaic acts of day to day living were violently challenged by steel and dynamite."[36]

On February 12, Mary Roberts, with the 56th Evac, was assisting in the operating tent when an enemy shell ripped through the canvas. Although she didn't waver in her duties throughout the 30-minute procedure, she later said, "I wanted to jump under the operating table, but before I could yield to the impulse I had to help lower litter cases to the floor. Then I noticed that a patient on the operating table had his helmet near him, so I put it over his head to give him that much protection. Two of our enlisted medical men were hit and I just did not have time to stop working."[37] According to Harry Noyes,

Roberts' leadership and example calmed the OR team. She handed her lantern to a medic, snapped nurses and medics out of their shock, and got them back to work, despite more shells. As fire spread and patients screamed, a nurse and two medics started to run but stopped when they saw Roberts standing by her post. The operations were successfully finished.[38]

Elaine Roe said, "We were so busy that we seemed calm. I kept telling our patients that it was our guns that they heard and I said it so loudly and so often, that I almost convinced myself."[39]

Ellen Ainsworth, also with the 56th, was wounded in the attack and died four days later. Before her death, she was visited by VI Corps surgeon Col. Rollin L. Bauchspies, who said, "Knowing that our best professional efforts were unable to save the life of this gallant nurse and that in a matter of hours she would pay the supreme sacrifice . . . brought not only sadness and a feeling of great loss . . . but vividly impressed on us the seriousness of our situation."[40] Ainsworth was buried on Anzio Beachhead "with the soldiers she served."[41]

Inez Combites was in surgery the night of March 29, when the 56th Evacuation Hospital was attacked again. "It was a very busy night," she said. "Doctors and nurses just put on helmets and kept on working."[42] The unit, later decorated with the Bronze Star, began their WWII service in North Africa and remained on duty until the end of the war.

In an article he wrote for the *American Journal of Nursing*, Red Cross Correspondent Frederick Clayton described his visit with the 56th at the Nettuno-Anzio beachhead. He told of ambulances and trucks driving with blacked-out lights, of corpsmen holding blued-out flashlights while setting up tents, of the "feverish activity" inside the tents, "the incessant, ominous undertone of guns booming," and of a floor filled with cots. Corpsmen typed admittance forms, handed out blankets, lit cigarettes, and held canteens of water "to parched lips of wounded men." In the preoperative ward, doctors selected cases while nurses took temperatures, gave injections, and administered blood plasma.

The surgical tent was minimal: supplies within easy reach, no poles to obstruct the work, a plank floor, and small portable stoves. The nurse in charge, Loretta Bass, seemed to be "everywhere at once . . . yet never going so far from the operating tables that she could not anticipate the need of the surgical teams." Six operating tables were being used at the same time with two surgeons, a nurse, a nurse anesthetist, and corpsmen at each one.

And the wounds—a complicated fracture of the femur, a hand amputation, a shell fragment deep in the thigh, a bullet wound in the head, a man whose lower jaw had been shot away. Even when a "lights out" was ordered, the surgical teams worked on. According to Clayton:

There was work to do and men who had been lying in foxholes could wait no longer. They might die if they were not cared for quickly. . . . So the skillful binding up of wounds went on through the evening, hour after hour; surgeons, nurses, and corpsmen drove themselves without rest until relieved by other teams who had slept earlier.[43]

Chief Nurse Dorothy Meadors said of their unit:

It's worth it. We can save so many. We already have reached our capacity. But we can still expand. We have to. Evacuation hospitals are geared to meet any circumstance—a normal flow of patients or an extraordinary emergency. The nurses thrive on the outdoor life; one of our girls worked from fifteen to twenty hours a day during the big pushes in North Africa and Southern Italy and never had a cold until she went on leave in Algiers and slept indoors in a real bed.[44]

Why weren't the nurses pulled out of such a place of danger? It was considered, said Sidney Hyman, but the units at Anzio were in a space so small that each knew what was happening to the other. The nurses, therefore, became not only the symbol of our "determination to hold what we had," but pulling them out would have "betrayed to the combat troops the gravity of their own plight."[45]

NOTES

1. Quoted in Wyatt Blassingame, *Combat Nurses of World War II* (New York: Landmark Books, 1967), p. 61.

2. Quoted in Major General Normal T. Kirk, "Girls in the Foxholes," *The American Magazine*, May 1944, p. 95.

3. Charles M. Wiltse, *Medical Service in the Mediterranean and Minor Theaters*, Series: U.S. Army in World War II, The Technical Services, The Medical Department (Washington, D.C.: Office of the Chief of Military History Department of the Army, 1965), p. 214.

4. Judith A. Bellafaire, *The Army Nurse Corps: A Commemoration of World War II Service* (Washington, D.C.: U.S. Army Center of Military History, no date), Pub. 72-14, p. 9.

5. Wiltse, p. 144.

6. Quoted in Lena Dixon and Aurelia R. Lehozky, *History and Modern Nursing*, 2nd ed. (Philadelphia: F. A. Davis, 1967), p. 153.

7. Bellafaire, p. 11.

8. Roberta Love Tayloe, *Combat Nurse: A Journal of World War II* (Santa Barbara: Fithian Press, 1988), pp. 28, 29.

9. Helen Pon Onyett, Interview with author, December 19, 1991.

10. Page Cooper, *Navy Nurse* (New York: McGraw-Hill, 1946), p. 130.

11. Tayloe, pp. 34, 37.

12. "Lt. Mary Ann Sullivan Wins Legion of Merit," *American Journal of Nursing*, December 1943, p. 1143.

13. Tayloe, p. 38.

14. Quoted in Philip A. Kalisch and Beatrice J. Kalisch, *Advance of American Nursing* (Boston: Little, Brown, 1978), p. 456.

15. Quoted in Dietz and Lehozky, *History and Modern Nursing*, p. 154.

16. 2nd Lt. Frances Wells, ANC, "North Africa," *American Journal of Nursing*, December 1943, p. 1130.

17. "Army Nurses in Ireland and India, New Caledonia and Africa," *American Journal of Nursing*, February 1943, p. 212.

18. "On Leave from Africa," *American Journal of Nursing*, June 1943, p. 559.

19. Wiltse, pp. 147, 162, 170.

20. 1st Lt. Mary Ann Harman, ANC, "Housecleaning in a Station Hospital," *American Journal of Nursing*, June 1944, p. 595.

21. Col. Raymond Scott, MC, U.S. Army, "Eleventh Evacuation Hospital in Sicily," *American Journal of Nursing*, October 1943, p. 926.

22. Henry Noyes, "Anzio Is Coming of Age for Army's Nurses." Series: Warriors of Mercy, Chapter 24, *The Mercury*, Fort Sam Houston: U.S. Army of Public Affairs, April 1994, no p. #.

23. *The Fighting Men of Texas: A History of the Second World War, A Memorial, A Remembrance, An Appreciation*, Vol. IV (Dallas: Historical Publishing Company, 1948), p. 1396.

24. *The Fighting Men of Texas: A History of the Second World War, A Memorial, A Remembrance, An Appreciation*, Vol. I (Dallas: Historical Publishing Company, 1948), no p. #.

25. Frederick Clayton, "Front-Line Surgical Nurses," *American Journal of Nursing*, March 1944, p. 234.

26. Quoted in Clayton, "Front-Line Surgical Nurses," p. 235.

27. Quoted in Robert Wallace, *The Italian Campaign*, Series: World War II (Alexandria: Time-Life Books, 1978), p. 146.

28. Quoted in Harry Noyes, "Evacuation from Anzio Never Gets Routine," Series: Warriors of Mercy, Chapter 24, *The Mercury*, Fort Sam Houston: U.S. Army of Public Affairs, April 1994, no p. #.

29. Harry Noyes, "Hell's Half Acre: Anzio Hospital Center Becomes Magnet for Stray Bombs, Artillery Shells," Series: Warriors of Mercy, Chapter 23, *The Mercury*, Fort Sam Houston: U.S. Army of Public Affairs, March 1994, no p. #.

30. Wiltse, p. 271.

31. Harry Noyes, "Easy Landing Gives Way to Bloody Struggle, Stalemate," Series: Warriors of Mercy, Chapter 23, *The Mercury*, Fort Sam Houston: U.S. Army of Public Affairs, March 1994, no p. #.

32. Wallace, p. 146.

33. Quoted in "Typical Army Nurse," *The Army Nurse*, April 1945, p. 6.

34. Noyes, "Anzio Is Coming of Age for Army's Nurses," no p. #.

35. Kenneth Dixon, "A Job Well Done," *The Army Nurse*, March 1944, pp. 2-3.

36. 1st Lt. Sidney Hyman, M.A.C., Historian, Medical Section, Headquarters, Fifth Army, "The Medical Story of Anzio," September 25, 1944, p. 11.

37. Quoted in Ruth Y. White, "At Anzio Beachhead," *American Journal of Nursing*, April 1944, p. 371.

38. Noyes, "Anzio Is Coming of Age for Army's Nurses," no p. #.

39. Quoted in White, "At Anzio Beachhead," p. 371.

40. Quoted in Noyes, "Anzio Is Coming of Age for Army's Nurses," no p. #.

41. Quoted in "World War II Casualties: Ainsworth, Ellen G., 2/Lt. ANC, N732 770," Center for Military History, Washington, D. C.

42. Inez Combites Hood Questionnaire.

43. Frederick Clayton, "An Evacuation Unit Serves under Fire," *American Journal of Nursing*, May 1944, pp. 453-455.

44. Quoted in Clayton, "An Evacuation Unit Serves under Fire," p. 455.

45. Hyman, p. 16.

Chapter 6

The European Theater

We saw it coming through the late 1930s. The reports from
Europe were like bulletins from an operating table. Yet,
America stayed in the waiting room, knowing that worse was
yet to come, knowing we would be drawn into it. Closer and
closer came the catastrophic crisis. Then, September 1, 1939, a
time for beaches and vacation, it struck and the dagger blow
was upon us with a terrifying swiftness that paralyzed the
world's statesmen: War!

—Harrison Salisbury
Foreword, *World War II: A 50th Anniversary*

Although Americans had watched Adolf Hitler's rise to power since the early
1930s, most were too preoccupied with surviving the Great Depression to
worry about the ravings of a tyrant so far away. Besides, the story he told
everyone outside of Germany was that he wasn't a "warmonger."[1]

The story he told his people, however, was different.

The Treaty of Versailles, which ended World War I, took territory away
from Germany, restricted the growth of the country's land and sea forces,
banned its air force, and forbade any expansion. The hardships of the years
that followed—poor economy, high unemployment, and crowded
conditions—made the Germans vulnerable to a leader who promised an end to
all their ills, and Hitler did just that. The Treaty of Versailles and Jewish
capitalism, said Hitler, were the roots of their problems. But they weren't to
worry, for he had the solution: Build up arms and take, by force if necessary,
the needed land—*Lebensraum* ("living space")—and use its current occupants
for forced labor. As one author put it, "It seemed, to many Germans, to make
sense."[2]

He began this expansion by crossing the Rhine River in March 1936, and putting German soldiers at the French border. Two years later, he sent his forces into Austria. Both feats were accomplished without resistance. Fearing that they were next, the Czechoslovakians planned to put up a fight, but the leaders of Britain and France didn't give them a chance. Believing Hitler when he said that he wanted only the portion called the Sudetenland (home to three million Germans), the two leaders let him take the area in September 1938. By March of the next year, Hitler had the entire country.

While Americans continued to watch, Hitler continued to expand— Denmark, Norway, Belgium, Luxembourg, The Netherlands, France, Yugoslavia, and Greece. Great Britain and Russia were also on his list, and some say the Americas and Africa were too.

Although many Americans still believed that the United States should stay out of the war, movements were made to enter it: the military was growing via the draft bill passed on September 16, 1940; defense plants began to speed up production of war materials; and on March 11, 1941, President Franklin D. Roosevelt signed the Lend-Lease Bill that supplied war materials to the Allies. Even as early as September 1939, the U.S. Atlantic Fleet supported the British Fleet under the guise of the Neutrality Patrol.

Before long, many U.S. citizens were feeling the effects of a war they still weren't supposed to be a part of. On September 4, 1939, the U.S. Navy was ordered to "shoot on sight at any vessel that threatened American ships or any ships escorted by American vessels."[3] On October 17, 1941, the USS *Kearny* was torpedoed, and though it didn't sink, 11 men became the first U.S. military deaths of the war. Even more men, 115, lost their lives when the USS *Reuben James* went down after being attacked by a German submarine on October 31, 1941.

From mid-1940 to mid-1941 Germany's U-boats and submarines so dominated the Atlantic waters that they called the period "Happy Time."[4] While Germany was determined to destroy U.S. and British ships and to prevent U.S. aid from reaching its allies in Europe and Asia, it was essential that they not succeed. The United States couldn't allow the Germans to sink all the supplies that Britain needed to stay out of Hitler's grasp or allow Japan and Germany to ship materials to each other. And, after December 1941, there was the need for the United States to send supplies and troops overseas for the invasions of North Africa, Italy, and Normandy.

Since the United States also needed land links for air routes, jumping-off points for military operations, and medical bases for patients on their way back home, it expanded its screen of defensive outposts "from the Arctic Circle to the Equator and from central Canada to the Azores."

Greenland, according to author Charles M. Wiltse, was "a potential stop on an air ferry route that could enable fighter planes to move from American factories to British bases under their own power." It was also "the only known commercial source of natural cryolite, invaluable as an electrolyte in the production of aluminum," and "the gathering point for storms that would influence air and naval activity in western Europe."[5]

Iceland, according to German geopolitician Karl Haushofer, was of such strategic importance that "whoever possesses Iceland holds a pistol pointed permanently at England, America and Canada." Thankfully, by the middle of 1943, the Allied bases in Greenland, Britain, Iceland, and Newfoundland provided so much air power that what had been "a virtual playground for the German subs" had become for them "a death trap."[6]

THE NORTH ATLANTIC

But Allied control of the seas was still two years away when American nurses began going overseas as Red Cross volunteers. In June 1941, Marion Blissett and nine other nurses, members of the Harvard Hospital Unit, were sent to England to establish a military hospital for American soldiers. They were crossing the Atlantic in the Norwegian ship, the *Vigrid,* as part of a convoy of 50 when, on June 23, the *Vigrid* developed engine trouble and was forced to lag behind. At 7:15 the next morning, they were 400 miles off the coast of Greenland when, Blissett said, "I was awakened by a terrific impact as the first torpedo struck without warning. The second hit as I reached deck. We found some sailors had put off in our lifeboat, but the second officer took all the girls in his boat." After the steamer went down, a German submarine surfaced, picked up the survivors, questioned them, and then offered the women passage on the submarine. The Norwegian officers declined.

Back on their own, the survivors rowed the small boats in the icy North Atlantic waters for 12 days. Daily rations went from one hardtack, a portion of a can of meatballs, and five ounces of water every 12 hours, to a half hardtack and saved rainwater. A lifeboat containing four of the nurses drifted away and was last seen on June 27. Those nurses became the first uniformed American women casualties of the war.

Rain, cold winds, and rough seas were almost daily companions, and some of the crew began showing signs of desperation and delirium by the time they were finally rescued by an American destroyer on July 5—200 miles from Greenland. Once aboard the ship the women were given the officers' quarters and "spoiled . . . with service and kindness."[7] Blissett was taken to Iceland where she rested for a few days before being sent back to the States. In March 1942, she joined the Navy Nurse Corps and spent the remaining war years in the Pacific.

Nurses arrived in Iceland in the fall of 1941, and worked immediately to make their surroundings more homelike. They turned packing boxes into furniture and made covers and drapes from whatever material they could find. "I cannot look at a packing box or crate any more without realizing its possibilities," said one nurse. "If I only had an opportunity to go into a Woolworth's store I wouldn't have a nickel left."[8] And their work paid off. One nurse described her hut as being "comfortable, cozy, and homelike."[9] Another said that the raging blizzard outside made "our Nissen hut with the large potbellied stove seem a cheery place."[10]

And the country's natural beauty wasn't lost on these women so far from home. "One does not miss the trees, for there are so many beautiful mountains to look at. Our hut has a double window on one side and we have a million dollar view."[11] Edna D. Umbach, ANC, said, "The view from our location is beautiful; high rugged mountains, capped with snow at this time of year, the colors changing constantly. The northern lights with their pale green streamers waving across the sky are very spectacular."[12]

But though they enjoyed summer and its picnics, sightseeing trips, and beautiful flowers, the winters were horrendous. "We had a gale that was really a hurricane. Our hut was banked recently, which I think is all that kept it on the ground. It shook and rocked so hard that books were thrown from the shelf and the stovepipe was pulled off. Muddy water from the road was blown all over the front of our hut, for we get the full force of the blast in our location. Sentries assisted the nurses to the mess hall, for it was almost impossible to walk alone. I made rounds with difficulty and lost my sou'wester."[13]

The number of military medical personnel on Iceland grew when the war started and then decreased when the danger of invasion lessened by the end of 1943. Patients included U.S. Army personnel, Icelandic citizens, members of the American Red Cross, U.S. civil service employees, and other Allied military personnel.

Medical personnel on Iceland saw few injuries and no combat wounds, and since there were very few insects on the island and "no diseases peculiar to the country," there were very few cases of disease and even a low incidence of venereal disease. Although there were jaundice and mumps outbreaks in 1942, respiratory ailments were the most common cause of hospitalization. Mental disorders were brought on by "isolation, boredom, lack of recreation, adjustment problems, and a feeling of contributing little to the war."[14]

But there was one time when many men owed their lives to the quick action taken by the nurses. As fire and smoke rose swiftly from the basement of a three-story wooden hospital, nurses moved the almost 100 patients to other hospitals or to the nurses' quarters, then moved them again when it looked like the fire would engulf these buildings too. "Every patient, doctor, nurse, and soldier was out of the doomed building within fifteen minutes" without "so much as a scratch or bad cold."[15]

GREAT BRITAIN

The United States sent troops to Great Britain to protect the island from invasion and to help with the efforts of the Royal Air Force Bomber Command's attacks on Germany. The United States also used Great Britain as a stopover point for troops going elsewhere in Europe and the Mediterranean. And because of the colossal buildup of personnel and supplies in preparation for the "largest and most complex land campaign of the Second World War,"[16] Operation OVERLORD, the invasion of Normandy, WWII Britain became the "biggest hospital on earth."[17] One person said that supplying all medical supplies and personnel for the European Theater was comparable to "shipping about 12 complete New York City Bellevue Hospitals, except the buildings."[18]

Hospital facilities included Nissen huts on concrete foundations, British hospitals, converted barracks and schools, and fixed hospitals (tents attached to existing hospitals). By January 1942, the British Churchill Hospital was renamed the American Hospital in Britain, and on July 15, 1942, it became part of the U.S. Army Medical Corps. (At that time many of the Red Cross nurses joined either the U.S. Army or Canadian Army Nurse Corps.) This hospital worked with the British Ministry of Health in treating and studying wartime diseases, particularly contagious diseases (always a problem in wartime when people are forced together and unable to maintain proper sanitary conditions).

But even as the first 1,500 American nurses were making their way to the British Isles, the British were making preparations for them—and not enthusiastically. According to Frank Stuart's article "Invasion by Angels," having strangers around is contrary to the English disposition. "We are secretive by nature. It is an English joke that an Englishman's greatest ambition in life is to have a railway carriage all to himself."[19]

And their concerns seemed quite justified. After all, the populace was already crowded and living on rations. How could they survive with an additional 1,500 bodies to house and mouths to feed? The locals feared that the nurses would buy all the unrationed items and take up all the seats in tea shops, on buses, and in movie theaters. And not only would the natives have to share their rations and bus seats, many would have to share their homes because many medical personnel would arrive without permanent assignments or housing accommodations. A nurse who arrived early in 1944 said, "The policeman took a group of you and walked down the street and said, 'One goes here and two go there,' and you walked into a stranger's house and that's where you stayed for about a month."[20]

So what happened when the American women finally arrived? One elderly lady complained royally when she was assigned a nurse—then later made the young woman her sole heir! Another family loved their nurse so much that they wanted her to stay with them after the war "as a daughter." Soon the nurses became commodities and "something very un-British happened," said Stuart. "Householders came scrambling for nurses, like prizes in a raffle. Some citizens were very annoyed because they woke up rather late and found there were no nurses left to distribute. One old lady produced her ration book and argued for quite a long time that she was entitled to her fair share of whatever was going. In the end they found her a little nurse from Virginia."

Because of the possible inconveniences to their hosts, the nurses had been given a list of dos and don'ts: don't crowd the buses, don't take over the civilian laundries, don't eat the rations offered in "private hospitality," and do go easy when buying British rations. One of the nurses, Ruth Jackson, billeted with the Stuarts who reported that Jackson was "so thoughtful, so considerate, so frightened of imposing on us, that we are embarrassed." Stuart added, "If she takes a cup of tea with us, she makes it last half an hour . . . when she is persuaded to take a cracker (biscuit to us), she makes that last half an hour, too. We never hear her come in or go out. She leaves the bath so clean after using it that we wonder how it is done. We can't do it like that ourselves."[21]

Eventually, the women were housed elsewhere and, according to Winona G. Comer, ANC, their lives in Britain boiled down to "fundamentals like work, play, eating, sleeping, and keeping warm." But, she added, "It is also possible to find comfort in many small ways and things such as hot water, books, radio, clean laundry, electric lights, and a conveniently located latrine. Most of us quickly make a satisfactory adjustment and feel our Army experience will be of value to us the rest of our lives."[22]

Army Nurse Genevieve Todd agreed. "[S]o many hours devoted to work, and so many devoted to play, but there have been experiences that have enriched our lives and memories we shall cherish for the rest of our days."[23]

Through the efforts of many people, primarily Mrs. Anthony Drexel Biddle, wife of the U.S. Ambassador to the Exiled Governments in Britain, nurses were able to relax in Red Cross clubs. The most popular of these was on Charles Street in London where nurses paid about a dollar a night for bed and bath and about 20 to 50 cents for meals. The club organized teas, dances, tours of London, and visits to big London hospitals. By early 1943, the Eighth Air Force was bringing its mobile movie unit to the club every Tuesday night.

Some of the nurses were among several groups invited to Buckingham Palace. "Only one who has lived the rough life of an Army nurse, no matter how briefly," said Irene L. Zwisler, "can appreciate what a pleasure it was to drink tea once more from a dainty china cup, to balance diminutive sandwiches on an equally dainty gold-encrusted saucer, engraved with the royal monogram." The nurses were the first group to be introduced to the King. "It was hard to realize," said Zwisler, "that we were face to face with a sovereign who governs five hundred million people and controls one-fourth of the earth's surface."[24]

And there were so many things to see. Nurses of the Presbyterian Unit from New York visited Samuel Johnson's birthplace and the Cathedral at Lichfield. They saw a production of *Hamlet* at the New Shakespearian Theater in Stratford-on-Avon and a sculptured memorial of Florence Nightingale in the crypt of St. Paul's. Roberta Love Tayloe described seeing "beautiful St. Paul's with great craters, the streets full of debris from a recent bombing. Fortunately," she said, "Westminster Abbey was still in one piece and it gave me chills with its beauty and history." She also went shopping and attended plays, dinners, and dances and experienced the famous "pea soup"[25] fog.

Because there was little activity in British military hospitals at this stage of the war, there were always some people—nurses included—who thought that if you weren't in the middle of combat, your work wasn't important. This attitude was obvious in Lt. T. B. Kemp when he visited the 150th Station Hospital in London to write a story about Army nurses. Disappointed to learn that the nurses performed, for the most part, the same type of nursing that they did in the States, Kemp said, "It didn't *sound* very interesting—for a war story, I mean . . . My mind had been filled with vivid pictures of heroic front-line nurses at Bataan and Corregidor. . . . Blood, bombs, guns, action." He even asked Chief Nurse Hazel Hawkins, "Do you mind—being here, I mean, doing ordinary sort of sick nursing? Wouldn't you rather be where there's more action and excitement?"[26]

Hawkins quickly responded. "No—I don't think so. After all they are all our men, and they are fighting for us. They need caring for when they're sick just as much as when they're wounded. Nurses are needed here as well as on the battlefields, and this is where we can serve best, I guess. I've never heard any of my nurses complaining. We're too busy to think about anything but the job we're doing."[27]

Immediately convinced, Kemp wrote, "It takes courage to nurse casualties under fire; but it takes no less courage to carry on day after day performing the same unexciting routine jobs behind the lines, away from the excitement and thrills and peculiar glamour that surrounds the battle front."[28]

These women may have served "away from the excitement and thrills and peculiar glamour that surrounds the battle front," but that didn't mean they were out of harm's way. Two U.S. hospitals in Great Britain were bombed: the 121st Station Hospital on April 19, 1944, and the 1st General Hospital on July 29, 1944.

And then there were the air raids. In her book *Combat Nurse: A Journal of World War II*, Roberta Love Tayloe recalled going underground and hearing what sounded like "a very bad thunderstorm. The ack-ack guns made such a racket, I wondered how they stood it, night after night, these brave people."[29] One nurse said that air-raid sirens meant that all nurses—on and off duty—had to report to stations wearing helmets and added that there were more casualties from people bumping into each other in the dark underground shelters than from enemy aircraft.

It was because of the very real potential for danger that nurses were taught to recognize the sounds of warfare: "how one plane attracted ack-ack while another dropped parachutists," and the difference in the sounds of German, English, and American planes.

And because of threats to security, the women were warned to be suspicious of "scratched or limping strangers carrying brief cases," and told that if a stranger asked them for directions they were to respond, "Where are you now?" and "Where are you going and where do you come from?" Street signs indicated only the global directions of north, south, east, and west; and military personnel were warned against going places in large groups because that might provide information about military unit sizes and locations.

The Army nurses had made such a good impression on the British that when 100 Navy nurses arrived in 1944, they were welcomed by throngs of flag-waving children. The women were stationed in Netley, on Southampton Harbor, and worked in the Royal Victoria, one of the first hospitals in England (founded circa 1862), and full of legendary tales. Not only did the front hall contain cases of china once owned and used by Queen Victoria, but legend says it once held a shawl embroidered by Victoria that was used to comfort dying soldiers.

The hospital itself looked like a place of legends—an "enormous and impressive weathered brick building with its early Victorian clock tower and handsome white arches . . . in an old and well-kept park at the edge of the water." One could see villagers playing cricket out a front window and the ruins of Netley Abbey off in the distance. Each of the hundred wards was heated by a tiny fireplace and held 10 beds. The nurses were housed in one of the wings.

As preparations for the invasion drew near, patients in the Royal Victoria Hospital were evacuated to make room for Normandy casualties. And the tension grew as the women:

saw equipment everywhere, in little woods, even in backyards, covered with camouflage nets. Ships were gathering in the harbor and leaves were canceled; no one was allowed to go up to London. In the middle of May groups of English and Canadian soldiers arrived and were isolated in a special ward. Their meals were served to them on the ward, by selected corpsmen and nurses, and they were not permitted to ask or answer questions. It was rumored that they had been briefed. For two weeks they came in and out. They were the only patients. The hospital was cleared of all others except members of the staff. The shock room was ready with sulfa, oxygen, plasma, whole blood, within hand's reach, and every bunk in the hospital was made up.

One nurse knew the time had come when she counted the bombers going overhead "until her eyes blurred and she gave it up somewhere beyond a hundred." According to Page Cooper in her book *Navy Nurse*, "By Monday night there could be no doubt that the invasion was actually on. The hum of planes overhead made a buzz like the noise of a sawmill. Most of the ships had cleared out of the harbor but it was full of activity."[30]

Within four days of the invasion, the nurses began receiving so many patients—many straight from the beaches with minimal first aid—that they could barely keep up. When numbers were tallied for June through September, the Royal Victoria had seen 10,000 patients, or one-fifth of the invasion casualties. By the end of September, the hospital was decommissioned and the Navy nurses sent home. Their commander, Mary Martha Heck, was given the Bronze Star, which she shared with her nurses. "Many of these boys would have died if we had not been there to give them immediate care,"[31] said Heck.

The staff of an Army transit hospital in south England was also expecting casualties and received the first ones by 8:30 the morning of the invasion. Because they'd been trained to treat patients direct from war zones, they were able to admit and process large numbers of patients quickly—most within 24 hours; 800 in one day. But those who were staying for a while received the TLC they so desperately needed:

[T]heir first concern was to get clean. There were showers for the ambulant, help in bathing from nurses and other patients for the handicapped. Some had beards a half inch long. It was not uncommon, as the days at the front increased, to use four blades in shaving one patient. Then there were hair cuts and a change of clothes. The next concern was food—hot fresh food in unlimited quantities and time to eat it! Their stomachs were like bottomless pits. The dietitians took special care that food was attractively served and that special diets, such as those for soldiers with jaw injuries, were adequate in nutritional value. In addition to being clean, the apex of luxury was a clean bed with white sheets. It is amazing how few narcotics are needed and the patients awaken only for food.[32]

When patients arrived at general hospitals, the fine work performed at the transit hospitals was evident: "most patients arrived . . . with fractures properly immobilized, wounds debrided and ready for secondary closure, and relatively little infection or gas gangrene. Patient deaths on the way to general hospitals, and after arrival there, were very few."[33]

EUROPE

The first nurses landed in Europe on June 7 and 8, and their hospitals—the 13th and 51st at OMAHA beach, and the 42d and 45th at UTAH beach—opened on June 10 and 11. Although they came over as field hospitals, they worked as evacuation hospitals on the coast until relieved. A few weeks later, one woman recounted her experience:

We landed on the beaches (France) just as everybody else had done. It was strange to think that we were walking up that beach and over the sand hills behind it without a moment's thought of any possible danger, when just a few weeks before men had died in hundreds as they fought their way through all the cruel obstacles and heavy fire . . .

When we first arrived and spent our first night in the field, we wondered if we would ever come through alive. Noise, noise, noise, overhead and all around! However, it's amazing how blasé one gets. We're in quite a safe spot now anyhow, and almost all the noise is ours—day and night it rolls on—supplies, supplies, supplies, troops, ammunition and overhead the constant roar of planes.[34]

An Army nurse identified only as Capt. M. M. was with the first medical unit in Normandy. When they arrived, she said, "all the patients had been flown back to England, except, one ward full. They were too sick to be moved. I really thought that most of them would never leave France, but then my nurses got busy—and what a change! Those men really took a new lease on life. In three days all but one were ready to be evacuated." Although she credited the doctors and aidmen for saving the men, she credited the nurses with much of the postoperative recovery. "The presence of nurses seems to lend an atmosphere of comfort and a feeling of safety and refuge—a touch of home. There is no limit to the amount of time and energy that both nurses and men are willing to give to the patients."[35]

The field hospital platoons on UTAH beach admitted the most urgent nontransportable cases, but between the attached auxiliary surgical teams and the three field hospital platoons, 30 major surgeries could be performed a day. According to Graham A. Cosmas and Albert E. Cowdrey, authors of *Medical Service in the European Theater of Operations*, the work was hard and demanding but "offered a high level of professional challenge and satisfaction."[36] Capt. M. M. agreed. "I doubt that any member of our hospital personnel would go home now if he had a chance. We are so desperately needed. It is what we have been training and waiting for [for] so long. We are rewarded constantly by look and word from our patients."[37]

In addition to wounds, there were outbreaks of diarrhea, respiratory ailments, and cases of vitamin deficiency caused by a diet of army rations. Some of the men who had served in the Mediterranean had recurring bouts of malaria. There was also an ever-increasing number of neuropsychiatric patients.

Claudia M. Draper, ANC, worked at a hospital in Cherbourg that had just been captured from the Germans the day before, and for 10 days the Americans were outnumbered by German patients and hospital personnel. "[I]t was hard to tell who were the prisoners and who the victors," said Draper. "It was certainly something that had not been covered by our training back in the states." But the German doctors were very cooperative and interested in American medical procedures, and when their patients were well enough, all were sent to England.

When they first arrived, the place was a mess. "Wards had been used as latrines, and half cans of food, pieces of used bandage, parts of bottles of liquor, all kinds of litter, were scattered throughout the entire place."[38] There was also propaganda: murals depicting German troops, mottos, and insignia.

But when clean enough to accept U.S. patients, the buildings and grounds were beautiful: tall, vine-covered stone walls; glassed-in, tiled porches; palm, walnut, and fig trees; hedges of hydrangeas; winding roads; beautiful roses; and pots of glowing red geraniums.

And, after a constant supply of K-rations, the food improved; and vegetables, dehydrated potatoes and onions, canned meats and beans were savored as if the finest cuisine. Soon there were bakeries and fresh bread. A dietitian remarked, "Our field kitchens are really coming along in fine style. Today we began eating on plates and using knives, forks and spoons, sitting at tables under a tent with sides rolled up—just another sidewalk cafe, quite stylish; and all this instead of eating out of mess kits, sitting on the ground in the broiling sun, battling with the bees for your food, mouthful by mouthful. We're really quite luxurious now, we think."[39]

Sometimes called "the Normandy breakout," Operation COBRA, which began on July 25, 1944, was the plan for getting the Allies away from the Normandy beaches and into mainland France. At the height of fighting to take Brest in September, there were 300 to 400 casualties per day, and those needing more than 10 days to recover were sent to England by LST or plane. During August, the field and evacuation hospitals had so much trouble keeping up with the fighting that they often played leapfrog with each other.

The 5th and 298th General Hospitals outgrew their predicted 1,000 beds and admitted both long- and short-term patients, thus acting as both general and station hospitals. Eventually, the 5th became a collecting point for patients with combat exhaustion and suspected self-inflicted wounds, and the 298th treated mostly mine accident cases.

The 108th General also had to reorganize for "mass casualty reception, emergency care, and evacuation" while working under less than desirable conditions:

Our own USA supplies had not come up from Le Mans, many of our surgeons and shock teams . . . were still away on detached service, no penicillin was available, the hospital communications systems had been destroyed by the retreating Germans, and we had no practical experience as a group in handling large numbers of casualties as an evacuation hospital. We used German paper dressings and other material they had left behind. . . .

We put dentists, chemists and bacteriologists to work in the wards with the medical men who were not giving anesthetics or assisting in surgery. We worked 36 hours straight, hoping to catch up, but were still 500 cases, needing operations, behind schedule. We then organized 12-hour day and night shifts and operated only upon the most severely wounded.[40]

On August 15, 1944, the Seventh Army landed in Southern France during Operation ANVIL, the counterpart of Operation OVERLORD. The two landings were originally planned to happen simultaneously, but too many of the ships and landing craft were needed for each to carry out such an objective. The goal of this second invasion—which included 1,300 planes, 880 ships, and 1,370 landing craft—was to join the Allied troops who'd landed in Normandy. Together they would "be in a position to advance in an unbroken front on Germany's homeland."[41]

And they succeeded. According to Rear Adm. Calvin T. Durgin, USN, "They now proved that they could wreck enemy forts, demolish his railroad and motor vehicle transport, and totally disrupt his transport and communications." Durgin also said that "German resistance became demoralized . . . and the triumphant armies swept on into France with the carrier planes still striking deep ahead of them up the Rhone valley."[42]

Medical support operated during ANVIL much as it had during OVERLORD, with units coming ashore with the troops and soon followed by field and evacuation hospitals. The first nurse to go ashore was Evelyn E. Swanson. Two others, Fern Wingird and Gladys Joyce, compared the French invasion to the Italian campaign where they'd gone ashore under fire, and said, "It just did not seem possible that any invasion could go so easily."[43]

Again the mobile units moved with the troops.

And though the roads were often bumpy and crowded, and while blackout precautions often contributed to accidents and lost routes, the nurses usually laughed it off.

Several evacuation hospitals made record-breaking moves, evacuating a full census of patients in less than five hours, packing, loading, and moving all equipment and personnel to new areas.   Much of this was accomplished in a blinding snowstorm along blacked-out roads, crisscrossing the upper Vosges Mountains.   Trained units, with months and months of experience in evacuation procedure, accomplished the task without mishap, each phase moving along smoothly and on schedule despite the fact that, as one nurse said, "the Germans were practically breathing down our necks."   One unit traveled in truck convoy 70 miles to new sites, but on arrival received instructions to go back to the setup they had just evacuated.   Observers thought the nurses were hysterical because they laughed at the prospect of unpacking and reopening the hospital they had just closed down that morning.   "It's all part of the job," was the response of the nurses.[44]

Sweeping across Europe

As the troops moved across Europe, nurses worked in Holland, Belgium, Germany, and other countries that many of them had seen only in books and magazines.   But instead of quaint villages and tourist attractions, they saw starving people and destroyed cities.   And whether they treated patients in a tuberculosis sanitarium or in a school that the Germans had converted into an obstetrical hospital for "Hitler Mothers," the women did their jobs.

The 24th Evacuation Hospital, one of the first at OMAHA beach, later moved from place to place along a stretch of road called "Hell's Highway," a single two-lane main road that saw constant traffic and periodic German attacks.   During the unit's first 24 hours in Bourg-Leopold, it received 512 casualties.   The next week the staff admitted more than 1,600 patients and evacuated 1,300.   With no reinforcements, the surgical staff worked 16- and 18-hour days and performed more than 540 operations.   Patients were evacuated to Diest, then on to Britain.   The unit found itself in Holland in October and "to the joy of the staff" took over a modern steel-and-glass hospital building in Nijmegen.   Though the building was nice, the location was close to the front and "constantly shaken—and occasionally hit by German shells aimed at the nearby Nijmegen bridge."[45]

The goal of Operation MARKET-GARDEN (initiated September 17, 1944) was to seize seven bridges over which Allied tanks could cross the Rhine.   This plan, the largest airborne operation of the war, put 35,000 paratroopers in harm's way and turned into a disaster.   More than 11,000 men were wounded or taken prisoner.

War correspondent Mary Jose spent a night with the nurses of the 110th in Luxembourg.   The hospital was an old three-story schoolhouse with 450 cots in the classrooms, extra ones in hallways, and 150 for ambulatory patients under tents in the playground.   The nurses lived across a driveway in a house that until recently had been a Gestapo headquarters.

Jose witnessed episode after episode of heroism, humor, sadness, and dedication.   She watched Wilhelma Tonnar treat a 19-year-old radio engineer who had been blown three feet in the air by a German shell, and a sergeant who had lost both hands and his eyesight during the same attack. She also witnessed one of the medical miracles that made nursing so rewarding:

Eleanor Aldrich, a blonde Minnesotan, instructs him. "Ernie, we're going to work with procaine just like a dentist does when he pulls a tooth. If we hurt you, nod your head so we'll know. Understand?"

Ernie nods immediate assent. She covers him up with a tent of sterile sheets so that only the top of his shaved head shows. He groans when the needle goes into his scalp. Eleanor runs supplies to the surgeon's tray; checks his pulse and blood pressure repeatedly. The hour hand of the big clock on the wall goes majestically past eleven . . . creeps up to twelve. Perspiration gleams on the doctor and his attendants as they pick the metal out of Ernie's head and clean away splinters of bone. There is a whisper under the tent—a half-unbelieving whisper that suddenly increases to a shout, "What d'ya know—I've got my voice back already. Hey, Doc, I can talk again!"[46]

Other nurses at the 110th included Ann Bunata, Bett Seib, Hilma Feistel, Valeria Murphey, Mary Margaret Grant, Mary Keily, Dorothy Johnson, Pauline Foy, Georgie Moss, and Dixie Diefenderfer.

In December 1944 and January 1945, the Allies and Germans engaged in the war's largest land battle fought by U.S. armed forces—the Battle of the Bulge. Thinking that the Germans were almost defeated, the American troops (most of which were new recruits) were scattered and taking a breather when a sudden German push took them by surprise. Had it not been for the extraordinary determination of *all* personnel—including non-combatants—and speedy troop reinforcement, Hitler might have achieved his goal of splitting the American and British forces at Antwerp and stabilizing the Western Front.

But the price was high. Between December 16 and February 22, the First Army's hospitals admitted more than 78,000 patients. The Third Army's admitted 70,000 in December and January alone. When the 44th and 67th Evacuation Hospitals were forced to leave their positions, five nurses with the 67th stayed overnight with 200 patients too weak to be moved. It wasn't until the next day that nurses and patients were rescued—just hours before they would have fallen into German hands.

In addition to receiving most of the American casualties from the southern part of the Bulge, the 110th Evacuation Hospital fed and housed thousands of troops separated from their units. They received approximately 300 patients a day and once had a surgical backlog of 300. Although the unit treated more than 5,000 patients a month, its mortality rate was a "little less than 1.5 percent among the over 2,000 admitted for surgery."[47]

The staff of the 750-bed 77th Evacuation Hospital at Verviers worked 18-hour shifts and kept operating and fracture tables busy day and night even while being attacked by artillery fire, V-1 attacks, and *Luftwaffe* raids. On December 20, the corner of the building was blown off and a Red Cross worker was killed. Even though the laboratory, pharmacy, nurses' quarters, and one ward were damaged, the 77th remained in service and was even admitting casualties from the bombed 9th Field Hospital a week later.

Wilma York, ANC, was chief nurse in a hospital in Belgium and very proud of the work her nurses performed during that cold and frightening winter. "Our hospital has been damaged twice by buzz bombs, our nurses' area strafed by enemy fire, and through it all they have stood steadfast, working their full quota of hours and more, enduring and enjoying the rigorous and rugged life of service in a hospital under canvas during a Belgium winter."[48]

The 103d Evacuation Hospital began receiving casualties from the Siege of Bastogne on December 27, 1944, and by the next day was treating more than twice its normal 400-bed capacity. But caring for the men was so important to the nurses that Chief Nurse Beth Veley, a survivor of Bataan, proudly boasted that her 40 nurses volunteered to work overtime. These were women such as Neola Thurneau, who "fairly beamed" when she saw the color come back to a patient's face and realized that he'd live after all, and women such as Mildred Briggs, who was able to turn down a patient's request for water because she knew the water would worsen his condition. She moistened his lips with a wet swab instead. These were women such as Olive Doyle, who stayed in France when she could have been home in the States at the moment that she became a grandmother. And these were women such as Helen Witzak, who said, "I won't leave until it's finished."[49]

And still they kept moving.

The 95th had come ashore at Salerno as a 400-bed hospital but expanded to almost 1,000. It later followed troops from southern France to the Rhine, leapfrogging on its way. While part of the hospital stayed behind to care for patients, another part moved ahead and into a complete tent city seven hours after arrival.

At one location, the 750-bed 9th Evacuation Hospital received 578 patients in 30 hours. In a little over two years, the hospital treated 41,923 Allied and enemy patients.

But it was hard work—and it took its toll.

The women knew that every time they heard the "big gun" (called "Alsace Alice" by the Allies), they'd soon be seeing young men torn apart—"young men with old eyes and old faces underneath beards and grime." Bernadine Sturniolo (called "Sturni"), of the 11th Field Hospital in Alsace, knew all too well what damage those guns could do. "When the clothes are cut away we see the torn thighs and buttocks, the multiple wounds from shell bursts, the shrapnel tears, the machine-gun perforations, the through-and-through wounds of rifle bullets."

Correspondent Dorothy Sutherland spent time with Sturni and described her as "twenty-nine but she looks thirty-five. Dark circles accentuate dark eyes and olive complexion, and there are streaks of gray through her black hair." Ordinarily an outgoing young woman, 30 months overseas and three invasions had taken their toll. "She goes out less, reads less, thinks more than she plays in her spare time, and wants to sleep the clock around —'just once'."

In Alsace, in February 1945, the fighting started every night at about the same time, yet each time it started the nurses hoped that this would be the last time—surely there had to be an end to the "days without end of slaughter, of round-the-clock nursing, of patients on litters in crowded hospital corridors or outside overflowing hospital tents."

But most importantly, they worried about the effect the nightly shelling had on their patients—men who jumped each time a bomb dropped or a shell burst, men who groaned in pain and flinched in fear. "Why doesn't it stop?" asked Sturni. "There are hundreds of them out there being hurt again."[50]

Into Germany

It was late in the afternoon when the tiny convoy began to move and the Belgian border was crossed at dusk.   The road left the plains and hedgerows to wind between steep hills covered with the dark forests of Germany.   The nurses were silent and serious for they realized they were engaged in a stern business. They strained their eyes half-expecting stray snipers to be lingering in the shadows. As the muddy road through the forest became narrower and more crooked, it became more difficult to see by the dimmed slit of the "cat-eyes" to which the ambulance lights were reduced. There was no moon, but artillery fire flashed like sheet lightning in the distance; and from the location and the sound, we could distinguish which were ours and which were enemy installations. At last the journey ended and, before the nurses could unpack their luggage, those designated for night duty began to care for patients who had already arrived.

Patients were cold, hungry, dirty, and wet. Many were in shock from loss of blood. They were covered with warm blankets and given transfusions, tracheotomies—whatever was needed—and taken to surgery as soon as they were ready.

The wards held 20 cots. Meals were served from a table at one end of the tent next to a 20-gallon can of drinking water. Tops of chests were used for treatment tables. Bedpans and urinals were cleaned and inverted on tent stakes in the ground to air. Vincoe M. Paxton, ANC, painted a picture of a field hospital in Germany in September 1944.

Wangensteen apparatus was made from intravenous solution bottles and plasma tubing. Other bottles were used as "water-traps" for closed drainage of sucking chest wounds. The nurses gave transfusions, plasma, and intravenous infusions. It was common to have ten or fifteen going daily in one ward. The bottles were suspended from the tent poles, a safety pin fastened to a seam in the tent or from an iron crook stuck into the earth. It was a feat of ward management to care for colostomies, Levin tubes, suprapubic drains, orthopedic appliances, burns, eye medications, delirious patients, and those on special diets, in one ward.[51]

The nurses worked 12-hour shifts, sometimes longer, and often suffered with backaches from bending over cots that stood only 18 inches off the ground. They slept on cots; had no heat or hot water for bathing; and had no light except from candles, flashlights, or lanterns. They stood in line to get their food and to wash their mess kits and spent their off hours washing clothes. And they could never completely unpack and feel at home because they rarely stayed anywhere very long. The few times they did, they enjoyed hot showers, mail call, movies, and a central laundry facility.

But always the patients made everything worthwhile, and Paxton recorded both wonderful and heartbreaking moments. One soldier insisted to his nurse that she make sure his captain was sent home; the nurse knew the captain was dead. One man thought he was back home on the farm and worried about feeding his livestock. A German saw the doctor draining his wounded chest and begged to be killed "rather than be bled to death by syringefuls!"[52]

When the First Army captured a railway bridge at Remagen on March 7, 1945, two elements of the 51st Field Hospital crossed over and were in operation within a week. Since many men were shot while trying to cross the Rhine, several evacuation hospitals were stationed near the west bank to serve patients on both sides. On March 13, the first nurses crossed the river: Chief Nurse Lois K. Grant, Ione C. Kinnick, Helen Johnson, Madalyn H. Andreko, Josephine J. Jennis, Beatrice Wachter, Mildred Juskins, Kay Watry, Florence Bestman, Frances M. Anderson, and Lois Judd. Although they dodged enemy strafing on their way to the bridge, their mascot, "Punch," didn't seem to mind. "The crazy little pooch wanted to jump out and watch the planes," said one nurse. "He's used to combat. He was born on the Normandy beachhead."[53]

By mid-March, the Seventh Army evacuation hospitals were sometimes moving every 10 to 14 days. Their clearing stations moved almost every day and the field hospitals every 5 days. And each move meant dismantling, packing, loading, unpacking, and setting up again—often with patients waiting.

One evacuation hospital, the 96th, became the first to move by air. The entire 400-bed hospital was moved by C-47s across the Rhine in April 1945. The nurses wore their full attire—gas masks, musette bags, pistol belts, canteens, and helmets—and even endured enemy shelling while they waited for their planes to take off. And they found it amusing that the pilots, "out of their element on the ground," dropped to the ground at every shell blast, even when they were inside the plane before takeoff. The medical personnel, on the other hand, were squeezed in so tightly that there was no room for them to fall, and "nobody wanted to be the first one to put his apprehension into overt terms."[54]

Easter Sunday 1945 was one that 10 nurses won't forget. Even though their lead jeep was marked with a white flag with the Geneva Cross, their convoy was ambushed near the town of Hanau by a company of the German 6th SS Mountain Division. The American equipment was confiscated and the personnel marched to a nursing home where they were forced to treat the German wounded. "The Americans did the best they could without any of their equipment, and the nurses worked calmly under enemy guns."[55] Luckily their confinement didn't last long; the U.S. 5th Infantry Division rescued them in nine hours.

The End of the War in Europe

As the end of the war grew closer and the Allies moved deeper into Germany, medical personnel were put in charge of caring for survivors—the Displaced Persons (DPs), Repatriated Allied Military Personnel (RAMPs), German POWs, liberated Allied POWs, and ordinary civilians. This meant taking care of everything from sanitation to food and water safety to medical care and disease control.

The 120th Evacuation Hospital took charge of 6,000 inmates from the Flossenburg Concentration Camp and later turned the SS barracks at Buchenwald into the camp's hospital.

The 116th and 127th Evacuation Hospitals treated the survivors at Dachau, called by one reporter "the first and worst of the German concentration camps." Although horrific, the situation created "a unique opportunity to study what happens to the human body, when the basic necessities of food and water are taken away, and how bodies can be recovered from the ordeal." And not just the effects on the body, but "the effect of starvation and torture and fear, on minds." In the reporter's opinion, the 38 medical officers, 39 nurses, and 207 enlisted men who worked at Dachau deserved "a mercy medal."[56]

Ann Franklin, ANC, heard survivors' horror stories as her unit traveled through France and Germany, but the stories and experiences couldn't prepare her for the reality. "I doubt if any person can portray to another what it was really like," she said. "There has never before in the history of the world been anything like it. . . . It doesn't make you sick to look at it. It is too stupendous for that. Your mind can't assimilate it that rapidly. . . . Many times it is difficult to carry on and you try fervently to squelch the feeling of revulsion that arises in you."[57]

The mortality rate was high at first. When attempting to administer penicillin injections, one nurse said, "I can't find enough muscle to get a hypodermic in." One surgeon said he couldn't operate because the shock would kill the patients. Another nurse said, "There is no disposition except death."[58]

But the persistence of the men and women of the U.S. military paid off, and eventually all the patients were cared for.

Regarding one patient, Franklin said, "We noticed something closely akin to worship for one nurse in particular and an immense liking for all the nurses."[59] The patient later told a doctor that he knew he wouldn't have survived without the care he received from the nurses of the 116th.

By June 1945, the POW camps became the biggest burden with each camp containing up to 160,000 louse-infected, sick, and wounded crammed into a space built for 20 to 50 thousand. And because they lived out in the open no matter the weather, some died of carbon monoxide from the small fires they built inside the foxholes they used for homes.

As for the American POWs, they'd been treated fairly well until war's end. One of the men said, "We marched, starved, froze, scratched lice, suffered from sickness and . . . marched some more. We lived in fields, slept in barns or fields, and dodged aerial strafings. We covered 600 miles in 87 days, and I had joined the Air Force so I wouldn't have to walk."[60] The men suffered from malnutrition caused by poor sanitary conditions and diet and many had been tortured. By the time they were freed, many of the men "were nothing more than wraiths of skin and bone, too weary to rise from their cots, and too emaciated to be able to eat a solid meal."

According to authors Cosmas and Cowdrey, "The European Theater was the healthiest in which Americans served." But the European Theater did have its advantages. There were no jungles and no tropical diseases, the area was relatively small and compact, there were friendly civilians, and the surroundings "possessed (even if in damaged form) all the physical substructure of industrial civilization."

But results are all that matters, and the authors wrote that "the theater could point to a superlative achievement in lifesaving under what were often most difficult circumstances. The job it did was of staggering size. . . . 'Of 393,987 battle wounded admitted to its hospitals, 12,523 died—a mortality rate of 3.2 percent, the lowest for any theater of operations'."[61]

NOTES

1. Quoted in Manchester Boddy, *War Guide* (Los Angeles: *Daily News*), no date, pp. 21, 20.

2. Elizabeth-Anne Wheal, Stephen Pope, and James Taylor, *Encyclopedia of the Second World War* (Secaucus, NJ: Castle Books, Div. of Book Sales, 1989), p. xii.

3. Theodore Ropp, "World War II," *World Book Encyclopedia* (Chicago: World Book-Childcraft Int'l., 1982), p. 391.

4. *World War II: Europe and North Africa*, Map (Washington, D.C.: National Geographic Society, December 1991).

5. Charles M. Wiltse, *Medical Service in the Mediterranean and Minor Theaters*, U.S. Army in World War II, The Technical Services, The Medical Department (Washington, D.C.: Office of the Chief of Military History Department of the Army, 1965), pp. 7, 18.

6. Quoted in Barrie Pitt, *The Battle of the Atlantic*, Series: World War II (Alexandria: Time-Life Books, 1977), pp. 136, 182.

7. Quoted in "Nurse's Log Pictures 12 Days in Lifeboat," Newspaper clipping sent to author by William G. Blissett, unidentified by paper name or date.

8. Quoted in Col. Julia O. Flikke, *Nurses in Action* (New York: Lippincott, 1943), p. 145.

9. "Army Nurses in Ireland and Iceland," *American Journal of Nursing*, November 1942, p. 1314.

10. Edna D. Umbach, ANC, "Christmas Overseas," *American Journal of Nursing*, December 1943, p. 1064.

11. Quoted in Flikke, p. 145.

12. Edna D. Umbach, "Army Nurses in Australia and Iceland," *American Journal of Nursing*, June 1942, p. 689.

13. Quoted in Flikke, p. 147.

14. Wiltse, p. 17.

15. "Heroism in Iceland," *American Journal of Nursing*, December 1943, p. 1143.

16. Graham A. Cosmas and Albert E. Cowdrey, *Medical Service in the European Theater of Operations*, Series: U.S. Army in World War II, Technical Services (Washington, D.C.: U.S. Army Center of Military History, 1992), p. 5.

17. Frank S. Stuart, "Invasion by Angels," *The Rotarian*, August 1944, p. 16.

18. Quoted in Cosmas and Cowdrey, p. 190.

19. Stuart, p. 14.

20. Quoted in Cosmas and Cowdrey, p. 114.

21. Stuart, pp. 15-16.

22. Lt. Winona G. Comer, ANC, "Somewhere in the British Isles," *American Journal of Nursing*, October 1944, p. 989.

23. Captain Genevieve Todd, ANC, "Memories We Shall Cherish," *American Journal of Nursing*, April 1945, p. 314.

24. Irene L. Zwisler, R.N., "Buckingham Palace Tea," *American Journal of Nursing*, March 1944, p. 257.

25. Roberta Love Tayloe, *Combat Nurse: A Journal of World War II* (Santa Barbara: Fithian Press, 1988), pp. 21, 22.

26. Lt. T. B. Kemp, Pro., "A Report from London," *The Army Nurse*, August 1945, p. 8.

27. Quoted in Kemp, p. 8.

28. Kemp, p. 8.

29. Tayloe, p. 22.

30. Page Cooper, *Navy Nurse* (New York: McGraw-Hill, 1946), pp. 122, 121, 124, 125.

31. Quoted in "Navy Nurse Receives Bronze Star," *American Journal of Nursing*, December 1944, p. 1180.

32. Vincoe M. Paxton, R.N., "ANC Reinforcements Land in France," *American Journal of Nursing*, January 1945, p. 13.

33. Cosmas and Cowdrey, p. 255.

34. "Excerpts from a M.D.D.'s Letter," *The Army Nurse*, November 1944, p. 13.

35. Capt. M. M., ANC, "From Normandy," *American Journal of Nursing*, September 1944, p. 914.

36. Quoted in Cosmas and Cowdrey, p. 233.

37. Capt. M. M., p. 914.

38. Capt. Claudia M. Draper, ANC, "From Normandy," *American Journal of Nursing*, October 1944, p. 989.

39. "Excerpts from a M.D.D.'s Letter," p. 13.

40. Quoted in Cosmas and Cowdrey, p. 340.

41. *The Fighting Men of Texas, A History of the Second World War, A Memorial, A Remembrance, An Appreciation*, Vol. IV (Dallas: Historical Publishing Company, 1948), p. 1395.

42. Rear Adm. Calvin T. Durgin, USN, "The Invasion of Southern France," *Battle Stations! Your Navy in Action* (New York: Wm. H. Wise, 1946), p. 282.

43. Quoted in "D-Day Plus 4," *Trained Nurse and Hospital Review*, December 1944, p. 450.

44. "A Report from the French Front," *The Army Nurse*, March 1945, p. 16.

45. Cosmas and Cowdrey, p. 310.

46. Mary Jose, "Night Shift in an Army Hospital," *American Journal of Nursing*, June 1945, p. 432.

47. Cosmas and Cowdrey, p. 409.

48. Capt. Wilma York, ANC, "Sink or Float?" *American Journal of Nursing*, October 1945, p. 850.

49. Quoted in Mary Jose, "Hi, Angels!" *American Journal of Nursing*, April 1945, p. 267.

50. Quoted in Dorothy Sutherland, "Nurses Also Cry!" *The Army Nurse*, May 1945, p. 4.

51. Vincoe M. Paxton, R.N., "With Field Hospital Nurses in Germany," *American Journal of Nursing*, February 1945, pp. 131, 132.

52. Quoted in Paxton, "With Field Hospital Nurses in Germany," p. 132.

53. Quoted in "Army Nurses in the ETO," *American Journal of Nursing*, May 1945, p. 387.

54. 1st Lt. Deborah Bacon, ANC, "Across the Rhine—By Air," *The Army Nurse*, July 1945, pp. 3.

55. Judith A. Bellafaire, *The Army Nurse Corps: A Commemoration of World War II Service* (Washington, D.C.: U.S. Army Center of Military History, no date), Pub. 72-14, p. 23.

56. May Craig, "Report From Germany," *The Army Nurse*, August 1945, p. 6.

57. 1st Lt. Ann Franklin, R.N., "An Army Nurse at Dachau. 1. Assignment to Dachau," *American Journal of Nursing*, November 1945, pp. 901-902.

58. Quoted in Cosmas and Cowdrey, p. 577.

59. 1st Lt. Ann Franklin, R.N., "An Army Nurse at Dachau. 2. We Care for Typhus Fever Patients," *American Journal of Nursing*, November 1945, p. 903.

60. Quoted in Cosmas and Cowdrey, p. 559.

61. Cosmas and Cowdrey, pp. 538, 559, 618.

APPENDIX 6A:
RAIN ON A TENT IN NORMANDY

It was raining—again. The time was fall after D-Day and the rain was getting cold, insistent. Was Nature still trying to reclaim Omaha and Utah beaches from all the blood? No use. Bloody wounds had kept coming, kept coming. It made no sense—especially to young nurses. We worked as hard as we could to patch up wounds only to see our G.I. patients sent back to the front to be wounded again, or worse. "Don't think. Just do your job." . . .

Four of us sloshed through the mud, boot deep. We were coming off duty for the evening. Long, olive drab hospital tents faded into grey drab against a filmy background. We saw it all through a blur of rain drops. On we sloshed to the Nurses' Quarters.

Stooping low to get through the flaps of our 16 x 16 pyramidal tent where the four of us bunked, we trailed in rivulets of dirty water on the concrete floor. Inside, the noise was louder, more pervasive, more intense. The clatter ruled out talk, and enhanced our weariness, our lethargy. Tonight we wouldn't bother with building a fire in the central pot-bellied stove, or even lighting the lamp. Save the oil. Flashlights would do. We were going right to bed—driven there by the rain.

Then it slackened a bit. The sounds became more rhythmic, somnific, hypnotic, like a monotonous metronome. Worrisome thought dissolved. Tapering off even more, the sound became a repetitious lullaby droning on and on, bringing peaceful meanderings to my mind. Was it Shakespeare who had compared God's mercy to the gentle rain? The muffled sound now seemed a benediction. We accepted it and let its soothing balm lull us into blessed anesthesia.

—Elizabeth Harman Masterson
Unpublished essay, 1988

APPENDIX 6B:
CHINA DOLL

He lay at military attention. His rigid limbs, white color, glassy blue-eyed stare, and glistening, shaved head gained him the moniker of "China Doll."

Would he have goose-stepped mechanically about the tent if he'd been able to get up from his hospital cot? We thought so. To us he was the epitome of a Nazi, lending credence to all the propaganda we had heard.

Disdainfully, he turned his face to [the] canvas wall when the Protestant or Catholic chaplain made rounds. He was even more haughty with the thirty-nine other Germans in the ward. No doubt a chess player, he considered himself a knight while they were mere pawns.

These pawns were older men and pitifully young boys, replacements to Hitler's army after the Russians had skimmed the cream the winter before. They were glad to talk to any chaplain. They called us nurses "Schwester" which also means "sister" in German. China Doll did not deign to use this appellation.

"Sub-lieutenant," he rasped, noting that I had lowly gold bars on my work fatigues rather than silver ones. His glinty stare was fixed on the syringe in my hand. It was yet another penicillin injection, and he had gotten one every three hours day and night. Unfamiliar with this newly developed antibiotic, he suspected torture.

"I demand my rights under the Geneva Treaty. I am senior officer here," he continued, trying to pull himself to full stature under the bed sheets.

I corrected him in my most Nightingale voice. "In medical matters, nurses outrank all patients. This is the same treatment given to wounded Americans." (No need to struggle with school-book German here; his English was better than mine.)

He bore the shot stoically, of course, and winced only later when, on turning back, his pillow shifted and out rolled a piece of bread squirreled away from his lunch tray. Embarrassment was fleeting; back came the impassive, expressionless mask.

When he needed blood, our ward officer arrived to administer it himself. China Doll's eyes took in the doctor's insignia, not his face, then shifted warily to the flask of dark liquid I was hanging on an I.V. pole overhead.

"From whom was this blood obtained?" He demanded, addressing the superior officer.

The doctor worked on methodically, taking his time. Then he gave his rather loud, off-hand reply to a nearby German.

"Tell him this was a fine young Jewish boy's blood."

"Juden blut, juden blut," chorused back through the tent, accompanied by ripples of suppressed laughter. The other patients knew we took blood for them from Germans in the stockade. They hadn't shared this, or much else, with China Doll.

"Aye, aye, aye," he whispered.

We knew better than to expect any improvement in his attitude or behavior from a transfusion. As his color grew pinker, he did, at least, appear more human—less like a China doll. But the name stuck.

—Elizabeth Harman Masterson
Unpublished essay, 1988

APPENDIX 6C:
THE GARDELEGEN BARN

We were unprepared for the sight and smell of our first atrocities. A large windowless storage barn stood alone in the middle of a field. At first glance there was no indication of its contents. As we drew nearer the unmistakable stench of burned flesh reached us and I thought of how it smelled like a thousand touches of the cautery needle.

First I saw what appeared to be a small rock at the edge of the foundation. To my horror a closer look showed it to be a burned head whose owner had managed to dig out this far before succumbing to the fire.

We peeked through the cracks in the boards and saw the entire scene. The floor of the whole barn was covered with blackened bodies, the faces not even recognizable as human. I believe the number who died there was counted as five hundred.

Later we heard most of the story which led up to this particular holocaust. Three Dutch prisoners who had escaped a few days prior to the fire had been taken to the Evac Hospital for care and protection. They told the following story:

A defeated German Army contingent was trying to hurry these prisoners along to get across the Rhine River ahead of the fast approaching American Army. The prisoners were in no shape to travel—starving, debilitated and ill, so the Germans contacted the local Burgomeister and informed him that the prisoners were being relinquished to his care.

The Burgomeister and Council were terrified that they had no secure place to hold these prisoners and feared reprisals should they escape.

It was then decided to lock them in the barn and burn them, which they did.

When the Americans arrived they ordered the townspeople to dig separate graves (they first tried to settle for one common grave) and bury these unidentified bodies.

During this time the Burgomeister attempted suicide by slashing his wrist[s] but was treated at the Evac and lived to stand trial for this mass murder.

One of the Dutch men who had escaped a few days before the tragedy told a heart-warming story of his two companions who hid out with him waiting for the "Liberators" to come. They became so hungry they decided to ask someone in town for food. They chose the house next [to] the Church which proved to be the parsonage. The minister fed them and hid them in his basement until the Americans came.

—Rachel Gilbert Francis
Unpublished Essay, October 22, 1993

APPENDIX 6D:
SECOND LIEUTENANT FRANCES Y. SLANGER

Of the more than 20 nurses killed by enemy action during WWII, perhaps the most widely known is Frances Slanger, who was wrapping Christmas presents in her tent in France when a German shell hit and killed her on October 21, 1944. She gained her celebrity because of a letter she wrote to *Stars and Stripes*, a letter that was printed less than a month after her death, a letter she wrote in response to words of praise for nurses sent in by GIs. The letter, said the paper's editor, "accomplished the impossible" because "in simple language she was able to put into words the feeling of American nurses for American soldiers . . . [and] unconsciously brought out the close professional camaraderie that exists among members of the Army Nurse Corps."[1]

A graduate of Boston City Hospital, Slanger was one of the first nurses to land on Normandy and was serving with a field hospital at the time of her death. She was the seventh Army nurse to die in the war and the first in the ETO. Before war's end, a hospital ship was named after her, "the largest and fastest American hospital ship afloat,"[2] the former luxury liner *Saturnia*.

Slanger's letter is printed here in its entirety and is followed by responses from two soldiers.

It is 0200 and I have been lying awake for one hour listening to the steady, even breathing of the other three nurses in the tent and thinking of some of the things we had discussed during the day. The rain is beating down on the tent with torrential force. The wind is on a mad rampage and its main objective seems to be to lift the tent off its poles and fling it about our heads.

The fire is burning low and just a few live coals are on the bottom. With the slow feeding of wood, and finally coal, a roaring fire is started. I couldn't help thinking how similar to a human being a fire is; if it is allowed to run down too low, and if there is a spark of life left in it, it can be nursed back. . . . So can a human being. It is slow, it is gradual, it is done all the time in these Field Hospitals and other hospitals in the ETO.

We had read several articles in different magazines and papers sent in by a grateful GI, praising the work of nurses around the combat areas. Praising us—for what? I climbed back into my cot. Lt. [Margaret M.] Bowler was the only one I had awakened. I whispered to her. Lt. [Christine] Cox and Lt. [Elizabeth] Powers slept on. Fine nurses and great girls to live with . . . of course, like in all families, an occasional quarrel, but they were quickly forgotten.

I'm writing this by flashlight. In this light it [the tent] looks something like a "dive." In the center of the tent are two poles, one part chimney, the other a plain tent pole. Kindling wood lies in disorderly confusion on the damp ground. We don't have a tarp on the ground. A French wine pitcher, filled with water, stands by. The GIs say we rough it. We in our little tent can't see it. True, we are set up in tents, sleep on cots and are subject to the temperament of the weather.

We wade ankle deep in mud. You have to lie in it. We are restricted to our immediate area, a cow pasture or hay field, but then, who is not restricted? We have a stove and coal. We even have a laundry line in the tent. Our GI drawers are at this moment doing the dance of the pants what with the wind howling, the tent waving precariously, the rain beating down, the guns firing, and me with a flashlight, writing. It all adds up to a feeling of unreality.

Sure, we rough it, but in comparison to the way you men are taking it, we can't complain, nor do we feel that bouquets are due us. But you, the men behind the guns, the men driving our tanks, flying our planes, sailing our ships, building bridges and to the men who pave the way and to the men who are left behind—it is to you we doff our helmets. To every GI wearing the American uniform, for you we have the greatest admiration and respect.

Yes, this time we are handing out the bouquets . . . but after taking care of some of your buddies; seeing them when they are brought in bloody, dirty with the earth, mud and grime, and most of them so tired. Somebody's brothers, somebody's fathers and somebody's sons. Seeing them gradually brought back to life, to consciousness and to see their lips separate into a grin when they first welcome you. Usually they kid, hurt as they are. It doesn't amaze us to hear one of them say, "How'ya, babe," or "Holy Mackerel, an American woman!" or most indiscreetly, "How about a kiss?"

These soldiers stay with us but a short time, from ten days to possibly two weeks. We have learned a great deal about our American soldier, and the stuff he is made of. The wounded do not cry. Their buddies come first. The patience and determination they show, the courage and fortitude they have is sometimes awesome to behold. It is we who are proud to be here.

Rough it? No. It is a privilege to be able to receive you, and a great distinction to see you open your eyes and with that swell American grin say, "Hi-ya babe!"[3]

—2nd Lt. Frances Slanger, 2nd Lt. Christine Cox,
2nd Lt. Margaret M. Bowler, 1st Lt. Elizabeth F. Powers,
Army Nurse Corps

RESPONSES

The editorial of November 7 was such as to bring a lump to a dogface's throat. It is more than touching to be told you are made of good stuff by somebody who ought to know, with such obvious sincerity as that of Second Lieutenant Slanger. Nobody turns down bouquets and we eat that kind up—but:

I wonder if the good nurse was deliberately overlooking the real reason for our deep-seated respect and regard for her and her sisters? Maybe in the throes of her passionate pen, she actually forgot the one factor which lifts her character above the level of the men she attends. Maybe it has never occurred to her at all. We want your respect, admiration and love, dear nurses, but we want it with your eyes open.

We men were not given the choice of working on the battlefield or the homefront. We cannot take any personal credit for being here. We are here because we have to be. You are here merely because you felt you were needed. So, when an injured man opens his eyes to see one of you lovely, ministering angels concerned with his welfare, he can't but be overcome by the very thought that you are doing it because you want to.

It does not matter that we lie in mud—yes, crawl in it, while you only "wade ankle-deep," or that you possibly enjoy a few more conveniences over here than we. The important thing is that you could be home, soaking yourselves in a bathtub every day, putting on clean clothes over a clean body and crawling in between clean sheets at night, on a soft, springy mattress. Instead, you endure whatever hardships you must to be where you can do us the most good.

I'd better stop now, because I'm getting sentimental, but I want you to know your "editorial" did not change, but only confirmed my deep respect for you modern Florence Nightingales. If the world had a few more people like you in it, there wouldn't be any more wars.[4]

—Pfc Millard Ireland, Inf.

What a grand group of women comprise the ANC. . . . At a time when duty in civilian life would bring the highest financial remuneration [they] chose to give up all the comforts of home and of the modern hospitals to give their services to the men of the armed forces. . . . [They] ask for no favors, want no special consideration, but rather face dangers to help some wounded man on his way to recovery.

I have had occasion to see many of the Army nurses in the ETO and they were always happiest when they were very busy because then they were really being useful.

Men, we owe these nurses the highest debt of appreciation and the utmost respect. They are really just women, like your sister, but they have proved beyond doubt that they have the "guts" of the best soldier.

All the praise, honor, and respect we can shower on the ANC cannot begin to compare to the glory each of them earns each day as a true American soldier.[5]

—1st Lt. Chester S. Wright, Jr.

NOTES

1. "Frances Slanger Killed in France," *The Army Nurse*, December 1944, p. 8.

2. "Hospital Ship Named for Frances Slanger," *The Army Nurse*, March 1945, p. 3.

3. "Frances Slanger Killed in France," p. 8.

4. Pfc. Millard Ireland, Inf., "More People Like You," *The Army Nurse*, December 1944, p. 2.

5. 1st Lt. Chester S. Wright, Jr., "True American Soldiers," *American Journal of Nursing*, February 1945, p. 149.

Chapter 7

The China-Burma-India Theater

The Army nurse is winning the war in Burma. . . . We're
used to thinking of beautiful girls in terms of beautiful clothes,
but these nurses in their work uniforms with their hair stringing
down looked perfectly wonderful. . . .

When the men were so tired they felt they couldn't go another
step, they'd see the nurses doing their job in the midst of the
downpour. They'd take heart and keep going.

—Chaplain (Capt.) John Henry Justus
"Chaplain Praises CBI Nurses,"
The Army Nurse, December 1944

Conditions in Burma were harsh, said Justus, "but the nurses were game" even
during the times when "soldiers and nurses were wet for days," and "shoes and
fatigues wore out in a month's time."[1]

As Hitler wanted *Lebensraum*—living space—so did Japan. Called the
"Great Space System" and the "New Order in Greater East Asia," the Japanese
plan was to conquer a fifth of the world's space and population. In September
1931, they seized the Chinese province of Manchuria. In July 1937, they
invaded China. In December 1937, they killed 250,000 civilians in Nanking.
By September 1940, Japanese troops were in northern French Indochina. By
the next year, they had military control of southern Indochina.

In order to prevent the Japanese plan of expansion, it was critical that the
Allies reopen the Burma Road, the "700 miles of dirt highway that represented
China's last overland link with the outside world,"[2] taken by the Japanese
when they occupied Burma in March 1942.

According to John Paul North, M.D., in his article, "The 20th General
Hospital—I.S. Ravdin, Commanding General," for the journal *Surgery*, the
20th General Hospital was located on the same 40 acres as the Ledo Road

(part of the main supply route, the Burma Road), a railroad, and a gasoline pipeline—all of which made it a tempting target. Fear of attack was so strong that the nurses kept their helmets on hand at all times and were told what to do should they become prisoners (give only name, rank, serial number) and what they could take with them if they were evacuated (whatever they could put into one musette bag). But even with such impending danger, said Dr. North, "everyone went on with the job without much concern."

Allies in this theater faced conditions similar to those in the South Pacific: wild forestation, insects, malaria, monsoons, problems with sanitation, and dangerous wildlife. North described a soldier's life in Burma.

He might then sleep soundly despite the uncomfortable rope charpoy and the nocturnal howls of jackals venturing into the hospital area. Scrawny cows, sacred to the Hindus, were apt to wander into living quarters and leave their calling cards. One became wedged in the entrance to a latrine, which had to be dismantled to release the beast. People returning to quarters late in the evening were occasionally startled by a large tiger stealthily heading for the hospital kitchens. On one occasion an 8 foot cobra invaded the nurses' ward.[3]

In her article "With the Army Nurse Corps along the Ledo Road," Agnes Gress also wrote of unwelcome visitors. "Some of the most common creatures that plague us as well as our equipment are snakes, scorpions, ants, termites, and the ever increasing colony of rats. In time we have learned to live in the presence of all these pests and disregard them. They are everywhere—in our living quarters, on the wards, and outside."

Another Army nurse, Matilda Dykstra, stationed in India, also lived with the sights and sounds of howling jackals, monkeys, snakes, and cows. The cows, she said, were everywhere, even in their huts. One nurse even had a pet goat.

One of Dr. North's nurses, Marion Kern, remembered mosquito nets that served a dual purpose: to keep out mosquitoes and to catch bugs or other creatures that fell through the thatched roofs. During the monsoon season, shelter halves were put over each cot to catch the rain coming through the roof.

Of the monsoon season, Gress said that it lasts from early spring through autumn and created problems with laundry because their clothes wouldn't dry. She described the rains as "steady, drenching downpours" and painted quite an uncomfortable picture: "In the summer the heat is intense, and the wet earth actually steams. The air becomes oppressing and rain is welcome and necessary or one could not exist. This goes on for months."[4] In another account, she wrote, "The continual rains, oppressive heat, and heavy mud were exhausting. Sometimes the wards were inches deep in water. We worked hard. Most of the time our clothes were drenched with perspiration. We had no time for midday siestas, which are the accepted rule of the tropical countries."[5] Gress also said that some of the women tried to grow gardens but the rains rotted the seeds or washed them away.

But the biggest problem with the rains were the accompanying mosquitoes and resulting malaria. In her pamphlet *The Army Nurse Corps*, Judith A. Bellafaire reports that the malarial rate in 1943 was 84 percent of total manpower, 120 sick soldiers for each wounded one. At the 20th, there were 7,236 admissions for malaria in a five-month period, and malaria caused one-third of all deaths.

Whereas the Chinese were often afflicted with a strain of malaria that could cause death in 24 hours, Americans were more often afflicted with a milder form. But since prevention was the best cure, personnel were required to take atabrine pills and wear protective clothing after dusk. The women also used Flit to repel the mosquitoes and one nurse said, "We used to cover ourselves with perfume to draw the men around; now it's Flit to keep from drawing mosquitoes."[6]

Spraying surrounding areas with DDT helped slow down the mosquito problem, but another problem soon followed—scrub typhus infections. Usually a result of working around mite-infested lanai grass, scrub typhus accounted for 578 admissions to the 20th General Hospital in a two-year period, required a high demand of nursing care, and had a 30 percent fatality rate; and even those who survived were sick for long periods of time. Other ailments included cutaneous diphtheria, hypohydrosis, peripheral neuritis, fungal infections, exhaustion, malnutrition, and amebic dysentery. There were also the problems of where and how to house psychiatric patients.

Winter temperatures brought other problems, and Gress said the winter of 1943 was an especially severe one.

We couldn't bathe the patients till around 11 o'clock after the sun took the chill out of the air. Even in winter the sun rays are warm. Only the night nurses and the wardmen know the agony of staying up all night without heat. Often their hands were so cold that they couldn't do the necessary charting. They wore all the heavy clothing that they could possibly put on—GI shoes, woolen socks, woolen underwear, top clothing, sweaters, scarves, and caps. Before morning they wrapped in blankets, hovering over shock lanterns which provided some warmth. What little wood we had was used in the daytime. The fuel situation was desperate. There was no coal and no saws to cut wood. We had a few axes for the entire hospital.

All the water for baths and treatment was heated in pails over a little Coleman stove which burns white gas. We never had enough. There was no running water in the wards and only a few faucets scattered over the entire area. The patients had cold showers if they could brave them. Often the patients' food was cold as the kitchen was several hundred yards away.

In spite of the discomforts our patients remained cheerful.[7]

Marion Kern was proud of her unit's low fatality rate and gave most of the credit to the surgeons and other doctors. Her patients included Japanese POWs, many of whom had malaria, dysentery, beriberi, and parasitic intestinal infections.

Since most of Matilda Dykstra's patients were Chinese, she had to adapt to their customs and habits—such as relatives sleeping on the hospital floor!

Especially troublesome were the patients who got up and wandered off whenever they wanted, refused to take medicine, and refused to stay isolated from patients with contagious diseases. And since the Chinese patients insisted on supplying their own food, nurses often found the floors littered with everything from orange peels and eggshells to chicken feathers. Agnes Gress said that the Chinese patients were always cooking, that some even grew garlic in little cans under their beds, and that most kept extra food supplies, which created a tremendous rat problem.

Most nurses lived in *bashas*, huts made from bamboo with palm leaf roofs. Some had two rooms for two women, one shared shower, and a ceiling fan that kept the temperature comfortable even in the hottest weather. The women added personal touches by hanging souvenirs and pictures on the walls and by combining homemade items (such as dressing tables made from boxes, lamp shades made by painting large coolie hats, and drapes made from unbleached muslin) with purchased items (reed chairs, small tables, and grass rugs).

With no laundry facilities, the nurses washed the hospital bedding and their own clothes. Heavy items, like fatigues, were washed in streams while light garments were washed in washstands outside their huts. While the items were wet, they were folded on the creases and hung out to dry. And since clothes and bedding were aired out whenever the weather permitted, Gress said that, "on sunny days our yards look like bazaars."[8]

Matilda Dykstra said they heated the laundry water over stoves made out of gasoline tins with wood that the women had gathered and chopped themselves. Marion Kern remembered bathing out of helmets and had only one complaint: the helmet's rounded top kept it from sitting well on the stove.

According to Kern, the 20th's mess sergeant tried his hardest to make decent meals out of corned beef, dehydrated potatoes, dried eggs, and dried milk. His attempts, plus their C-rations, caused Kern to lose 30 pounds in two years. Eventually, the 20th started a vegetable garden that produced at least one fresh vegetable a day for the patients and sometimes enough for hospital personnel. They also raised pigs and geese.

The better conditions in India meant better food—iced grapefruit juice, tea, cocoa, and coffee served with treats like apple pie, fried chicken, and hot biscuits. "It's remarkable what the cooks can do with their gasoline field stoves,"[9] said Dorcas Avery.

There was always a scarcity of eggs and fresh vegetables at the 14th, said Agnes Gress. "We have never had fresh milk here. Fresh meat (no steak) is rationed to us only twice a week. The rest of our food is canned and dehydrated. Recently, after twenty-three months, we received our first bottle of cola. We shall always remember our childlike enthusiasm for our first ice cream. If there were any of these luxuries in this theater before, they never reached us."

For recreation, the nurses listened to the phonograph, played bridge, and traded letters, books, and magazines. They also enjoyed dances, parties, shopping in neighboring villages, swimming, hiking, picnicking, and fishing.

One day when Agnes Gress and some friends went searching for orchids, they got lost among the tall, leech-infested elephant grass. "We were near panic as we saw dozens of them [leeches] reaching out from the grass crawling up our shoes and socks, and attaching themselves to our legs. They seemed to be everywhere, so we took off to a clearing where we deleeched ourselves, touching them with lighted cigarettes."

But despite the malaria, drenching rains, and frightening encounters, Gress found good things to say about life along the Ledo Road:

Though one USO troop of entertainers called our basha an "old dump," we have been very happy here in the clean atmosphere of the jungle, away from the disease-filled cities. After a rain, the foliage shines with freshness. At night the stars and the moon appear at their best through towering trees overhung with vines. The night is alive with insect noises and night prowlers. We awaken in the early morning to the music of birds or the noise of a band of monkeys.[10]

The nurses in the China-Burma-India theater didn't receive the attention that nurses in other theaters received, but they performed the same duties and lived through the same dangers and primitive conditions as nurses anywhere, often worse. According to *YANK* correspondent Sgt. Bob Ghio, the women exhibited "the usual feminine interest in rumor-swapping and bull-shooting and they show a remarkable military talent in the soldierly art of griping," but they griped about the mud and insects—not about their duty. "They lead a rugged life, the nurses of Assam. But they don't grumble about it. And the Army sure as hell doesn't grumble about having them there. They're as fine a bunch of GI's as you can find anywhere."[11]

NOTES

    1. Quoted in "Chaplain Praises CBI Nurses," *The Army Nurse*, December 1944, p. 4.
    2. David W. Hogan, *India-Burma*, Series: The U.S. Army Campaigns of World War II (Washington, D.C.: U. S. Army Center of Military History, 1992), p. 3.
    3. John Paul North, M.D., "The 20th General Hospital—I.S. Ravdin, Commanding General," *Surgery*, Vol. 56, No. 4, October 1964, pp. 616, 619.
    4. 1st Lt. Agnes D. Gress, ANC, "With the Army Nurse Corps along the Ledo Road," *The Army Nurse*, February 1945, p. 11.
    5. 1st Lt. Agnes D. Gress, ANC, "The 14th Evac on the Ledo Road," *American Journal of Nursing*, September 1945, p. 705.
    6. Sgt. Bob Ghio, "The Ladies of Assam," *YANK*, September 13, 1943, no. p. #.
    7. Gress, "The 14th Evac on Ledo Road," p. 704.
    8. Gress, "With the Army Nurse Corps along the Ledo Road," p. 11.
    9. Capt. Dorcas C. Avery, ANC, "Army Nurses in India," *American Journal of Nursing*, August 1943, p. 769.
    10. Gress, "The 14th Evac on Ledo Road," p. 706.
    11. Ghio, no. p. #.

Constance "Connie" Sansone, Army Nurse
Corps. (Courtesy of Constance Sansone)

Janina Smiertka, Navy Nurse Corps,
Chelsea Naval Hospital, Chelsea,
Massachusetts. (Courtesy of Janina
Smiertka Davenport)

Rachel Gilbert, Army Nurse Corps, Bolling Field, D.C., 1941. (Courtesy of Rachel Gilbert Francis)

Marion Blissett, Navy Nurse Corps. (Courtesy of Lt. Col. William G. Blissett)

Inez Combites, Army Nurse Corps, Korea.
(Courtesy of Inez Combites Hood)

Alice Lofgren (in uniform), Navy Nurse
Corps, and sister. (Courtesy of Alice
Lofgren Andrus)

Ruth Claff, Army Nurse Corps. (Courtesy
of Chester E. Claff, Jr., Ph.D.)

Juanita Hamilton, Army Nurse Corps. (Courtesy of
Juanita Hamilton Webster)

Dora Cline, Navy Nurse Corps, and husband. (Courtesy of Dora Cline Fechtmann)

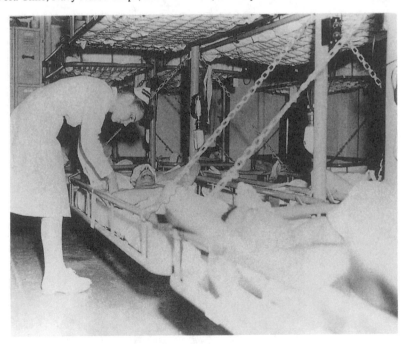

Navy nurse treats patient aboard USS *Samaritan*. (Courtesy of Navy Bureau of Medicine and Surgery)

Navy nurse uniforms during World War II. (Courtesy of Navy Bureau of Medicine and Surgery)

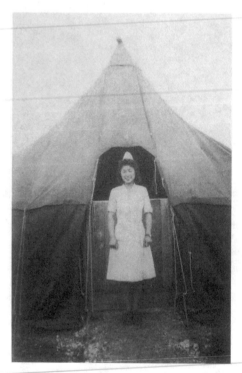

Helen Pon, Army Nurse Corps. (Courtesy of Helen Pon Onyett)

Easter Sunday, 1943. Left to right: Mary Ranous, Red Cross; Selma Moody, Army Nurse Corps; Mildred Thorell, Army Nurse Corps. (Courtesy of Selma Moody Brawner)

The 128th Station Hospital Staging Area, Camp Columbia near Brisbane and Ipswitch, Australia, February 1944. Note: Ruth Shadewaldt, ANC, is at tip of pyramid by tent opening. (Courtesy of Ethel Lane, Ruth Shadewaldt's sister)

Gay Nineties Party. Note: Ruth Shadewaldt is on the right on the back line. (Courtesy of Ethel Lane)

Santo Tomas, Manila, Philippines. (Courtesy of Ethel Lane)

9th U.S. Army nurses, Christmas, 1944, 91st Evacuation Hospital, Valkenburg, Holland. Left to right: Mildred Knoll, Ruth Barr, Neva Rohar. (Courtesy of United States Army)

804th Medical Air Squadron, 1943, Archer Field, Brisbane, Queensland, Australia. (Courtesy of Armed Forces Institute of Pathology, United States Army)

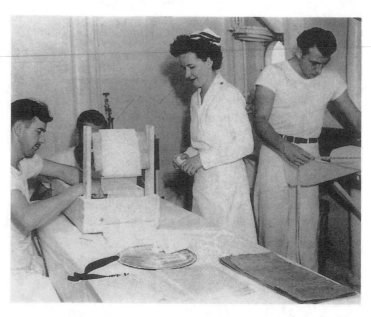

Navy Nurse Beatrice Rivers supervises preparation of plaster casts, 1945. (Courtesy of Navy Bureau of Medicine and Surgery).

Navy Nurses stroll through residential section of Colon, Republic of Panama. Left to right: Mae Kennedy and Navy Maddio. (Courtesy of Navy Bureau of Medicine and Surgery)

Chapter 8

The United States and Western Atlantic Minor Theaters

Among them were the amputees, the blinded, and the cord cases who would require special treatment. Most of them remained only long enough for preparation for transfer to the hospitals nearest their homes which could provide the orthopedic or other special care needed by each one. Inadequately staffed for the first massive wave of patients, nurses were torn (as had been all nurses close to the lines) between the urgent physical requirements and the deep-seated emotional needs of their patients. A hypodermic for pain could be given quickly, but reassuring a suffering patient and helping him to decide how he would break the news of extensive injury to his family or sweetheart required more time.

—Mary M. Roberts, R.N.
American Nursing: History and Interpretation

So much publicity was given to the combat nurses that women who couldn't meet the criteria sometimes felt inferior, but they shouldn't have because their services were desperately needed in all the veterans hospitals, debarkation stations, military bases, hospital trains, and air transports within the United States (also known as the Zone of Interior) and its chain of minor theaters. There was also a civilian population that couldn't be ignored: the families of military personnel, people in relocation camps, and workers in factories and on farms. Marguerite Regina Mella, ANC, summed it up. "All the skill of surgery and the swiftness with which it is accomplished is of no avail if when these patients return to the States they are neglected because of lack of nursing care."[1]

Nurses, such as Maren Frye, quickly realized the importance of stateside duty. "When I took my Oath which made me an officer in the U.S. Army

Nurse Corps, my only thought was to get into this thing and get 'overseas' as fast as possible. There, I felt, was where I could 'do my bit'." But when a year went by and she was still stationed in the States, Frye saw her role differently. "I have learned that the part to which I have been assigned in this total war is just as important as that of my sister nurse who serves on foreign soil. And, I believe, that glory which I hold deep inside me will in every way equal that which will be shown on the outside by overseas ribbons, medals, etc."

Frye saw this glory in her patients, such as one young man who lost an arm during training and who, like her, would not be going overseas. "From his indomitable courage and good spirits," said Frye, "I learned that not all of the real fighting is done at the front lines. His appreciation of the care given him by our nurses made us proud to be caring for our men on the home front."

Another patient was a paratrooper who was rejected from service because of what appeared to be a mental disability. From her talks with him, Frye discovered that he had hit his head during one of his jumps and needed brain surgery and a long recuperation. He recovered fully. "This to me," said Frye, "is a worthwhile victory in itself."[2]

In his book *The Medical Department: Hospitalization and Evacuation, Zone of Interior*, Clarence McKittrick Smith produced the figures that proved the need for medical personnel in the States: From January 1942 through August 1945, approximately 8,900,000 patients were admitted to hospitals in the Zone of Interior. During that same period, 639,900 other patients were being transported *to* those hospitals.

During the war, there were four types of Army hospitals in the Zone of Interior: general, regional, station, and convalescent. By June 1945, many of the general hospitals had been designated as special treatment centers for one or more fields—amputations, neurosurgery, orthopedic surgery, thoracic surgery, trench foot, or vascular surgery. This concentration of specialists meant that treatments could be tested and evaluated easier, and therapeutic approaches and personnel could be more effective. Attempts were made to send patients to the extended-care facility nearest their home.

Convalescent hospitals, which began in the U.S. Army Air Force hospitals, proved so effective that the AAF initiated a program for their fliers in overseas hospitals and opened seven centers in the United States. The program included some sort of physical exercise that could be started while the patient was still bedridden then extended and expanded as the patient recovered. According to the Commanding General of the Army Air Forces in January 1944, "Every known facility is being used to aid these physically and psychologically wounded soldiers to make a new place for themselves in military or civilian life. Our interest and responsibility do not stop at the moment our men drop their bombs on the target."[3]

And though they weren't exposed to enemy fire, home-front nurses still found themselves in situations where extraordinary courage was needed. When a hospital stove exploded, Edith Greenwood, ANC, removed 15 patients before their ward burned to the ground. Afterward, she provided medical treatment to a young private who had helped her with the evacuation. She and the private both received the Soldier's Medal for heroism, Greenwood being its first female recipient.

The second woman to win the medal was Margaret Decker who saved a soldier from drowning then gave him first aid and accompanied him to a station hospital. The third medal recipient was Orah Stephenson who, although suffering from burns to her face and hands and partially overcome by smoke, dragged an unconscious nurse to safety.

Janina Smiertka was in the Navy Nurse Corps from 1938 to 1943. One of her wartime assignments was the Washington, D.C. Navy Yard Dispensary from which she was occasionally sent to the Accostia Ammunition Plant in Bellevue, Maryland. During her 3 to 11 shift at the plant on July 20, 1942, "somebody was careless with Tetryl powder and just as I was entering the plant at 9:30 p.m. to check on some of my patients, an explosion occurred, a low boom, and everybody was running out past me shouting 'the money isn't worth it'. . . . One man was killed outright . . . and the woman worker next to him died the next day as the powder had ricocheted into her lungs."[4] Smiertka was awarded a Navy Commendation.

According to Mary Roberts in her book *American Nursing: History and Interpretation*, nurses at debarkation centers often saw men who "had been wounded so recently that they were still in battle uniforms."[5] Nurses at Mitchell Field near New York City treated men with all types of injuries. Among them were a young man from Texas who had been hit by a mortar shell that exploded two feet behind him, a man from Chicago who suffered from a two-day-old machine gun wound to the head, a boy who had lost an arm after helping to pick up wounded buddies in Germany, and an older man who had lost a leg when walking in a mine field.

But returning home proved miraculous.

Morale is really high when they are established on home soil. Injuries, though often severe, dwindle in importance with the joy of being at home and of breathing American air again. The warmth of the hospital, the familiar home-side food, contribute to the psychological and physical comfort of care at home![6]

On their very first day back, the men enjoyed beds, baths, and shaves. By the second day they'd had haircuts and a shampoo. They made phone calls, sent telegrams, and enjoyed hot coffee and good meals for the first time in months.

After a few days in the debarkation ward, the men were taken—by airplane, ambulance, or bus—to the general hospital nearest their home or to a specialized hospital for surgery or prostheses.

They were also moved by train. Equipped with a medical unit car, operating room, and kitchen, each ward car carried 32 beds. Five or six nurses, along with doctors and corpsmen, were assigned to each train. Mildred Lamar, ANC, described the first time she nursed on a train:

Did you ever serve a tray while a train is going about sixty miles an hour down grade with a few very sharp turns thrown in for good measure? When all the patients were fed, one teaspoon and fork were still unaccounted for, one white uniform was soiled, and several nurses were trying to figure out why patients must eat. . . .

The nearest we came to a casualty was when the mess sergeant fell as he got off the train to obtain ice for the kitchen. One patient, on crutches, left the train against orders and almost found himself left behind.

Reaching our destination early in the morning of the fourth day, we unloaded the patients to be transferred to the hospital; the beds were stripped and coaches cleaned and we were off again.

Lamar added, "Any time that Uncle Sam needs nurses to convoy his soldiers, I know five Army nurses who are ready and eager to go."[7]

In addition to their hospital ships and bases around the world, the Navy ran 36 hospitals and seven convalescent hospitals in the continental United States. Dorothy Main worked with incoming wounded at the U.S. Naval Hospital on Mare Island in California.

These boys who are being carried into the ward on stretchers, with all their worldly possessions in a paper bag, needing a shave and haircut, look as though they had been bled, starved, and thoroughly mistreated. The nurse knows what has happened to them since they sailed away from home many months ago. They have been fighting in the tropics, which means sleeping, fighting, eating, and dying in the jungle mud. There they lived with a fox hole for a bed and a bomb for an alarm clock. Malaria, dengue, and dysentery made most of them sick before they were wounded.[8]

Another nurse said, "We all feel that admitting these boys from the war front is one of our most important jobs. And it is. Not only do we do our duty as doctors and nurses, but the entire staff of the hospital becomes a combined reception and welcoming committee."[9]

Mary Towse, a commander in the Navy Nurse Corps from 1918 to 1945, felt herself fortunate to be stationed at a beautiful Spanish building on 80 acres—the Naval Hospital in San Diego. Nurses were housed in a converted exposition building in Balboa Park and taken to and from the hospital by bus. In one four-month period the patient population grew from 3,000 to 4,000. "Our patients are cheerful and eager to get back to the battlefront," reported Towse in an article she wrote for the *American Journal of Nursing*. "Every day here is interesting to me as I see these men progressing. Most interesting of all is the reconstructive surgery."[10]

And the reconstructive surgery was nothing short of miraculous. Thumbs were "grown" from fat in the abdomen and new eyelids made that the patient could "bat as well as the one he lost." One marine's paralyzed face could move again after tissue from his thigh was transplanted to his cheeks. There were, of course, instances when operations didn't go as planned. Author Page Cooper tells of a humorously painful incident in her book *Navy Nurse*:

A new lip must be grown from the other because the lip is the only part of the body that grows skin with color. This boy's upper lip was attached to the lower. For three weeks, while the graft was becoming attached, the boy could neither speak, smile, nor eat except through a tube. He begged for a radio and was so restless that Miss Jones gave him a set of earphones. That was an error. He listened to a Bob Hope show, burst out laughing and tore his lips apart.[11]

Even the nurses who went overseas usually worked in a stateside hospital before or after their overseas tours. Before going to the Pacific, Lillian Dunlap, ANC, spent six months at Camp Young in California, where she treated patients with traumatic injuries, gastrointestinal diseases, asthma, burns, and psychiatric problems. Patients with the mumps were a particular problem because they weren't supposed to be moved, so during air-raid drills they were—as gently as possible—put under their beds.

After completing tours on hospital ships and in North Africa, Helen Pon, ANC, was stationed at Camp Patrick Henry in Virginia, and put in charge of the neuropsychiatric, venereal disease, and infectious hepatitis wards. She also worked with German POWs and learned enough of their language to say, "No work, no eat."[12] This knowledge, however, made the prisoners think that she understood them and they quit talking in front of her.

Sarah O'Toole began her Navy career at a naval hospital in Florida and then took care of newborn babies at a dependents' hospital before being put in charge of her own ward. Later she became an assistant to the chief nurse, then became the chief nurse at a small naval air station dispensary where she often treated crash and accident cases.

A particular event at Fort Story, Virginia shows the courage it takes to be a responsible nurse. Louine Connor, ANC, was preparing to assist in the amputation of a young GI's leg when she noticed a pulse in the limb. Her training had taught her that sensation meant amputation wasn't needed, so Connor told the commanding officer that she wouldn't assist in the surgery. Since the military frowns (to put it mildly) on disobeying orders, Connor was transferred to the U.S. Hospital Ship *Acadia*, which happened to be exactly what she wanted. Thanks to her convictions, the surgery was called off and the young man kept his leg.

Nurses stayed in shape and kept busy. The U.S. Naval Hospital in San Diego even initiated a fitness program whose motto was "Keep fit to keep fighting men fit,"[13] and sports were a good way to not only stay in shape but enjoy friendly rivalry with nurses from other hospitals. And almost every sport was included: softball, bowling, golf, tennis, archery, swimming, and volleyball, even horseback riding in the park.

The women also took advantage of the many clubs around the country that gave them a place to relax, get exercise, and entertain guests. Most included dining rooms and kitchens, private rooms, living rooms, libraries, playrooms, and canteens. Depending on the location, there were golf courses, horseback riding, swimming, tennis, and hiking.

"When we were off duty, a few of us nurses would put on our dress uniforms, take the local bus to Oakland, and then the 'A' train to San Francisco," said Alice Lofgren. "There we would happily spend all day sightseeing, eating at favorite restaurants, shopping, or maybe seeing a movie until it was time to start the long journey back to the base again."[14]

WESTERN ATLANTIC MINOR THEATERS

The defense of the Americas was the longest, most uneventful, and least heralded military campaign the United States conducted in World War II.   Yet it was fundamental to Allied victory against the Axis coalition, for it guaranteed the security of the base that President Franklin D. Roosevelt earlier termed the "arsenal of democracy." It likewise guarded the Americas from attack while the United States raised and trained its armed forces.

Expecting war, political leaders in the Americas began making preparations in the mid-1930s. And while Germany was winning in Africa, they were particularly concerned with protecting the southern hemisphere, the area they thought the most likely for German invasion. According to author Charles E. Kirkpatrick, if the Germans reached the western edge of Africa, they could jump from there to Brazil. Because of this threat, American nations agreed to work together whenever any aggressive acts threatened any one of them. In 1939, the Panama Conference of Latin American Nations proclaimed a neutrality zone that excluded hostile warships.

Because the United States had made arrangements with many countries— Natal, Newfoundland, Bermuda, the Bahamas, Jamaica, St. Lucia, Antigua, Trinidad, and British Guiana—to use their territories for military bases, it had established two arcs of defense: the Pacific, which ran from the Aleutians, through the Hawaiian Islands, to Panama; and the Atlantic, which ran from Newfoundland to Bermuda to Puerto Rico to the Windward Islands by Panama. These bases were land links in the major transatlantic air routes, jumping-off points for future operations, and stopover points for patients being evacuated back to the States.

On September 11, 1941, President Roosevelt issued a "shoot-on-sight policy"[15] for any aggressive acts within 50 miles of these coasts, and at first there was reason for concern. From mid-1940 to mid-1941, Germany ruled the waters of the Atlantic, and in early 1942, their U-boats prowled the waters off the U.S. eastern shore and sank thousands of tons of Allied shipping.

Even though it was obvious by the middle of 1942 that America's bases were safe from invasion, nurses were still needed to take care of the military personnel stationed there. Although there was a mysterious strain of fever and there were skin allergies from eating certain fruits and touching certain trees, most patients were victims of accidents and venereal disease. But there were also the heartbreaking cases: the 19-year-old Seabee whose body had been smashed by a bulldozer, and the survivors of a torpedo attack who had drifted for three days without food or water.

And while some nurses saw their assignments as less important and less colorful than those of the battlefront nurse, many found delight in their posts, such as the Navy nurses in Guantanamo Bay in Cuba.

The long, screened porch of the attractive quarters that overlooked the bay, the lawn abloom with poinsettias, jasmine, roses and delicate pink hibiscus, the bridle path along the edge of the beach, the shops full of alligator bags, perfumes and mahogany chests from Haiti, made the tour of duty in Cuba seem like a tropical holiday.[16]

Alice Lofgren also remembers good times when her ship was docked at Guantanamo Bay.

We seldom had patients to care for although one nurse was required to be aboard at all times in case of any emergency. We certainly enjoyed the leisure time in such a sunny, beautiful countryside. People on the base were very friendly. In fact, when some of us enjoyed going for long walks, it was rather difficult when we were frequently offered rides by people driving by; some found it hard to believe that we preferred walking.

One time a few of us had fun singing as we walked along and felt lucky on the way back when we finally found enough coconuts fallen by the roadside so each one had a coconut to take back.

With a marking pen, I wrote an address on the outer husk of my coconut and mailed it to my dad in Utah. He later wrote how he had finally managed to break the outer shell open, and then the inner one. It was a challenge he enjoyed.

Another time several of us arranged to have a whole stalk of green bananas for a long time as they gradually ripened one or two at a time.[17]

Three Navy nurses stationed on the Caribbean island of Curaçao worked in a dispensary and took care of the men guarding the oil refineries. There they lived "a Cinderella life" and were always in demand for parties, teas, and receptions. They were later sent to Trinidad.

Here in a little valley on a compound surrounded by jungle, the girls lived in "monkey cage" quarters set up on cement stilts. The furniture was of Trinidad mahogany, slat chairs made by the natives, beautifully grained but guaranteed to catch your garter every time you tried to get up.

This was the tropics; it rained so hard that the girls couldn't hear each other speak across the dining table. A few feet beyond the compound they could pick wild limes and bananas and avocados. Yet in spite of the abundance, marketing was a problem. Most of the ships had been taken from the Caribbean to ferry troops to England so there were no fresh vegetables from the States. The officers soaked native lettuce in a weak solution of potassium permanganate and ate it, but the chief nurse didn't want her girls to take a chance.[18]

While military personnel who served in the United States or one of the minor theaters never got the attention and glory of their overseas counterparts, winning the war took the efforts of every one of them. After all, without a healthy civilian population to produce everything needed for wartime, how could the U.S. military personnel be effective? Without knowing their families were well cared for, how could the fighting men concentrate on the task at hand? Without good nurses to train other nurses, how could the tremendous demand be met? As one author put it, those in the States "provided the tools that gave the Allies victory."[19]

NOTES

1. Lt. Marguerite Regina Mella, ANC, "From the Home Front," *The Army Nurse*, December 1944, p. 5.

2. 2nd Lt. Maren A. Frye, ANC, "From the Home Front," *The Army Nurse*, September 1944, pp. 3, 4.

3. "Army and Navy Hospital Facilities," *American Journal of Nursing*, March 1944, p. 246.

4. Janina Smiertka Davenport, Letter to author received December 1993.

5. Mary M. Roberts, R.N., *American Nursing: History and Interpretation* (New York: MacMillan, 1955), p. 349.

6. "Nursing in a Debarkation Ward," *American Journal of Nursing*, February 1945, p. 134.

7. Quoted in "Army Hospital Trains," *American Journal of Nursing*, June 1943, p. 566.

8. Ens. Dorothy Lucille Main, R.N., USN, "Sailors and Marines Come Back," *American Journal of Nursing*, April 1944, p. 356.

9. Quoted in Main, p. 355.

10. Cmdr. Mary D. Towse, R.N., NNC, "Naval Hospital in San Diego," *American Journal of Nursing*, March 1943, p. 269.

11. Page Cooper, *Navy Nurse* (New York: McGraw-Hill, 1946), pp. 221, 222.

12 . Helen Pon Onyett, Interview with author, December 19, 1991.

13. "Navy Nurses Keep Fit," *American Journal of Nursing*, September 1943, p. 817.

14. Alice Lofgren Andrus, "Navy Experiences," Unpublished memoirs, November 1993, p. 3.

15. Charles E. Kirkpatrick, *Defense of the Americas*, Series: The U.S. Army Campaigns of World War II (Washington, D.C.: U.S. Army Center of Military History, 1991), pp. 3, 9.

16. Cooper, p. 111.

17. Alice Lofgren Andrus, "Random Navy Memories," Unpublished personal essay, November 1993, pp. 1-2.

18. Cooper, p. 115.

19. Theodore Ropp, "World War II," *World Book Encyclopedia* (Chicago: World Book-Childcraft Int'l., 1982), p. 408.

APPENDIX 8A:
NURSING IN A STATESIDE BURN WARD

Many of our patients were undergoing a series of reconstructive plastic surgeries to repair damage done earlier, but between operations, they were ambulatory. They helped us taking care of bed patients and admitting new patients. Their friendly joking and assistance soon made new patients feel welcome. Some wanted to talk about their experiences, like the barely 18-year-old sailor, whose oil tanker had gone down, with burning oil engulfing everyone trying to escape. The young sailor was severely disfigured by burns on his face, head, arms and body. Talking about it seemed to be his way of trying to accept the fact that he really was scarred and nothing would ever be normal again for him. Another patient had only moderate burns, but he had been told that his blindness could not be changed; he would never see again. While he was despondent and wanted to be left alone, occasionally other patients quietly visited briefly at his bedside, gradually making him feel one of the group. He was still depressed, but he did not feel alone, as the other patients gave him moral support and understanding.

Another patient had been confined to bed for some weeks. As he began to feel better, he wanted to get up and walk around, but his orders as a bed patient remained. Finally one day, with nearby patients as look-outs, he sneaked into the bathroom and was almost back to his bed when he was "seen" by a corpsman. When the doctor was told of this adventure, he laughed. When patients are determined enough to sneak out of bed, he explained, they are well on their way to recovery. This improved the morale of the whole ward.

Some of our patients, between operations, were encouraged to get passes and take the bus into Oakland to get used to being among civilians again. Some, who had gone once, refused to go again. They said that some children and many adults would stare at their scars, crutches, or bandages, and whisper, point, and even laugh at them. Since they were in full uniform, it was obvious that their wounds were a result of the war, but many people reacted in a cruel, unthinking way of ridiculing anyone who looked "different" in any way.

Once when I was working a late shift, all but one of our patients who had been out on passes were back in bed. Suddenly, the door to our ward was jerked open, and in walked our Marine patient. He was tall, strong, good-looking, and a little unsteady on his feet. He was angry and mumbling something I couldn't understand. As he stood in the hall, his fist suddenly punched a hole in the plasterboard wall. This was entirely out of character, as he was a friendly, good-natured person whom I had never seen angry before. Quickly, I called the corpsman, who with the help of another patient, soon had our Marine peacefully in bed, sleeping.

In the morning, he was embarrassed to see the hole he had made in the wall, and explained that he had been out with a buddy who had noticeable scars. They were enjoying a fine evening until several civilians began making crude, ridiculing jokes about them. Since getting into a fight could have caused serious medical problems, especially for his buddy, they controlled their anger and walked quietly away. However, the anger and frustration remained. All of us in the ward understood, and no one seemed to notice when the wall was soon mended without comment.

—Alice Lofgren Andrus, "Navy Experiences"
Unpublished essay, November 1993, p. 1

Chapter 9

Wild Blue Yonder

The flight nurse, having checked her passenger list, supervises the loading. She sees that each man is safely settled and made as comfortable as possible in one of the stretcher bunks, quadruple-decker tiers of which line the huge plane's cabin.

Then, as a preparation for the take-off, she checks the adjustment of the safety belts. Once in the air, it is she who will give the men their meals, chat and perhaps play a few hands of cards with them, and, of course, administer whatever medical attention may be necessary.

—"Air Evacuation . . .
Returning Wounded Fly Under Care of Army Flight Nurses"
The Army Nurse, March 1945

By the end of the war, 1,176,048 casualties had been evacuated by air, most under the watchful eyes of an Army or Navy nurse. And their services were certainly appreciated. As Army Nurse Geraldine Dishroon-Brier said of the men evacuated from Normandy, "Even if it was a minor injury, you were doing something for them because you were taking them off the beachhead. And believe me, they were very glad to leave."[1]

But a high price was paid. One nurse, Reba Z. Whittle, spent time in a German POW camp after her plane crashed behind enemy lines. Thirteen nurses were killed in weather-related crashes, and four were killed in action.

The first call for Army Air Forces nurses came on November 30, 1942. Between February 1943 and March 1, 1944, 4,152 applications were processed by the Procurement Branch of the Personnel Division of the Office of the Surgeon General. Recruits had to be members of the Army Nurse Corps, spend six months in an Army or Army Air Forces hospital, then request assignment to the Army Air Forces Evacuation Service. They had to be between 62 and 72 inches in height, between 105 and 135 pounds in weight, and between 21 and 36 years of age. All who were accepted were volunteers who could return to their previous assignments at any time.

According to Mae Mills Link and Hubert A. Coleman in their book *Medical Support of the Army Air Forces in World War II*, the first 39 women who attended Army Air Forces flight nurse classes at Bowman Field, Kentucky were "poorly housed and had completed a program of instruction that was definitely in the experimental stage."[2] One nurse said that there were "no books . . . nothing for our training whatsoever. It was improvised. . . . We were given the material as fast as they could get it."[3] When she went through the course in May 1943, Agnes Jensen said, "No one really knew how we would operate overseas, but they (the staff) continually reminded us that we were pioneering air evac and they were assuming we would be working and living very near the combat zone and tried to prepare us to take care of ourselves in those conditions."[4]

The four-week course included training in aeromedical physiology; principles of air evacuation operations; tactics and logistics; first aid and field sanitation; loading and unloading planes; crash procedure and survival in various climates, terrains, and the ocean; gas-mask usage; parachute packing; ward management; operating room technique; and orientation to military social service. In October 1944, the school became part of the School of Aviation Medicine at Randolph Field, Texas, and simulated altitude practice with oxygen equipment was added to the curriculum. To receive real in-flight experience, nurses performed air evacuation inside the Continental United States.

The first class of Army Air Forces nurses graduated on February 18, 1943. They were given their diplomas by General Fred S. Borum (Commanding General, First Troop Carrier Command) and addressed by Air Surgeon David N. W. Grant.

Your assignments will probably take you closer to the front lines than any other group of women personnel. You can expect that your plane may sometimes be the target of enemy aircraft. You will be called upon to carry out your work with quiet, purposeful action when all about you may be the excitement of battle. You will, I am certain, serve with the same heroic endeavor as the nurses on Bataan and Corregidor.[5]

Each woman then became part of a Medical Air Evacuation Squadron (MAES) that consisted of 1 surgeon, 24 flight nurses, 1 hospital corps officer, and 24 medical corpsmen. One nurse and one corpsman were in charge of the patients on each flight. The average patient load was 25 and the average flight took 19 hours.

Army nurses flew in planes that weren't protected with the Geneva Red Cross because the aircraft were also used to drop off troops and supplies and, therefore, were subject to attack. Geraldine Dishroon-Brier, the first nurse to receive her wings, said that they "were just another airplane . . . an open target."[6]   One plane, the C-46, was even nicknamed the "flying coffin"[7] because its heaters often exploded during flight. (Pilots often endured the cold rather than turn on the heaters.)

But the danger didn't deter thousands of young women from eagerly volunteering. Women such as Elsie Ott, the first woman to win the Air Medal. Not even a flight nurse at the time she was selected, Ott was given only hours to prepare for her first flight. Her mission? To collect five patients in India and take complete charge of them until they reached Washington, D.C. This included not only nursing, but feeding and housing and making sure all the luggage made the trip with them.   Ott won accolades and proved the advantages of air evacuation.

Danger didn't deter Helena Ilic either. Ilic became a nurse because the airlines required that their hostesses be nurses, but when she graduated from nursing school and saw a recruiting ad for flight nurses, she joined the military. After flight training at Bowman Field, Kentucky, she flew with the 801st MAES in the Pacific.

Eugenie Rutkowski joined the Army Nurse Corps in May 1943; trained at Bowman; became a part of the 807th MAES; worked in North Africa, Italy, Sicily, and Albania; and was the recipient of numerous awards including two Bronze Stars and a Battle Star for Air Combat Balkans. As an instructor at Randolph Field, Rutkowski was responsible for the indoctrination, flight training, and coordination of personnel on training flights.

Lucy Wilson saw flight nursing as a way to care for the wounded better than she had been able to when stationed on Corregidor. "After watching men suffer and die on Bataan and Corregidor because of lack of medical facilities, it gave me the greatest satisfaction to realize that these men were being flown to the finest hospital care within a few hours."[8] Already a recipient of the Presidential Unit Citation for her service on Bataan, Wilson received the Air Medal for combat flying.

The Navy had been evacuating men by air in the Pacific since 1942, but flight surgeons had been the only crew members trained in flight medicine. When Navy nurses were given the opportunity to fly, they chose it above all other assignments, even that of duty aboard a hospital ship or at Pearl Harbor. But the admission requirements were so demanding that "not more than a fifth of the girls who volunteered [were] accepted." *Navy Nurse* Author Page Cooper paints an amusing picture of the first graduating class:

Miss [Mary Ellen] O'Connor helped select the first group on the basis of physical fitness and character reports without first seeing the girls, but when the class assembled at Alameda, the air officers at the station wouldn't believe that she hadn't mixed her qualifications with those for Miss America. Indeed, from Lt. O'Connor to the newest recruit, the group was as outstanding a collection of pulchritude as one could find in a day's flight.[9]

Navy flight nurses were also teamed with a corpsman, called a pharmacist's mate. Unlike their sisters in the Army, however, Navy flight crews flew in two-engine Douglas Skytrains marked with the Geneva Red Cross. The planes could hold 24 litter patients or 27 walking wounded.

Navy nurses flew three main routes: from target areas to forward hospitals, such as Guam; from Guam to Pearl Harbor; and from Pearl Harbor to the continental United States. They also transported men within the United States to equalize the patient load in hospitals. They rotated between combat and noncombat flights and were not allowed to fly more than 100 hours per month.

Nurses and pharmacist's mates attended the Navy Flight Nurse School, which opened at the Alameda Air Station in December 1944, and then went through a special flight indoctrination course with Naval Air Transport Stations (NATS) at Oakland, Seattle, or Olathe. The first class of 24 nurses and 24 pharmacist's mates graduated in January 1945.

Training was similar to that given to Army nurses, but with a greater emphasis on water survival. The women had to be able to swim under water to escape burning oil, climb onto a life raft, and inflate "Mae Wests" (life jackets). According to Page Cooper, by the time the women passed their tests, they could swim a mile, tow or push a victim for 220 yards, and swim 440 yards in 10 minutes.

Day-to-day living for flight nurses meant adapting to a lack of privacy, irregular hours, and poor food and housing; and such conditions eventually manifested in diarrhea, constipation, bladder infections, and skin problems. But, according to author Judith Barger in her dissertation, "Coping with War: An Oral History of United States Army Flight Nurses Who Flew with the Army Air Forces in World War II," the women "continued to work despite their discomfort, often to the point of exhaustion."[10]

The privacy factor loomed large when it came to personal hygiene and toilet facilities—or the lack of both. If a plane had toilets, they weren't enclosed. You were "practically on display," said Army Nurse Adele Edmonds. But most planes didn't have them at all. According to Dorothy White, ANC:

If you were lucky, and you had a long flight, there might be a pail in the back that we had to use. It is possible for a nurse with slacks on to aim at the pilot's relief tube, but, believe me, it's very difficult, and you have to hope that the plane is going to fly steady while you're there.

Army Nurse Frances Sandstrom remembered a scheduled 90-minute flight that lasted seven hours because of fog. "The worst part of it was that we had no place to go to the little girl's room . . . I can remember that was very uncomfortable, to say the least." Barger said that the women learned to control their food and fluid intake. "We just dehydrated ourselves; it took care of that,"[11] said Sandstrom.

And their uniforms often bulged with toilet paper and sanitary napkins. "Our menstrual cycle was irregular and more frequent," said Lucy Wilson. "Supplies of every sort were in short supply. We learned to always carry a pad with us during a flight or we might have to tear off our shirt tail to use for a pad. Most of the time pads were cloth diapers which we took over with us and we would wash them to reuse, but they eventually wore out."[12]

The only water available during a flight was the canteen. Even when they were at a base, water was often rationed, so the women often washed their clothes in the ocean.

In regard to living conditions, Jocie French recalled her quarters in Europe: "We were put in this old abandoned mess hall . . . the vines were growing inside through the windows, and there were mice all over the place. . . ."

Ivalee Holtz, stationed in the Pacific, said:

[W]e all lived in this one big Quonset hut, and we had an outdoor latrine, and they were still finding Japanese around. . . . So when we got to the back door of the Quonset hut to go to the bathroom at night, . . . you'd call, "Guard!" And he'd come and walk you to the latrine. I bet he loved his duty during the war![13]

The flight nurses of the 802nd landed in Oran, North Africa, on February 21, 1943, and "spent the night sleeping on cold hard floors in our bedrolls, eating C- and K-rations for dinner." Their next home was in Maison Blanche, Algiers: "an old French barracks building with flowers around it, cold showers, an indoor bathroom, dayroom, double deck bunks and housed four people. . . . Personnel bombs were dropped on our base at night, thus we were cautioned never to pick up fountain pens, pencils or cigarette lighters."[14] According to Army Nurse Ivalee Holtz,

We all complained about the food constantly, because it was mostly stuff shipped from Australia, and the meat, we called it Australian bully-beef. It was really canned meat of some sort, but it really was tasteless, so we got to the point we didn't eat that anymore. And I think once they even sent us canned liver, but I'm not sure of that. But I know most of us survived on peanut butter.

But most took the inconveniences in stride. Army Nurse Sara Jones said, "I didn't expect to be carried around . . . [or] have all the comforts of home. . . . How could you have everything plush when there was a war going? That's ridiculous!"[15]

Since the first days of flight, pilots have been seen as dashing and daring, but the flight nurses of World War II were just as courageous and proved it time and time again.

Ann M. Krueger, of the 817th MAES, pulled all 27 patients out of a downed plane before it burst into flames.

Jeanette Gleason was on a nighttime flight over mountainous terrain when the plane's motor failed and the pilot gave orders to jump. Landing, alone, on a mountaintop, Gleason slept in her parachute, ate a chocolate bar for breakfast, then walked down the mountain to a hut where a Chinese family fed her rice and took her to the nearest town.

When the Fourteenth Air Force was forced to abandon some of its bases in eastern China, it appeared that there would be no way to evacuate the wounded, but the C-47 transport planes took on the task. Patients were put in every available space and the nurses—some of the last personnel to leave the bases—performed their duty. According to an article in the *American Journal of Nursing*, all wounded and sick were evacuated "without a hitch."[16]

Having become separated from the rest of their crew when their plane crashed, three nurses of the 807th MAES—Wilma Lytle, Ann Maness, and Helen Porter—hid across the street from a German camp. They used a tunnel to move from one cellar to another each time the Germans searched the houses until eventually escaping the town disguised as Albanian peasants. After an 800-mile journey across several mountain ranges, the nurses, with the help of partisan guides, reached the coast and were picked up by an Allied torpedo boat. A plane trip that started on November 8, 1943 ended on March 22, 1944.

Mary Louise Hawkins was on her way to Guadalcanal with 24 litter patients when the pilot decided to land in a 150-square-foot clearing on a small island because the plane was running low on fuel.

During the landing, a propeller tore a hole in the side of the fuselage; patients and crew were uninjured except one man who received a severe cut in his throat which severed the trachea but missed the jugular vein. Lieutenant Hawkins devised a suction tube from various accessories including an asepto syringe, colonic tube, and the inflation tubes from a "Mae West." With this contrivance she was able to keep the man's throat clear of blood until aid arrived nineteen hours later. Radio contact brought glucose and plasma, parachuted to the stricken plane. A U.S. Navy destroyer picked up the island castaways the following morning and brought them into Guadalcanal.[17]

The first Navy nurse to fly an evacuation mission in the Pacific was Jane "Candy" Kendeigh, and her story was recorded in words and pictures by Lt. Gill DeWitt, USN, in a booklet, *The First Navy Flight Nurse on a Pacific Battlefield*. Her 700-mile, 15-hour journey began when she boarded a C-47 around 2 a.m. at the Agana Airfield on Guam. When they spotted Iwo Jima,

an off-shore bombardment was in progress and we had been ordered to circle the field for 90 minutes, until it was over.

We circled and circled the small island and watched the bursting shells beneath us like firecrackers on a fourth of July. The front line was so easily distinguished by the trail of smoke and dust across the north end of the island.[18]

According to the *American Journal of Nursing*, "The plane landed at a southern air field under mortar fire and Kendeigh and the crew were sheltered in foxholes while carrier planes finished an attack on enemy positions north of the field."[19] Kendeigh said, "I don't remember being frightened while we were on the ground. There wasn't time to think about anything except getting these wounded men on board. But now we are safe, in the air again, I find my knees are shaking so I can hardly stand up."[20]

Flight nurses also transported POWs, and the presence of one young German showed Eugenie Rutkowski how war affected normally moral men.

Locating the plane, I noticed the cabin door was missing. This didn't seem to bother the crew. The pilot said, "Yeah, we lost it on the way up." The attitude seemed to be "you do with what you have." In flight, the British became aware of the German prisoner. Eyeing the open door, talk started on how best to assist him to walk home from seven thousand feet over the Mediterranean. These seasoned troops were not joking. I was not sure how to avert the situation. It occurred to me that I outranked them. I let loose with an angry barrage of words and threats. One statement seemed to have reached them, "They were soldiers and not murderers." They realized what a can of worms they had opened and started to laugh. Everyone seemed to relax and the situation was diffused. Their attitude is understandable. Just a few hours before, they were in battle with German soldiers. To change mental gears, that for them the battle was over, was not easy. Their home was also a battleground. These men were tough. I liked them and was glad they were on our side.[21]

Jenevieve Boyle knew the hazards of transporting POWs and took steps to prevent them.

[H]ere you'd have a German soldier lying right alongside of someone who had been trying to kill him, and that he'd been trying to kill just a matter of hours before. . . . I always put the German soldier up closest to the bulkhead, and I covered him up and told him as well as I could to be quiet and not to move his covers. . . . "Don't ask for anything" so that no one would know that he was a German soldier. . . . I also didn't want to cause any incidents. So I would just cover them up with the blankets, and hot or cold, they stayed that way until they got back.[22]

Since the women spent many days and nights on the ground, they sometimes ran into family members and often made friends with locals. Helen Ilic had two brothers and seven cousins in the service and happened to be treating her cousin George when she found out that another cousin, Tom, was on nearby Guadalcanal. She and George wrangled the use of a jeep and driver and paid Tom a visit. Her friendship with a family on Tinian inspired their daughter to become a nurse.

When Dorothy Rice landed in Kirawagi, New Guinea, she and her fellow passengers were met by friendly villagers, but the women were especially fascinated with the American woman. According to Rice, they "swooped down upon me. . . . As they reached for my hands, they discovered my bright red fingernail polish. This was too much! The loud chattering rose to a crescendo."[23]

Lucy Wilson remembered how the natives helped carry supplies and construct buildings and airfields, even a church that they gave to the Americans. But their services were especially valuable because they provided information about enemy locations and downed Allied crafts and personnel.

Flight nurses were expected not only to perform ordinary nursing duties but to handle those medical emergencies caused by the high altitudes and the possible lack of oxygen, conditions that cause the brain content to expand and the volumes of gases in the intestinal tract to double or even triple. The nurse had to alleviate the expanding gas to prevent abdominal sutures from popping open and make sure the gas didn't push the diaphragm up against the lungs and heart. Morphine was often given to patients so they'd sleep through the flight. This was particularly important for patients whose jaws were wired shut because if they became nauseated and vomited, they would very likely choke to death.

There were always, of course, those patients whose conditions "often touched the flight nurse's spirit, requiring unusual fortitude,"[24] said Judith Barger. These were the blind, the men whose faces were nearly destroyed, and those who'd been burned or had lost more than one limb. Psychiatric patients were not only heart-wrenching but challenging because of the lack of adequate restraining devices.

Lack of equipment made one flight hard for Ivalee Holtz.

He started bleeding under a makeshift cast, and we didn't have any cast cutters, and I had to cut this cast off with the bandage scissors. That's all we had. . . . It was terrible. I had the navigator come back and try to help me, because, you know, it really got very hard to cut this hard cast off, and yet I could see the red creeping through the cast, and I knew I had to get to it to put pressure on it.

Losing a patient was, of course, the hardest experience, as Louise Anthony recalled.

But as they brought the last patient in . . . I could see he was dying. . . . So as soon as we were airborne, I went up to tell the radio operator . . . as soon as he could, radio and ask a doctor to be waiting. I didn't know whether or not this patient would live until I got him to England, and a few minutes later he did die over the Channel. . . . The other patients did not know that this one had died. I did not cover his face, I turned his head, I adjusted his pillow, I checked his pulse. I pulled the blanket back to check his dressings, the same as all the rest of the patients. And then when . . . we landed, the door was opened so quickly, and the first one on was the doctor. And I said . . . "This is the patient I wanted you to check." He checked him and took a quick look and could see that he was dead. . . . And so no one knew anything.[25]

Looking back at the World War II years, it's hard to imagine flight medicine being in its infancy, but it's not hard to imagine how important it was—and still is—to get wounded personnel out of harm's way. As the editors of the *American Journal of Nursing* wrote, "Several minutes away from the field, the men, previously silent, begin to kid one another, and there is a feeling of great relief. They realize they are now free from snipers, air raids, and bombardment."[26]

And they were so grateful to the nurses, according to Congresswoman Frances Payne Bolton,

Ask the men sometime what they think of those flight nurses! I've talked with hundreds of them and in only one instance did I hear anything but praise and a gratitude beyond all words—the kind that wells up in the eye and runs down the cheek as the lips smile tremblingly.[27]

NOTES

1. Quoted in Capt. Becky Colaw, "An Operation Called Overlord," *Airman*, June 1994, p. 25.

2. Mae Mills Link and Hubert A. Coleman, *Medical Support of the Army Air Forces in World War II* (Washington, D.C.: Office of the Surgeon General, USAF, 1955), p. 370.

3. Quoted in Judith Barger, Ph.D., "Preparing for War: Lessons Learned from U.S. Army Flight Nurses of World War II," *Aviation, Space, and Environmental Medicine*, August 1991, p. 774.

4. Agnes Jensen Mangerich Questionnaire.

5. Quoted in Ruth Y. White, "Army Nurses—In the Air," *American Journal of Nursing*, April 1943, p. 344.

6. Quoted in Colaw, p. 25.

7. Quoted in Judith A. Bellafaire, *The Army Nurse Corps, A Commemoration of World War II Service* (Washington, D.C.: Center for Military History, no date), Pub. 72-14, p. 14.

8. Lucy Wilson Jopling, R.N. *Warrior in White*, (San Antonio: Watercress Press, 1990), p. 85.

9. Page Cooper, *Navy Nurse* (New York: McGraw-Hill, 1946), pp. 167, 170.

10. Judith Barger, B.S.N., M.S.N., "Coping with War: An Oral History of United States Army Flight Nurses Who Flew with the Army Air Forces in World War II," Dissertation, The University of Texas at Austin, December 1986, p. 97.

11. Quoted in Barger, "Coping with War," pp. 99, 100.

12. Jopling, pp. 87-88.

13. Quoted in Barger, "Coping with War," p. 91.

14. Clara Morrey Murphy, Dottie Lonergan Jouvenat, Harold Carter, John Matrise, Catherine Laver, Charles Bybee, Leona Benson, Anne Wilson, Barb Clay, Jane Faulkner, and Vito Tursi, "History of 802nd MAES," *The Story of Evacuation, 1942-1989*, Compiled by the World War II Flight Nurses Association (Dallas: Taylor Publishing Co., 1989), pp. 70, 71.

15. Quoted in Barger, "Coping with War," p. 94, 101.

16. "Army Flight Nurses in China," *American Journal of Nursing*, January 1945, p. 64.

17. "Army and Navy Nurses Tell Us," *American Journal of Nursing*, June 1945, p. 489.

18. Lt. Gill DeWitt, USN, *The First Navy Flight Nurse on a Pacific Battlefield* (Fredericksburg, TX: The Admiral Nimitz Foundation, 1983), no p. #.

19. "Navy Flight Nurses in the Pacific Area," *American Journal of Nursing*, April 1945, p. 318.

20. Quoted in Wyatt Blassingame, *Combat Nurses of World War II* (New York: Landmark Books, 1967), p. 133.

21. Eugenie Rutkowski Wilkinson, Letter to daughter, no date, no p. #.

22. Quoted in Barger, "Coping with War," p. 110.

23. 1st Lt. Dorothy M. Rice, R.N., ANC, "Flight to Kirawagi," *American Journal of Nursing*, January 1945, p. 10.

24. Barger, "Coping with War," p. 113.

25. Quoted in Barger, "Coping with War," pp. 111, 115.

26. "Navy Flight Nurses Serve the Pacific Bases," *American Journal of Nursing*, October 1945, p. 795.

27. Frances Payne Bolton, "Home from ETOUSA," *American Journal of Nursing*, January 1945, p. 7.

APPENDIX 9A:
TALES OF AN AIR FORCE NURSE

Eugenie Rutkowski Wilkinson, of the 807th MAES, had several adventures while a flight nurse. Many years after the war, she put them together in a letter to her daughter.

We disembarked and were quartered in large tents in a bivouac area. Dinner was different from the food on the ship [which she said was "excellent"]. K-packages were distributed. After sunset, I decided to attend an outdoor movie near my tent area. It was pleasant sitting on the grass and watching the film. I don't remember what had been shown because, suddenly, all hell broke loose. Alert alarms were blasting, planes droning above, and antiaircraft guns bombarding the sky. Talk about being scared, I sure was. I started to run toward my tent area foxhole. Next thing I knew a hand grabbed my arm and a British voice yelled "keep pumping." I ran as fast as I could to keep up with him. He guided me to a Nazi bunker. I noticed he was a British lieutenant. The bunker was made and used by Rommel's people before they were rousted out of Africa. The lieutenant had made himself comfortable in the bunker. He had a cot, table, two chairs, and a large opening in one wall. It was situated in front of French antiaircraft guns which seemed to be shooting continuously. Every fifth bullet was a tracer. The lieutenant was very casual about the noise and activity. He offered me a chair, a glass of wine, and a view. It looked like the Fourth of July fireworks. I needed that drink of wine because my stomach was upset and my hands shaking. I hesitated to lift the glass until I had control of my hands. I could not believe this introduction to war.

When Rutkowski started working evacuation flights, C-47s, out of an area north of Catania, Sicily, her first flight was to Bari, Italy.

We did not work in teams as planned. There were many Americans need[ing] to be evacuated. Effort was made to remove them from the battle area as soon as possible. Flying to Bari, I was in the cabin alone. Looking out the window I saw fighter planes approaching us from the rear. It took just three leaps for me to cross the cabin into the cockpit to let the crew know about the fighters. They had seen them and had been notified that British fighters would provide escort. The escort didn't last long. The fighters were notified of a raid in Bari. They went ahead to tangle with the Nazi Luftwaffe. Our pilot descended to a lower altitude, reduced speed to give the fighters time to clear the area so that we could land. The landing was uneventful. We loaded the plane as quickly as we could with army soldiers and flew to Algiers.

On the return trip . . .

A short time into the flight we ran into thunderstorms. The radio operator, a Sgt. D. Lebo, from Harrisburg, Pennsylvania, reported contact with their home base was lost. We continued to fly. It seemed a long time. An airfield came into view. The pilot was making an approach to land when bullets with tracers were coming around the plane. Looking down on the field there were swastikas on the parked planes. Our pilot started to climb and ducked into heavy clouds. Gasoline was running low; he found a flat area in the mountains and crash-landed—wheels up.

We learned after landing that we were in Nazi-occupied Albania, north of Berat. An Albanian guided us to Berat during a heavy rain. The Albanians extended a friendly greeting and we were lodged in various local homes. The next day we were assembled in a hall. Mr. Hozie, the Albanian leader, spoke [sic] through an interpreter, gave a speech. He spoke of Albania's problems and what help they could give the Allies. They assumed we were an advanced unit [sent] to prepare for an Allied invasion to rid Albania of the Nazis.

During the two-month sojourn in Albania we engaged in hide-and-seek with the German military while walking 800 miles trying to escape. The supply of food was meager. The mainstay was hand-crushed corn mixed with water and a little salt. It was baked on the floor of the fireplace with a metal lid over it and covered with hot coals. Gastric distress was an ongoing problem. The bathroom was the great outdoors in the cold and snow. The most troublesome were fleas and lice. The daily walks of 15 to 25 miles wore holes in the soles of our boots. Feet would get wet and cold from the snow.

General Twining and his 15th Air Force, and a British Wellington bomber, tried to extricate us but the Germans moved tanks to the edge of the airport. Not to be deterred, the Army Air Corps dropped an OSS officer, a Major Lloyd G. Smith, who escorted us to the coast and eventually Allied-occupied Italy.

Chapter 10

Life at Sea

I could visualize the floating hospital steaming into a distant harbor, gleaming white, bearing the Red Cross of mercy, like a messenger from the folks at home, offering such luxuries as clean beds, delicious food, American nurses to care for them, and efficient doctors to treat them.

—Ruth Young White
"The Solace Plies the Tasman and Coral Seas,"
American Journal of Nursing, June 1944

When patients couldn't return to their posts even after being treated by the men and women near the front lines, they were sent to general hospitals or back to the United States—and most often by ship. One vessel, the *Solace*, began wartime duty the very day the United States entered the war. Having joined the Pacific Fleet in Pearl Harbor on October 7, 1941, the *Solace* was dropping lifeboats and picking up wounded exactly two months later.

Since hospital ships were protected from attack by the Geneva and Hague Conventions, they had to meet specific criteria. They were painted white, had horizontal green stripes on each side, and red crosses on each side and each funnel. The crosses were lit at night and the entire ship had to have the capability of being lit from sunset to sunrise. They could not carry cargo, not even ambulances or mail; and since the radio couldn't be used, captains had to navigate by the stars. Ships could carry medical personnel and equipment, but absolutely no military troops; and they had to have segregated areas for patients with mental problems or communicable diseases.

Although ships had been used as medical facilities for centuries, the United States was frighteningly wanting for hospital ships in 1941. The Army had none and the Navy had only two—the *Solace* and the *Relief*. Since it took 18 months to build a hospital ship, and since the need was so great, some wounded were sent home on transport ships or ambulance transport ships. Although this solution was undeniably practical—the ships could carry patients to the States and bring fresh troops back to war zones—their use was a source of disagreement throughout the war. One of the most ardent dissenters was the Chief Surgeon of the European Theater, General Paul R. Hawley, who said that "no officer or soldier who is unable to care for himself in the event of enemy attack upon the vessel in which he is a passenger, be evacuated on any but a plainly marked and regularly operated hospital ship."[1] Hawley was so unyielding in this opinion that he refused to put men on the transports even if the ships sailed half-empty and the wounded languished in overseas hospitals.

Many nurses spent a lot of time at sea, either as personnel or as passengers on their way to and from assignments. But even when traveling as passengers, the women usually helped out in the ship's sick bay. Army Nurse Helen Pon always wanted to help, but she was a tiny woman and the bunks were five tiers high, so she usually recruited a corpsman. "I can't reach the top two," she'd tell him, "but I'll do the middle two if you'll do the top two and the bottom two."[2]

As men and women have done through the ages, nurses fell in love with the sea. Navy Nurse Catherine Shaw shared her feelings with readers of the *American Journal of Nursing*.

[T]here's ecstasy to be found in the ever-changing miracle of sea. There are blues, rich and deep and royal, or verdant green, to be churned to turquoise in the wake; clear-shimmering depths, rainbow crested waves, pearls in the foam. There is the benison and kiss of spray, the cool and rough embrace of wind, penetrating sun. And then at night there is pearly moonlight, a million scattered stars reflected in black marble seas, a phosphorescent wake. No wonder this was life we loved![3]

Most women soon thought of the vessels as home. Page Cooper recalled this attachment in her book *Navy Nurse*, as she described two nurses who'd just finished a tour on the *Solace*: "Forgetting all the times that they had wanted shore duty at home they stood on the Golden Gate Bridge to watch for her, lonesome and a bit homesick for her now that they had been detached. When at last she came along and passed beneath them, her lights blazing, they cried until she was out of sight."[4]

And sometimes only those nurses who had previously served on land could truly appreciate the comforts of shipboard nursing. When Mary Mixsell, an Army nurse who had lived in tents during other assignments in the Pacific, began duty on a hospital ship, she said, "I felt that I was really back in civilization again."[5]

Another Army nurse, Roberta Love Tayloe, was very impressed with the luxury of the former liner *Monarx*, particularly the dining room with its china and cloth napkins. "A tin spoon, I discovered later, will never taste the same as a silver one."[6]

Nurses adapted easily to the ship's routine, even the water rationing. Helen Pon remembered unheated saltwater showers and said they took many a "spit" bath: a little water and a lot of cologne. And since there were only certain hours when one could bathe—an hour in the morning, a short time at noon, and an hour before dinner—the nurses used the time to their advantage. According to Shaw:

We filled the basin, hot water bottles, and jugs with extra water and those who had bathtubs were nicely set. . . . By clever use of water containers we managed to splash a little at bedtime and to polish our teeth. And somewhere in those precious "washing hours" we tackled our clothing! You had to duck a dripping clothesline in every stateroom.

Life at sea also meant becoming acquainted with:

the sound and meaning of the horns, the siren, and the bells, to distinguish fire and collision drills from "general quarters" and "abandon ship." . . . We were drilled, timed, and checked. We learned to put on life jackets with dispatch, all strings secured, the collar well in place, and we stood in orderly rows along the boat-deck, by our station, with bandannaed heads and bulky jackets ("Mae Wests"), the pockets bulging with essentials. In those pockets were sometimes knives . . . flashlights, cold cream, toothbrush, vitamin pills, or packages of peanuts.[7]

Those bells and sirens could signify danger, and no one knew that better than the nurses who had survived the sinking of the hospital ship *Comfort* because six of their friends and co-workers had not: Margaret M. Billings, Frances O. Chesley, Evelyn C. Eckert, Ida M. Greenwood, Florence Taylor Grewer, and Dorothy M. Stanke. American Army Nurses Ruth Hindman and Anna Bess Berrett also knew how dangerous the seas could be. They were among the lucky survivors of the sinking of the British ship *St. David*.

But even discounting the danger, it took a special breed to work aboard a ship, as Army Nurse Doris Schwartz wrote in her article for the *American Journal of Nursing:*

[T]he limitations of being entirely surrounded by ocean are confining, to say the least. Living conditions are crowded, and hours off duty are necessarily spent in the company of the same doctors and nurses as the hours on duty. In such a set-up, there is no room for unfriendliness, lack of courtesy, or selfishness.

And the appreciation of the men made everything worthwhile.

"Real sheets—Hey, this set-up is O.K."
     "Hot water—electric fans—everybody doing things for ya—it's almost like home!"
     "Almost like home" is the atmosphere that the *Marigold's* staff . . . tr[ies] to establish for their patients. For on a hospital ship, the transporting of newly wounded men is a task which combines the finest of medical and surgical care with an opportunity to give patients their first taste of peacetime contentment. The long-awaited hot baths and back rubs and the specialized nursing are so integrated with the long-awaited Coca Colas, swing records, and Red Cross books and magazines that it is hard to tell which is most appreciated.[8]

By the end of the war, the Army had 29 ships that were either converted, newly built, or in the process of being converted. The number of medical personnel on each varied according to the number of patients, but a 500-bed ship usually carried 8 doctors, 33 to 35 nurses, and 99 enlisted men. Additional personnel included dentists and dietitians, and sometimes supplementary units of doctors, nurses, and enlisted men.

The Navy ended the war with 12 hospital ships, each with an average crew of 19 medical officers, 3 dental officers, 30 nurses, 5 hospital corps officers, 2 American Red Cross workers, and 254 hospital corpsmen. And as fine as the first six hospital ships were, the second six were described by the Navy as being "the finest of their type sailing the seas under any flag."[9] The new ships were completely air-conditioned, had a patient capacity of 800+, four elevators, and two milk emulsifiers, which could make enough ice cream "to satisfy the craving of a thousand wounded sailors."

The following stories are about some of these ships and the women who served on them.

On December 7, 1941, the Navy hospital ship *Solace* had just returned to its home base at Pearl Harbor from its shakedown cruise—a trip down the Atlantic Coast and through the Panama Canal. Newly refurbished with the latest equipment, it "carried medical supplies to last a year and provisions for six months, refrigerators full of frozen meat, and Birdseye cabinets with fresh fruits and vegetables, and enough strawberries and raspberries for ice cream every day."[10]

But their return to Pearl Harbor wasn't what they had expected.

Bombs were dropping on the *Arizona* and machine guns were killing men on the *Nevada,* but Chief Nurse Grace Lally was too busy setting up emergency wards to absorb the horror happening in front of her unbelieving eyes. Before the first flight of Japanese planes had disappeared, lifeboats had been lowered and patients were coming aboard. A doctor stood at the top of the gangway shouting assignments to a nurse who hurriedly filled out stretcher tags, and soon there were patients in every inch of space. And the sight must have been sickening. Chief Surgeon Capt. George Eckert said that "many were so seriously burned as to be unrecognizable."[11]

Page Cooper described what must have been a surrealistic scene:

All morning the nurses in the operating rooms sterilized trays of instruments and gave anesthetics while the doctors set fractures, amputated, and probed for shrapnel. In the burn wards the floors were slippery with tannic acid with which the corpsmen drenched dressings. In every ward, nurses and doctors were giving plasma. Everybody wanted to help the supply officer make the rounds with towels, toothbrushes, toothpaste; the chaplain gave spoonfuls of water to those who could take it; seamen brought pails of fresh water and carted away caked, oil-soaked clothes and reeking dressings. When a second flight of bombers attacked the *Oklahoma* and the *Nevada*, nobody looked up.

Almost three hundred men were treated on the ship that first day, and nightfall brought no relief. "Even the patients who had minor injuries went into delirium or shock when the anti-aircraft guns sounded. And this in spite of general anesthesia. But the shock of seeing their friends blown to shreds before their eyes left them so stricken that they could not make the effort to recover."

The nurses made a rule that they didn't "talk shop" in their off hours. Instead, they tried to joke and make the times more pleasant for everyone. According to Cooper, "Within twenty-four hours the *Solace* was a cheerful ship."[12] Grace Lally had nothing but good words to say about her nurses: "There never was a finer group of women anywhere. The excellent care they gave to the patients and their unselfish and uncomplaining devotion to duty deserve the highest praise."[13] Thirteen of these women were awarded the commendation ribbon.

The *Solace* soon headed for duty in the South Pacific where it made round-trip runs to support General MacArthur's campaign in New Guinea. News of the good food aboard the ship—especially the ice cream—attracted men from all corps wherever she was docked. According to Cooper:

Dirty, bearded, parboiled, they sat in the boats happily spooning it up, exchanging wisecracks with the nurses and envying the patients who had come aboard and were already eating a hot meal. The patients also asked for ice cream even after a huge breakfast. Sometimes the nurses protested mildly that they wouldn't want their lunch, forgetting that during the months of existing on Spam and dehydrated potatoes they had constantly dreamed of ice cream.[14]

Catherine Shaw spent a year on the *Solace* treating patients from Guadalcanal and Bougainville. Although she was assigned to the mental ward, the ship carried men with all types of wounds and disabilities. Each time they docked, men were brought out in motor whaleboats, launches, or flat-top barges. After being carried on board or assisted up the gangway, they were tagged, given pain medication if needed, and sent to the proper wards. Those needing emergency operations were given anesthetic and sent to surgery. A writer for the *American Journal of Nursing*, Ruth Young White, described the disciplined and experienced surgical routines.

Even when the seas were rough and the engines of the ship were turning over hard as they battled the force of the waves, the doctors operated calmly, seeming to be able to calculate the heaving as they did their delicate repair-work. Everything in the operating room was tied down and the procedure was uniform: the corpsmen assisting the surgeons with the instruments and the nurses bracing their feet, as they stood at the patients' heads, watching the pulse and ready to give blood plasma or saline solution in case of shock. Lieutenant Shaw told me that she had seen doctors take foreign bodies from men's eyes, while the ship was all but turning upside down during hurricanes in the Tasman Sea.

The psychiatric patients needed "rest, quiet, fresh air, good food, and pleasant companionship," and most were so weak that they had to be strapped onto their stretchers. But the main thing many of them needed was a chance to talk to someone and be "reminded of the strain they had endured and . . . assured that theirs was a natural emotional reaction that would not last."[15]

For the nurses, days aboard the *Solace* were full of lifeboat drills, teaching corpsmen, assisting in surgery, preparing hypodermics, checking on patients, and, sometimes, visiting foreign ports. Twice a day everyone enjoyed ice cream, milk shakes, and soft drinks; and patients and crew members usually put on informal shows or sang in the afternoons. The nurses tried to find time to talk to the men and write letters for them, finding the latter a good way to learn of their problems.

But if their days and nights ever began to seem routine, something usually happened, such as the early morning in November 1943 when the *Solace* was zigzagging her way to the Ellice Islands.

[T]he girls who were on night duty heard a distant boom of guns so loud that it brought the whole staff on deck. Orange bursts of fire hung in the sky and the red arcs of tracer bullets crisscrossed the horizon. As the light grew they could see a string of little islands containing a few rows of pine trees and before them the dim shapes of battleships and cruisers. White moving specks of foam, Higgins boats, darted back and forth from the beaches. As the *Solace* dropped anchor off a tiny island called Abemama, a submarine surfaced not more than a quarter of a mile away and began to shell one of the islands. Now they were on the very edge of the battle. The whole sea was cluttered with battleships of every sort, all pounding at the largest of the islands, Tarawa, someone said. So the *Solace*, the first American hospital ship to serve under fire, took part in the third day of the costliest battle the Navy had fought. But there was little time to watch; no sooner had the *Solace* dropped her anchor than the casualties began to come aboard.

With stretchers all around them, some of the new nurses had to withdraw for a few minutes because the tragedy made them sick, but they returned and were "able to smile at the boys waiting on the stretchers and give them a cheerful 'How you doing bud?'"[16]

One nurse, Ann McLaughlin, "adopted" a marine who'd been almost completely paralyzed by a bullet that had entered the front of his neck and come out his back. She took charge of his care to the extent that other patients teased her. "Whenever we want her she's always in the emergency waiting on the gyrene."[17] By the time they reached San Diego, McLaughlin had calmed the man's fears about how his wife would react to his disability, and a relieved McLaughlin later received a letter from the couple in which they said that the marine felt McLaughlin had saved his life. She kept the letter as a memento "to read on black days when she feels that no one can be of much use in a world preoccupied with slaughter."

The *Solace* also participated in a battle with the *Relief* as each served at opposite ends of the island of Eniwetok. According to Page Cooper:

They arrived at the beginning of the battle and were actually in the harbor where the nurses could see its progress. The big ships began to fire in the morning and bombarded the island all day long; the girls watched the palm trees going down as though they were being mowed by a giant sickle. At night the shells burst on the island, making the heavens look like a glorified Fourth of July. Nobody could have slept even with ear plugs, the tension was so great. The marines, everyone knew, would land sometime before dawn; one could almost feel them gathering in their landing boats out there in the black harbor. In the morning when it was light enough to see, they were ashore, protected by a wall of fire thrown in front of them by the big guns. By afternoon there wasn't a palm tree left standing on Eniwetok.

For several days the hospital ships stayed in the neighborhood while the nurses and doctors operated on and cleaned up their patients, then hastened to a base hospital to unload and be ready for the next battles, Peleliu, Guam, Saipan. Always it was the same pattern, the bombardment, the landing of the marines in the black hour before dawn, the small boats running back and forth all day long with the wounded. At Guam the amphibious boats went onto the beach and brought casualties directly to the ships. Always the nurses and doctors worked day and night, without sleep, without rest, until the casualties were taken care of, then relaxed and stored up fresh energy in the lull that came after their wounded were delivered to a shore hospital.[18]

A 1992 issue of *Navy Medicine* includes a story by LCDR Christine Curto about the hospital ship *Relief,* "the first ship of the U.S. Navy designed and built from the keel up as a hospital ship."[19] The *Relief* that saw action through World War II was the sixth hospital ship to carry the name and was serving as a base hospital and part of the Atlantic Fleet when the United States was drawn into war. Cruising a route from Charleston, South Carolina, to Argentia, Newfoundland, *Relief* served the Atlantic until it was sent to the Pacific in 1943. There it worked with other ships picking up casualties and delivering them to shore hospitals or other hospital ships.

Even though the ship was supposedly safe from attack and even though it stayed close to shore during the day and moved out at night "with lights ablaze,"[20] the *Relief* was almost attacked by Japanese planes, so blackout precautions—even smoke camouflage—became the norm.

Curto said that patient traffic flow was very organized and that some of the wounded were brought on board within 30 minutes of being hurt. One time they picked up 691 patients in 1 hour and 15 minutes.

Navy Nurse Georgia Reynolds described life aboard her ship, the *Bountiful,* for the *American Journal of Nursing*:

Imagine receiving approximately five hundred fresh casualties within the space of a few hours! Yet, thanks to planning and organization, it is accomplished smoothly and speedily. . . .

Between trips with patients we hold "Field Day"; the wards and special departments are given a thorough cleaning, airing, and repainting if necessary. Supplies are made, packaged, and sterilized and all hands relax, rest, and do odd jobs.

Before we leave the ship we expect to see further action, and perhaps take part in the final invasion before victory. When back ashore we shall be able to look back at our sea duty and have the satisfaction of work well done.[21]

The *Refuge* was the only Navy ship to serve in the Atlantic, Mediterranean, *and* Pacific. It took casualties from Normandy to Norfolk and from southern

France to Naples, and took German prisoners of war to Naples and Italian prisoners from North Africa to the States. Page Cooper described one trip:

On Christmas Eve they found themselves somewhere off the Philippines in the midst of a battle. All night long they sat blacked out listening to the noises about them. By daylight when the LSTs began to bring out the wounded, they were so close to Leyte that they could see the shore. The wounded were both Army and Navy from the island and the ships that were taking a beating from the Jap planes. They hadn't even been given first aid, nothing but dressings, and they cried when they saw white sheets.

All day long the LSTs kept ferrying the wounded, fifteen at a time. Occasionally in a lull the nurses slipped up to the wardroom, washed their faces, powdered and smoked a cigarette until they heard a shout, "Throw over the lines on the starboard side." Then they ran down again, knowing that the big cable was swinging over the homemade, boxlike elevator that was quicker than the hook and stretcher.[22]

The nurses on the *Refuge* were very proud of their ship and liked to brag about it being one of the first to own a Burman locator—a pencil-looking instrument that could locate any type of metal in a patient's body, thus saving time and cutting. The women experimented with the machine by hiding pins and then looking for them with the machine.

Not only did these nurses have to cope with war and its effects, they also had to live with Mother Nature and the realization that there is no place to hide when you're in the middle of an ocean. In her book *Heads in the Sand*, Edna Lee Glines tells the story of her sister's service. Pauline (Polly) Glines served on the Navy hospital ship *Benevolence* and experienced Mother Nature at her fiercest when a "two headed monster typhoon split in two" in June 1945. One of the "heads" attacked the *Benevolence* and another hospital ship. As the nurses were being told to report to sick bay because the ship might be hit by "very rough water and hurricane winds,"[23] Glines was thrown across her room by the impact of a giant wave. In a few moments she was escorted to sick bay (where beds and patients were both anchored) by a corpsman after he tied a rope around both of their waists. Although the ship wasn't suited for such weather and was in danger of capsizing, all turned out well, but it was an experience Glines wasn't to forget. "I have never been so scared before, and hope never to be so scared again!" she said.

When the final glorious moment occurred and the terms of surrender were being signed on the *Missouri*, the *Benevolence* was nearby picking up American POWs. One of them, General Jonathan Wainwright, is quoted as saying, "The sight of the beautiful navy nurses was the best medicine an American could have."[24]

Alice Lofgren witnessed Mother Nature's wrath from aboard the *Consolation*.

Everything was "secured" as we plowed through high waves that rocked the ship, rolling side to side as well as pitching fore and aft. No one was allowed topside without authorization since the unwary could easily be washed over the side and lost. We made good use of handrails in the passageways as we moved from one part of the ship to another.

During storms, mealtimes were mostly sandwiches. In this heavy weather, the corpsmen served us each a plate with a sandwich. The large tables were bolted to the floor, but as we sat in our chairs, and the ship started to roll, some of us instinctively grabbed our plates as our chairs slid several yards to the right. Others had a firm hold on the table, so their chairs stayed in place, and their plates slid promptly to the floor. Soon the ship rolled to the left, and we slid back to our places at the table.

With remarkable efficiency, the corpsmen soon brought more sandwiches and cleaned up the spills. But some teasing and laughter continued for days afterwards. We had quickly learned how to cope with eating in stormy weather.[25]

One of the first nurses to serve on the *Consolation*, Lofgren was at the commissioning ceremony on May 22, 1945, and also on board when the ship made its first run to Wakayama, Japan, to pick up American POWs. These newly freed men had been transported from the POW camp by train and had walked the rest of the way. And they were a sad sight. "Many were emaciated and weak, some limping or using makeshift crutches. . . . Soon our few corpsmen hurried up the road with stretchers and carried back the weakest ones."[26] The nurses hurriedly bathed the men and gave them clean pajamas so they could board the ship and get the much needed medical care and rest.

The *Consolation* left Wakayama a few days later and took the 1,062 patients to Okinawa from where they would be taken to the States. A sister ship, the *Sanctuary*, was also in Wakayama. Between the two ships, approximately 3,000 men were evacuated.

Lofgren said that the food on the *Consolation* was "very good" and fondly recalls the day that she and another nurse were treated to a surprise birthday party that included two cakes and gifts. Lofgren later wrote her mother, "You would be surprised how fast the cakes disappeared."

Mail call at sea meant waiting to dock, then getting quite a backlog. As Lofgren wrote to her mother, "Hope I get mail soon—it's been quite a while since our last mail call so we should have quite an accumulation by now."[27] And when mail call time came around, "even getting an advertisement was better than nothing," she said. "Some people were very popular, receiving a handful of letters, occasionally perfumed. . . . It was sad to see that some never seemed to get any mail, and they would usually avoid mail call."[28] Lofgren was lucky to come from a letter-writing family, but since her mother had five children, she used carbon paper and made five copies of each letter.

During the invasion of Italy, the *Acadia* served as a mobile surgical hospital. Men were brought on board directly from battle, treated, then sent to hospitals in North Africa. A former transport ship, the *Acadia* had only three small operating rooms.

Major Edith A. Aynes visited the *Acadia* and wrote about it for the *American Journal of Nursing*. At the time, 29 of the original nurses had just completed their twelfth crossing of the Atlantic and there were 776 patients on board. As on other hospital ships, the nurses had too much leisure time en route to a war site and none on the way back, often working nine-hour daytime shifts and 12-hour nighttime shifts. While in port, two nurses covered the daytime shift and one nurse covered the nighttime shift. The ship was divided into four decks, and nurses took care of all the patients on their assigned deck.

The nurses filled their leisure time sewing, crocheting, playing cribbage, rummy, and solitaire, and watching movies every other night. But who would have thought a simple hobby such as knitting could cause trouble? According to Louine Connor:

We put the socks and things that we knitted in the color Army olive drab; they were meant to keep water out so we wouldn't get frozen in the water. I had a big ball of olive drab line. It was so big, it was about the size of a mine. I lost it overboard and it floated because it had a lot of wool [in it]. I think that the Navy sent the Coast Guard out, but they did come out and shoot at it. I heard later, I don't know how true that was, but they got hold of my knitting directions and they were trying to decode them.

Other items thrown overboard made amusing stories. When drinking cups were ordered, D-cup bras were delivered instead, and Connor said, "They didn't know what to do with them; I guess they threw them overboard. I don't know what happened to them or who found them." When bedspreads and mattress covers were delivered by mistake, they were also thrown overboard, but some people found uses for them. "The Arabs . . . wrapped them around themselves. . . . They loved them. . . . They could make tents out of those [bedspreads]. They could dress the whole family."[29]

"The *Acadia* has been very fortunate in never having been the 'innocent bystander' during all of the activity she has seen," reported Major Edith A. Aynes in her article for the *American Journal of Nursing*. "The nearest thing to it happened when flak that had been fired at a reconnaissance plane sprinkled down on the deck of the ship. No one was injured, however. The ship was in the Palermo harbor only two hours before the bombing of that port city took place; later the nurses could hear the blasting of the bombs and see the fiery flashes from their position at sea."[30]

Louine Connor might disagree. "Sometimes the enemy subs would come in underneath us. Although hospital ships were supposed to be safe from hostile fire, we knew, when we were empty and riding high, that we made an easy target and were expendable by even our own forces. If it meant the difference between saving thousands of our sailor's lives to get that sub, using us for cover, we knew we could be blown out of the water."[31]

Another time: "[W]e went up to help the English in the Adriatic and the British hospital ship had been sunk by the Germans by accident and they needed help badly." Because of the stringent rules of the Hague and Geneva Conventions and the fact that there was a Merchant Marine on the bridge, no one could tell the *Acadia* where the mines in the area were located, so the ship spent four days in that spot moored to an ammunition ship. "That was just an invitation being tied up to her," said Connor.

Complying with Hague and Geneva Conventions' requirements meant reporting their position every four hours, yet "they'd [the Navy] tell us not to give it and the Germans were picking up on that position of the ship. . . . We were ordered to never turn the red lights off, or the red crosses, but in reality we turned them off many times, we blacked out many times. This didn't happen when we had wounded on board. So that was kind of the feeling—that we were expendable and we knew that." She added, "Of course, we weren't allowed to wear helmets and life jackets, yet we knew that the men on the bridge all had helmets and life jackets on. We'd see them and knew that we couldn't put them on because it would frighten the patients. We had them but we had to hide them so the patients wouldn't see them. We could reach them if we needed them, but it seemed pointless because you couldn't move very long. No one would come pick you up, if you had to sit there, no one would stop, they couldn't because they would be marked, they would be a target."

Overall, however, Connor said the morale was high.

We went kind of numb lots of times; most of the time we were because there was always that feeling that it wasn't exactly the safest place in the world to be. But we weren't frightened, just numb. We accepted it. We didn't think of the people back home or our families because, I think like every soldier, if you thought of home, you were homesick or something like that, you weren't going to be able to do your job. If you thought of the people back home when you were in combat, you turned; so you depended on the people, the person next to you. You developed close bonds but you never got homesick or worried. . . . The minute you started that, you were glad to be down and you will be a target. . . . We knew that instinctively.[32]

The *Comfort* was built by the Navy for the Army in 1943, and christened by Eunice Hatchitt and Beth Veley, both veterans of Bataan and Corregidor—an appropriate choice since the *Comfort* was one of the ships chosen to liberate the Philippines. The ship had a fully equipped 700-bed hospital and was staffed with 17 medical officers, 37 nurses, a dietitian, 2 Red Cross hospital workers, and 154 Medical Department technicians. Most of the nurses were already veterans, an aspect that increased the admiration between nurse and patient.

The nurses participated in a special training program with the medical officers and corpsmen that included first aid, lessons in treatment of war injuries, teaching corpsmen, and a question-and-answer session with a Navy nurse from the *Solace*. Calisthenics, military drill, and swimming were added to keep personnel in shape.

Although brightly lit and clearly marked, the new ship was seriously threatened on April 28, 1945, at 8:58 p.m. The following account is provided by Dietitian Edna M. Raybourn.

We were out of port about four hours when the plane circled over our ship, giving us the friendly signal. It was only a matter of a few minutes when we were aware of the fact that it was not a friendly ship but a Jap suicide plane. It did damage to the upper ward room and officers' quarters on the bridge deck, demolished the operating room, dental clinic, X-ray, offices, wards, and hallway on the superstructure deck. On the main deck, it completely destroyed three wards, main diet pantry, elevator shafts, passageways, and telephone exchange. On second deck, the stoves were damaged. Of course all of this was not done by a falling plane alone. It was assisted by two bombs which were dropped during action.[33]

The attack resulted in 63 casualties including 29 deaths but "within two minutes of the explosion . . . the uninjured nurses were taking care of patients. 'There was no panic among the nurses or patients. It was remarkable'."[34]

The *Marigold* became an Army hospital ship on February 24, 1944. Previously called the *President Fillmore*, the vessel had accommodations for 763 patients and carried 10 doctors and 37 nurses. It saw action in the European and Pacific Theaters and covered a route more than 65,000 miles long. Its crew saw as many as 800 patients in a day; 739 boarded in four hours in Naples, Italy. Patients also included casualties from the Southern France invasion, Pacific natives, and German POWs. Sometimes the ship ran the "ferry jaunts" and treated men recently wounded, and other times it took men to the States.

In her article for the December 1945, *American Journal of Nursing*, Doris Schwartz described some details about the ship.

Attached to each bed is a cleverly designed metal stand which serves as a table. Separate spaces in it hold bath basin and toothbrush mug at bath time, or water glass, ash tray, and personal belongings during the day. It is necessary, of course, to have some such arrangement to hold articles securely, for in rough weather the ship lurches considerably. At mealtime, the chow trays fit neatly over the whole, offering a secure and comfortable dining table. The only drawback to this practical gadget is its bulk. The narrow aisles between the bunks are so well filled with bed trays that they necessitate navigating the ward with the "Marigold Crawl," a sort of snaky, weaving, hula motion recommended only to the slenderest of nurses.[35]

Ruth Claff, ANC, took the *West Point* from San Francisco to Milne Bay. It took two days, she said, to rid herself of the "curious unbalanced feeling in my head and stomach that wasn't quite nausea or dizziness," and found "to my delight" that she wasn't afraid of the water and that she loved to travel. "I can't understand why it took me so many years to discover I was born for wandering," she said. They were at sea, unescorted, for 20 days "trusting to blackout, radar, zigzagging, and our speed to keep us out of trouble." But the time was enjoyable: two meals a day, snacks of ice cream and cokes, movies every other night, bridge, and watching the water kept them happy and entertained.

Crossing the equator meant being initiated; seeing flying fish; enjoying a calm sea, a hot sun, and double and triple rainbows; and dancing under the Southern Cross "in the shadows of the big guns." The images were unforgettable ones, said Claff, particularly evenings "dreamily watching in the water the big chunks of phosphorus that looked like drowning stars fallen from the sky. Nothing is more impressive than taps at night on a dark ship in the middle of an ocean." The men gave the nurses doughnuts and coffee "at sunrise on the upper deck every morning that we got up in time" and took them on tours of the ship. "It was a glorious glamorous trip."

But there were a few fearful days. Arriving in Milne Bay, New Guinea, on March 10, 1944, they sat in port for three days. "We traveled the width of the ocean in terrifying darkness, just to sit three days in the harbor in a regular spotlight. They seemed pretty confident that the Japs couldn't get back that far—we certainly hoped they were justified in being so sure—what one little yellow bomber could do to 10,000 boys, not to mention a couple hundred of 'us girls.' I wouldn't say we felt too comfortable about being so conspicuous."

Claff also made a trip on the *Tasman*. "I was in a trance with the trip," she said. "The ship was a clean dazzling white, with bright red crosses fore and aft and on all sides and all decks, and we traveled fully lighted, with floodlights on the crosses, very conspicuous. Our only protection was our faith in the Jap observance of international law covering hospital ships. No arms, no ammunition, no troops, no guards, no lookouts, no zigzag."

On the voyage to Hollandia the women slept in "clean, airy and comfortable" wards and enjoyed listening to the radio and sitting in the open and covered decks. But while the continuously rough weather kept many below deck "groaning in their bunks," Claff said she "spent the time on the pitching deck, getting drenched in the spray and the howling wind." But the weather caused problems when the ship made stops at various islands to drop off nurses. "There was a bad storm," said Claff, "and the waves were breaking as high as the top deck, leaving flying fish floundering there, and our hearts were in our throats as we watched the girls transferring to the landing boats. One second the bottom of the ladder would be crashing into the barge and the next second be fifteen feet above it."

Claff's next sea voyage was on the Navy ship *Hope* where waiters served them a Thanksgiving dinner that included shrimp cocktail and mince pie served on real linen with silver and china. "There was a welcome address written by the navy to the army on the menu (oh, my yes, naturally menus!) that sounded as if they were just a little sheepish about faring so much better than we did. Well, they did, of course, but they were very generous with us when they got the chance to be, and they gave us full credit for our hardships."

While the ship was anchored and in the center of the fleet, it was blacked out and, therefore, subject to attack. And one particular night:

[I]t sounded as if all hell had broken loose, and the ship rocked at anchor as if we were in a heavy sea.

The air was crisscrossed with ack-ack fire, searchlights, tracer bullets—quite a show. For three hours we loaded patients, mostly burned cases. The raid was one of the first of the dread kamikaze raids, though they were just called suicide raids then. There were a lot of them that night.

And the next morning, "a plane flew by low, and in a few minutes came back—and dropped a bomb so near my porthole that I thought we were hit, and the ship seemed to stop in its tracks for a second. . . . The nurses, after the first stunned moment, coolly cleared the decks and got everyone back into his own ward in case of strafing."

Claff's love of life aboard ship and at sea are evident throughout her wartime experiences, *Lady with the Flashlight*.

The sound of the bosun's pipe was always a thrill, and general quarters call at dawn of each day was exciting. I would awaken to the sound of the shrill whistle and the patter of little feet past my door as everyone scurried to his post. . . .

Another thing that always delighted me was the solemn "Now hear this" that preceded all orders over the PA system. . . . And the order "Sweepers, man your brooms. Clean sweepdown fore and aft," uttered as dramatically and impressively as if the order had been "Fire when you see the whites of their eyes." I loved it, loved it, loved it.[36]

Nurses of the 95th Evacuation Hospital spent the night before the Italian invasion on board the *Newfoundland*. The doctors and corpsmen went ashore with the invasion troops on September 9, 1943. If the women were kept on the ship for safety measures, the plan backfired, because early the next morning, the ship was bombed by a German plane. Six British nurses were killed and three American nurses were wounded. Survivors were picked up by the British ship, *St. Andrew*, and taken to North Africa.

The resulting absence of the 95th's nurses erased any doubts as to the necessity of women in combat medicine as evidenced in a diary: "The fact [that] our nurses are not with us is costly . . . [and] has proved a serious handicap to our medical and surgical staffs."[37] The men were certainly relieved when the women joined them two weeks later.

Juanita Hamilton's unit, the 153d, took the *Parker* to New Guinea in March 1942.

Shortly after embarkation I began to have a very curious sensation. The black and white bathroom floor blurred, the water in the commode moved, and I started 5 days of seasickness. With every roll of the ship I was nauseated. When I finally got nerve enough to go to the dining room, the soup moved back and forth in the plate, and several of us hit the GI cans conveniently placed by the doors. I was sick all the way from New York to Panama. The Atlantic Ocean is very rough in March, and this was the days before Dramamine and other motion sickness remedies.

I lived on ripe olives and saltine crackers for those five days—staggering up on deck once a day for fresh air, and trying to keep my eyes on the horizon. Some helpful sailor told me to watch it, because it did not move—never to watch the water. In addition to rough water, the convoy had to zig-zag and change course every so often to hopefully avoid a torpedo in case of attack. The German submarines were operating freely in the North Atlantic at that time. Finally—into the calm of the Panama Canal Zone. What a beautiful sight—peaceful, still, blue water. My seasickness left and I was back among the living.

After a trip through the Panama Canal, they were on the Pacific where they continued to zigzag and maintain blackout conditions. And since only two meals were served each day, Hamilton said they all came to appreciate the cheap cigarettes and candy bars. Time on board was spent playing Chinese checkers, reading, chapel services, nursing, and lifeboat drills. "Sure glad we never had to use those creaky old life boats. I don't think they would float," she said. When two weeks went by and they all feared they'd never see land again:

The loud speaker played Hawaiian music and we all dashed topside. What a beautiful sight! It was land! A truly tropical island: palm trees, coral reef, white surf and all. The colors of the South Seas defy description. There must have been a dozen shades of blue in the water hitting that coral reef.

Then, out came the natives, in the typical outrigger canoes. They brought coconuts, beads, grass skirts and coral to sell or trade to us. I got so excited I traded one of my precious white uniforms for a string of beads and a grass skirt. Lend lease in reverse!

They had landed at Bora Bora, south of Tahiti, and though the nurses weren't supposed to leave the ship, Hamilton talked an officer into taking her ashore. "I jumped out, planted my feet firmly in the sands of Bora Bora, then back in the boat, and hurriedly to the ship. All the time he was muttering, 'You're going to get us both court martialled'. But, of course, we weren't, and I can say I did step on a South Sea Island."

A turkey dinner with all the trimmings had been planned for the last meal at sea, but Mother Nature had other plans. As they crossed the Tasman Sea, a storm came up and Hamilton's seasickness returned. "No celebration for me on my last night aboard ship,"[38] she said.

In 1923, a Navy nurse wrote to the *American Journal of Nursing* to report that an assignment aboard a ship was "much coveted by all who are good sailors." In 1934, another nurse wrote, "Every nurse relinquishes duty with a new source of misgivings—will she ever like the humdrum of land-living again!"[39] These sentiments were echoed again in 1944, by Mary Mixsell:

Although I might have chosen to stay at home and help the war effort there, I wouldn't trade my present job with anyone else on earth and I hope they don't send me home until the war is over for good. I like to be in the thick of it, have my information first-hand, and hear another American say, "Gee, it's good to talk to an American girl!"[40]

NOTES

1. Quoted in Graham A. Cosmas and Albert E. Cowdrey, *Medical Service in the European Theater of Operations*, Series: U.S. Army in World War II, Technical Services (Washington, D.C.: U.S. Army Center of Military History, 1992), p. 104.

2. Helen Pon Onyett, Interview with author, December 19, 1991.

3. Lt. (jg) Catherine Shaw, NC, USN, "We Traveled by Transport," *American Journal of Nursing*, November 1943, p. 1023.

4. Page Cooper, *Navy Nurse* (New York: McGraw-Hill, 1946), p. 85.

5. 2nd Lt. Mary Mixsell, ANC, "We Improvise and Economize," *American Journal of Nursing*, March 1944, p. 290.

6. Roberta Love Tayloe, *Combat Nurse: A Journal of World War II* (Santa Barbara: Fithian Press, 1988), p. 11.

7. Shaw, pp. 1022, 1023.

8. 1st Lt. Doris Schwartz, R.N., ANC, "Nursing Aboard a Hospital Ship," *American Journal of Nursing*, December 1945, pp. 996, 998.

9. Quoted in Cooper, p. 212.

10. Cooper, pp. 16, 213.

11. Quoted in Jan K. Herman, "Navy Medicine at Pearl Harbor," *Navy Medicine*, Bureau of Medicine and Surgery, Department of the Navy, November-December 1991, p. 17.

12. Cooper, pp. 19, 20, 22.

13. Lt. (jg) Grace B. Lally, NC, USN, "What Nurses Do," *American Journal of Nursing*, August 1943, p. 724.

14. Cooper, p. 79.

15. Ruth Y. White, "The Solace Plies the Tasman and Coral Seas," *American Journal of Nursing*, June 1944, pp. 552-554.

16. Cooper, pp. 87-88.

17. Quoted in Cooper, p. 89.

18. Cooper, pp. 91, 209.

19. Quoted in LCDR Christine Curto, NC, USN, "Nurse Pioneers and the Hospital Ship *Relief*," *Navy Medicine*, May-June 1992, p. 21.

20. Curto, p. 24.

21. Lt. (jg) Georgia Reynolds, NC, USN, "On a Navy Hospital Ship," *American Journal of Nursing*, March 1945, pp. 234-235.

22. Cooper, p. 211.

23. Edna Lee Glines, *Heads in the Sand* (Los Angeles: Authors Unlimited, 1990), p. 42.

24. Quoted in Glines, pp. 42, 51.

25. Alice Lofgren Andrus, "Random Navy Memories," Unpublished essay, November 1993, p. 1.

26. Alice Lofgren Andrus, "A Moment in History," Unpublished essay, March 1993, no p. #.

27. Alice Lofgren Andrus, Letter to parents, May 30, 1945.

28. Alice Lofgren Andrus, "Navy Experiences," Unpublished essay, November 1993, p. 6.

29. Louine Lunt Connor Peck, United States Army Nurse Corps Oral History Program, Interviewed by Col. Clara Adams-Ender, A.N., Major Wynona Bice-Stephens, A.N., ed., North East Harbor, Maine, August 31, 1986, pp. 27, 51.

30. Major Edith A. Aynes, R.N., ANC, "The Hospital Ship *Acadia*," *American Journal of Nursing*, February 1944, p. 99.

31. Quoted in Nan Lincoln, "Captains Courageous," *Bar Harbor Times* "Selects," February 21, 1991, p. B2.

32. Peck oral history, pp. 23-24, 26.

33. Quoted in "A Report from the USS *Comfort*," *The Army Nurse*, July 1945, p. 10.

34. Quoted in "Army and Navy Nurses Tell Us," *American Journal of Nursing*, June 1945, p. 489.

35. Schwartz, p. 996.

36. Ruth Claff, *Lady with the Flashlight*, Unpublished memoirs, 1947, pp. 16, 17, 27, 38, 39, 40, 43, 44.

37. Quoted in Wyatt Blassingame, *Combat Nurses of World War II* (New York: Landmark Books, 1967), p. 71.

38. Juanita Hamilton Webster, Unpublished memoirs, no date, pp. 7-8, 9, 10, 11, 12.

39. Quoted in Curto, p. 21.

40. Mixsell, p. 290.

Chapter 11

Camaraderie and Romance

It would be hard in the States ever to imagine a dance where everyone wore the same clothes—men and women alike. A suntan world, slacks and shirts. It sounds drab, but when one stopped to notice it, it was pretty spectacular. And there were moments—a Filipino orchestra playing plaintive Hawaiian music, while you danced with a man who was on his way out— your heart would burst with emotion, purely impersonal, and yet, and yet—it was like losing a part of yourself when they went. We were so closely united, there was a feeling—Oh, help me someone, with the words, but let it be someone who was there, because it cannot be imagined.

—Ruth Claff
Lady with the Flashlight

When speaking to World War II veterans, it's easy to see the mature and seasoned men and women of today and forget that these were once very young people, vulnerable and eager to sample all that life had to offer. Added to their natural vigor was a righteous cause for which to fight. How could one *not* feel energized and invincible? How could one *not* want to enjoy and savor every moment? Although older than the average Army nurse when she joined, 42-year-old Ruth Claff was filled with such excitement. "I might find that the biggest reason [to join the service] was a hunger for adventure, and an escape from a dull life—an urge to be myself at last and at all costs. . . . After all, everybody knew the war would be over in a few months!"[1]

Thousands of young Americans left the safety and familiarity of their homes to travel thousands of miles away and often into perilous situations. They grew lonesome and homesick. When young men and women are thrown together, especially in such circumstances, it's only natural that they seek out friends and lovers. Most just wanted someone to dance with on a starry night, perhaps a temporary romance. Some found lifelong marriages and some suffered heartbreak. Relationships between male and female military personnel fell into many categories.

First and foremost was nurse and patient.

To most soldiers and sailors, nurses made such a difference in their lives that the men soon began calling them "angels." Seven GIs even composed a compilation of tributes to battlefront nurses that they titled *They Brought Us Back*. Private Michael Geoghegan called them "G.I. Janes" and said that they restored the confidence that many men lost after being injured.

She taught him that he was still a soldier, still fighting a battle, still with an idea that must be maintained. Yes, she taught him to banish the clouds of eternal inner suffering, self-pity, and self-consciousness. Instead, she helped him find the cheerful, warm, radiant sunlight of self-assurance which will remain with him until he has ridden in his last jeep.[2]

A colonel who served on Bataan said, "I can't begin to tell you how wonderful they were. . . . I'll never forget little Miss _____ [*sic*] in our ward. She never lost her smile! Sticky from the heat, grimy with dust from the bombardment, dressed in an oversized Army coverall that she bunched up into 'a new style bustle,' her cheerfulness was like water in a desert."[3]

Private Gerald Dominguez landed successfully in Holland on September 17, 1944, but during a battle over one of the bridges, his right foot was torn off by a shell fragment. Shortly before he was hit, Dominguez had given his only morphine to a German he'd just shot, a humanitarian act that left Dominguez without the much-needed drug when he needed it himself. But by the next afternoon he was on his way to an evacuation hospital where he received the care and attention of nurses. He particularly appreciated the compassion of one nurse on those nights when his pain was almost unbearable. "Nights I couldn't sleep she'd sit 'n' talk to me. She was, well yeah, you could call that nurse an angel."[4]

After being wounded in North Africa, Sgt. Frank Day sent the *Stars and Stripes* a poem he'd written, part of which was printed in the August 1943 *American Journal of Nursing*:

> You never see her on parade,
> Like WAAC's and WAVES and such;
> She's much too busy working hard
> To keep away Death's touch
>
> . . . .
>
> I won't forget her tender skill,
> From Pvt. Joe to Capt. Bill;
> My thanks to you! I wish folks knew
> The hell you've seen and waded through;
> I'd like to tell the universe;
> God bless you, keep you, Army nurse.[5]

Even a British soldier wrote to President Roosevelt about the American nurses:

Dear Mr. President:
   I am a British Tommy and I have taken this great liberty in writing to you to express my sincere and heartfelt thanks, through you, to the doctors and nursing staff of the _____ [*sic*] Station Hospital, USA, who are somewhere in North Africa, and who, through their wonderful skill and patience, have made it possible for me to be a fit man once more. Especially to Doctor Major Brody and Lieutenant Longyear.
   How can I ever thank you enough for all that you did for me—and the nurse of ward 27, who I only knew as Miss Connie? Nothing was ever too much trouble for her to make our pain and wounds easy to bear.
   The treatment that I received in my six weeks stay at this hospital will forever live in my memory, and there is one British soldier who really means it when he says "God Bless America."
   In closing, I should be very grateful if you could convey my sincere and heartfelt thanks to the medical staff of the above-mentioned hospital.
   I am yours sincerely,[6]

As Commanding Officer Col. Paul Martin said, "We can't do without nurses, even in the combat zone. We have good corpsmen, but you can't make a doctor or a nurse out of a layman in one year. It takes training to develop the inborn sense of sterility a nurse has. In the operating room every tray to her is an individual problem. She doesn't have to look for an instrument. She knows where it is. If she didn't have anything more to do than mingle with the patients she'd be doing a great service. The patients' morale goes up 100 per cent when they know a woman is looking after them."[7]

And the nurses returned those feelings. According to Army Nurse Juanita Hamilton, "The soldiers were the best patients in the world. In fact, [after the war] it was harder for me to adjust to the care of women and children and the complaining paying patient."[8]

These women loved their patients and never suffered more than when they couldn't save a life, relieve suffering, or even give enough attention. When a nurse in the Pacific heard planes leaving a nearby base, she prayed, "Dear God, please bring those boys back to us alive and well. But if they are hurt, give us strength, courage, and wisdom to be ready to help them." And when the men did arrive needing help, she said, "it made me feel mighty proud to do my little bit in helping to take care of them."[9]

"Nothing gave our nurses a keener sense of accomplishment," wrote Alice Goudreau in her article "Nursing at an Advanced Naval Base Hospital," "than to be able to bid Godspeed to a paralyzed marine who was leaving the hospital after several weeks of care, with his wounds healing and the rest of his skin intact."[10]

American nurses were so dedicated to their patients that when Hattie Brantley and the other nurses were taken prisoner in the Philippines, they tried to wait for their men, and did so until forced at bayonet point into the trucks that took them away.

And while they purposely maintained a confident and cheerful spirit when with their patients, in private they often broke down. Louine Connor, ANC, said, "We were comfort. The fact that we weren't emotional or showed too much concern for them, was also a comfort to them—that we seemed almost indifferent (we weren't but we were protecting ourselves) by the fact that you couldn't take each one into an internal level, since that would upset your ability to function. You had to do that first."[11]

Navy Nurse Alice Lofgren said, "Sympathy is the worst thing in the world for most people. I learned that growing up—sympathy gets you nowhere. . . . You did the best you could at the time [then] it's in God's hands."

These women cared so much for their patients that more than 50 years after the war, memories still tug at their hearts and make them cry.

Alice Lofgren:

One young sailor was so small. He said he was just under 18, but he didn't look more than 16. His ship sunk, a tanker I think, and there was flaming oil everywhere. He was a mass of scars, and some of his fingers were burned off. Most of his body was burned. He was the most pathetic thing you ever saw, but it didn't make me sick because I knew I could talk to him and the other patients would crack jokes with him.

But the most tragic thing, and some of them were badly disfigured, was that some of them never had any word or any response from their family. Some of them had family who'd visit them and be so happy to have them back. If they were missing a leg or needed more surgery, they didn't care; they were glad to have them back.[12]

Retired Brig. Gen. Lillian Dunlap:

One morning I went on duty and was getting the change of shift report at the nursing station. One of the patients from my wing came to me and said another patient wanted to see me. . . . The patient who wanted to see me was a great big strapping Marine who had his right arm amputated and both legs amputated. He had had a brain injury too and, as a result, hadn't been able to speak although he was alert. . . . When I walked down . . . he looked at me and said, "Hi, Tex." The patients were just so excited about it because it was the first thing he had said—"Hi, Tex." Now, how can you ever forget anything like [that]?[13]

In the April 1994 issue of *The Mercury*, author Harry Noyes quoted Grace Newton, an Army nurse with the 93d Evacuation Hospital in Anzio:

I can't ever forget one young soldier whose bravery collapsed in a last desperate cry as the medical officer walked away, unable to . . . save him. "Nurse, don't let me die." Kneeling beside his cot, I could only hold him as he died. What little we had to offer! Sometimes only a prayer that God would grant a quick death.[14]

As Alice Goudreau wrote, "Even the toughest marine, when wounded, was just another homesick American boy yearning for home and his loved ones."[15] Women could provide the feeling of home that men couldn't, and the nurses went out of their way to do the little things that often made a big difference. One Easter in the Aleutians, nurses embroidered each officer's name onto a dinner napkin and used egg dye and decorations to make favors for the patients' trays. The women also made goodies for the men when supplies permitted—chocolate milk, milk shakes, eggnog, fudge.

Rita E. Beauregard, ANC, managed to turn the painful act of getting a penicillin shot into a parade—marching into the ward holding the instruments while a sergeant held the sterilizer, a private carried the sponges and needles, and another noncom carried the penicillin. When Beauregard and the men stopped to give a shot, they performed with such pomp and circumstance that the patient was barely aware he'd been stuck!

And it was because they felt so bad about giving so many shots that the nurses often gave the men that little bit extra. Louine Connor even received a letter from a patient telling her how much he missed her back rubs because the nurses at Walter Reed didn't given them. Rachel Gilbert remembered a little verse on the subject:

> Bless all the nurses cause they rub your backs
> That's a lot more than you'll get from the WACS.[16]

But there were many people who didn't think women belonged in the military, especially overseas.

While serving in the Pacific, Ruth Claff became ill and was sent home aboard the USS *Hope*, as the only female patient. As she was hoisted up the side of the ship, the doctor saw her and said, "My God, a woman—what next."[17] Another part of her trip was made as the only female onboard. The "old salts," wrote Claff, believed that women on a ship were bad luck, and it didn't help when a patient fell overboard and the ship stopped to rescue him. As if it had been her fault, Claff said, "I got some dirty looks from the uneasy personnel and passengers and I smiled indiscriminately and apologetically."[18]

But they usually won respect.

When a nurse in Germany overhead a soldier saying, "It's not right. It's bad enough for men, but this is no place for a woman," the nurse asked, "Do you think there would be any difference here if there were no nurses?" When the young man quickly answered, "Oh, my, yes," the nurse said, "Well, then that is the reason we're staying."[19]

Since part of the nurse's job was to train corpsmen, this became an important wartime relationship, and for the most part, it went smoothly. Navy corpsmen often bragged that they could outnurse the army medics. There was, however, occasional resentment, and with good reason. After all, the women were volunteers—and instant officers—while the men could not only be drafted, they usually came in as privates, and even those who were nurses in civilian life were not always assigned to the medical corps. Those who did serve in the medical corps often spent months performing all nursing duties only to be relegated to subordinate positions when the women arrived. In *The Army Nurse Corps*, Judith A. Bellafaire quotes someone as saying that when the women arrive at a base, "the morale of the corpsmen plummets."[20]

On Tinian, Navy Nurse Sarah O'Toole said, "[A]t first we detected a certain amount of resentment toward us. When they realized that we admired them and had no feeling that they could not get along without us, they were no longer resentful and are now giving wholehearted co-operation."[21]

The traditional military phrase "hurry up and wait" meant that a lot of young American men and women had a lot of free time on their hands, but they used it to have fun and get to know each other. Favorite activities included listening to the radio; playing cards, baseball, and checkers; dancing; and swimming.

Lillian Dunlap remembered taking patients outside to watch the nurses play softball, then being teased by the men with comments like "You swing that bat like a rusty gate!"[22]

Louine Connor remembered laughing at the skits the men performed aboard ship. Hitler was usually the subject of their gags but no matter the topic, Connor said, "It was hilarious. We would sit there and laugh and laugh and laugh." She also recalled the time the men broke open a huge case of condoms, blew them up, tied the ends with string, then threw them—thousands of them—into the Mediterranean until "the whole bay of Naples was full of them."[23]

Army Nurse Ruth Shadewaldt remembered sitting outside on wooden planks to watch movies even when it was raining. "You'd go there with your raincoat on and a big poncho over your head. Then you'd sit there with your boyfriend under the poncho watching the movie."[24]

Ruth Claff enjoyed her train trip from Chicago to Florida—singing with the many enlisted men and celebrating a fellow nurse's birthday. An unrelenting romantic, Claff described watching a couple as they sat together and shared a meal. Then, writes Claff, "as night drew on . . . sleeping with her head cozily resting on a khaki shoulder. That's my kind of democracy! I wish it had outlasted the war."[25]

Juanita Hamilton recalled fun times aboard ship—playing softball, telling jokes, and playing cards. "Once we even dared strip poker," she said, "but we had so many earrings, watches, etc., to take off [that] we never got down to the bare facts."[26] After dinner they often gathered on the deck to sing and watch the flying fish.

And, as it has throughout history, the communal activity of eating served as a way to interact. Ruth Claff put it all together in one quote, "Imagine getting beef and butter and 100 men all at once!"

Army nurses quickly learned that the Navy had the best food and the women rarely refused an officer's dinner invitation. According to Claff, meals aboard ship were good "even by Stateside standards" and the women often returned back to their units with goodies—"an egg here and there, or a pound of butter or a cold piece of meat. Even a whole chicken and a couple bottles of Coca Cola once, and one lovely bottle of Australian beer—the champagne of beers."[27]

Flight nurse Ivalee Holtz agreed. "We were invited out lots of times to dinner by the Navy and it didn't matter who invited you, you always went, because they always had the good food. . . . They would give us canned stuff . . . Vienna sausages or Spam or something to bring home with us, and that was really great!"[28]

On a trip aboard the USS *Monticello*, Helen Pon mentioned that it was her birthday and was surprised with a cake. While she was aboard the USS *Anderson,* the men brought her a Coca Cola and sandwich during each of her 12-hour shifts.

The men on the USS *West Point* were the same. According to Lillian Dunlap, "They took good care of us. You only got two meals a day, but when we'd come through [the mess line], our enlisted men would see to it that we had plenty. The took good care of us the whole time we were together."[29]

Janina Smiertka was a Navy nurse stationed at the Naval Academy Hospital in Annapolis, Maryland, and said that her happiest memories are of sailing with the Midshipmen. "[T]he nurses would prepare the sandwiches and the Midshipmen got the Cokes into a net, [and] threw it overboard to keep the drinks cool."[30] The men invited the women to formal balls and the women invited the men to their quarters for home-cooked meals. She also enjoyed meals at the officers' clubs.

Nurses always found themselves outnumbered—and they rarely complained about it! After all, being on a ship with 10,000 men meant that there was always someone wanting to dance with you, always someone giving you compliments. "What a way to go to war!"[31] wrote Roberta Love Tayloe in her memoirs, *Combat Nurse: A Journal of World War II.*

Two nurses stationed in the Aleutians, Kathryn Kavotovich and Lois Naftzger, said of their male/female ratio, "Speaking of mail, there is a wide variety of male stationed here too—and very little competition!"[32]

But since the women weren't allowed to date enlisted men, being outnumbered didn't guarantee finding a date. The USO, organized to help enlisted men, realized this and organized some clubs for the nurses. The one in Falmouth, Massachusetts organized dances and afternoon tea "dates." The director of a club in El Paso organized ballroom dancing classes and horseback riding lessons. A club in Fitchburg, Massachusetts invited civilian men to the dances they held for Army nurses.

Dancing was definitely a favorite pastime, and dancing was what many Navy nurses had been doing on the decks of the USS *Arizona* on the last night of America's innocence, December 6, 1941. Genevieve Van de Drink ("Van") has fond memories of the doomed ship sharing its decks with two bands and dancers wearing their finest attire.

Ruth Claff recalled someplace in the Pacific where their dance floor was a piece of canvas spread over the sand and their lights were jeep headlamps. "But," she said, "there was a full moon and a four-piece orchestra of sorts, and GI sandwiches and 3.2 beer." She also recalled a night she danced with a good-looking young major. "[W]hen George danced he floated, dreamily and beautifully. There came to me suddenly the realization that this was one of those rare and precious 'perfect moments'—so hard to tell about, but that second out of all time was timeless, fixed in my memory as a still picture, as the figures are frozen in a movie scene when the projector is stopped."[33]

In her letter to the *American Journal of Nursing*, Matilda Dykstra, ANC, told of being stationed in India where she and the other nurses were invited by British tea planters to dinners, teas, and dances. "[W]hen all of us went," she wrote, "the very walls bulged!"[34]

In an article for *The Army Nurse*, Rosemary Forsythe recalled a memorable night.

I can still hear the exciting melodies of the Filipino Infantry string band as they played the New Year in under the gaily colored lanterns in our club, built native-style. The scene that evening could belong in any authentic travelogue of the South Sea Islands. Wisps of clouds covering a tropical moon drifted overhead, a soft southern breeze stirred the lanterns, and the sound of the rippling mountain stream blended with the music. Couples danced against this background.[35]

Whether at a dance or elsewhere, love found its way into many hearts during the war.

Lillian Dunlap dated but never married after her paratrooper fiancé died during the war. In an article written for the *San Antonio Express-News*, Dunlap is quoted as saying, "You think, 'Maybe this one will be the one,' but then you get involved with your work and your friends and it doesn't happen."[36]

In the midst of all the pain and suffering on Bataan, Lucy Wilson became engaged to Daniel Jopling, who gave her a carved ivory bracelet for an engagement ring. But instead of a day of joy, the proposed wedding date, April 9, would become a day of sadness—the day Americans on Bataan surrendered to the Japanese.

Juanita Hamilton met Doug Webster in Australia, but since he wasn't an officer the two weren't supposed to spend time with each other, but as soon as he spotted Hamilton, Webster swore that he would marry her. Even when she rejected his requests for dates, he told her, "You might as well give in, for I'm not going to give up."[37] But Hamilton was already attracted to the young man with his "narrow waist, broad shoulders with muscles that rippled under that smooth khaki, a sassy swagger in his walk, and the bluest eyes I had ever seen."[38] The couple married in Brisbane in May 1943.

Ruth Claff wrote very honestly about her loneliness and vulnerability in her memoirs, *Lady with the Flashlight*. The unwritten rule of "forty nurses and forty officers" spelled danger. But there was also the very real danger that a young man who said he won't be back, won't be back. "You couldn't just laugh at the boys," she wrote. "They were so sure sometimes that they wouldn't come out of their next advance—and they were so right so often . . . But some of them went overboard in trying to whitewash their quite natural feelings, and some of the girls took it seriously too, which was bad. What they couldn't see was that the nurses were substitutes for the women at home. We were symbolic of all that meant home to them." But wartime romance was a reality. "If there was a little necking under the desert stars, it was with our feet firmly on the ground, and with full knowledge that with the end of the war, it was over—and neither of us cared too much."

But even Claff lost sight of her common sense and fell in love several times. One man told her he was a widower. "I believed him—why not? I fell in love—he warned me how things were in the army, here today and gone tomorrow, but I wouldn't listen. I was plenty old enough to handle any heartbreak that might come my way—yeah!" Eventually, Claff's officer told her that he was married and they parted. "It hit me harder than anything had in many years,"[39] she wrote.

In her book, *Navy Nurse* Page Cooper wrote,

At first they were sympathetic when an officer phoned with a long sob story about his being away from civilization for years and longing for the sight of a girl from home. Wouldn't she dance with him that evening? If she was ironing, she left it half-done, if she was washing her hair, she tied a kerchief around it and went to cheer up the lonely officer only to discover that he had been in a New York night club two weeks earlier.[40]

When one patient swore they'd get together after the war, Alice Lofgren, NNC, knew that he was reacting to his circumstances. He did write to her a few times, she said, but the tone grew more and more impersonal. "Just as I'd expected. So many of them hadn't had anybody who was clean and doing nice things for them so they were very impressed."[41]

Many women tried to avoid entanglements. A flight nurse, Dorothy White, said,

Most of us had been injured or hurt romantically in the early stages of the war. My friend was missing, still to this day missing . . . we were part of the war, and you had to shield yourself from getting any personal involvement in it. Otherwise you'd fold up. You couldn't because it was all around us. So having a lot of brothers was a much easier way of handling it. . . . We had to be careful, because we had to do our work. And you certainly couldn't work if you were madly in love with somebody, and they'd go and get killed.[42]

Sadly, there were incidents of unbecoming conduct.

For example, there were times when the nurses' quarters had to be guarded to protect the women from unwelcome intruders. In the Solomon Islands the women lived in metal Quonset huts surrounded by a camouflaged fence made of chicken wire, barbed wire, and camouflage tape. In addition to a sentry posted at the gate, the women were escorted to and from the hospital and couldn't leave their quarters during off-hours unless they were part of a group. Although the official reason for the extra security was that there were isolated Japanese guerrilla patrols still roaming the islands, the real reason, according to Judith Bellafaire, was to "discourage incidents of sexual harassment and fraternization."[43] According to Mary H. Staats, NNC, "We hardly knew what to think of this set-up, but we gladly took refuge behind the fence. It screened us from the frankly curious eyes of the servicemen who had been dreaming about their women folks at home for twenty or thirty months." Staats was quick to add that the men soon became accustomed to the women being there "and realized we were sent here to do a job."[44]

But the precautions didn't always work.

In Milne Bay, New Guinea, some of the men dug under two rows of fences to get to the women.

In Hollandia, New Guinea, a nurse was hit over the head while returning from the latrine in the middle of the night. And though she saw that the man wore patient's pajama trousers, she couldn't identify him and he was never caught. Another time in Hollandia, one nurse was awakened by a man who, when she ordered him to leave, promptly crawled under her cot. When later asked if he thought he could have gotten away with forcing himself on one of the women, he answered, "No. I could have talked someone into something."[45] According to Ruth Claff, "Maybe he was a little more nuts than the rest of us!"

And even as much as she enjoyed the company of men and joked about being outnumbered by them, Claff sometimes found their numbers a little scary, especially at night aboard ship.

They lay all over the deck, and we had to pick our way blindly between them, trusting to luck that they would think we were men. But they usually knew. Once, and only once, I essayed it alone. I got halfway through before my hair brushed against a GI and I was surrounded and held while they got pretty cute, until I swore I'd scream my head off if they didn't let me through. Not exactly fresh or nasty or vicious, just having a little fun (those seabees!) they finally escorted me mockingly to the door of the lounge. Thereafter I went accompanied by an MP or the major.

Claff also wrote about a truly horrifying event that took place on New Guinea when a couple of nurses were out with a group of officers and enlisted men (off limits, out past curfew, and on a deserted beach), and another group of men made unwanted advances toward the women. When their escorts resisted, they were hit on the head and the women were attacked. Afterward, all nurses were restricted to their base and given a lecture that Claff said made them feel "like a band of not too intelligent prostitutes." Their restriction was finally lifted but the women had to travel in groups of four (two nurses and two armed male officers), they had to have a specific destination, and they weren't to leave the highway or stop the car before reaching their destination. Under no circumstances were they to leave their stockaded area during the night without an escort, and guards were posted at each latrine door. Six nights of the week their curfew was 10:30 p.m.; one night it was midnight.

When the commanders felt sorry for the women and wanted to give them a place to have some privacy and relax, the nurses acquired an island that could be reached only by boat and was for only nurses and their dates. While Claff and a few women went to the island for the purpose it was designed—to swim and picnic—there were mostly those who used it for romance, which, according to Claff, "anyone with any sense would have expected." While there one evening, Claff said, "we didn't dare use a flashlight, and couldn't walk two feet without stepping on someone." The nurses lost their island after only two weeks—"a wicked error in judgment that was soon corrected,"[46] wrote Claff.

Helen Tynan had an unsettling experience when walking with two sailors and an island's chief. Tynan was paying more attention to her surroundings than to what was being said until she realized that the sailors were bartering with the chief—about her price! Surely they were joking, she told herself, but she didn't know the sailors very well. . . . To her relief, the sailors finally told the chief that Tynan was government property and couldn't be sold.

In her essay "The Court Martial," Elizabeth Harman wrote about a nurse who "polished brass two ways" and teased the enlisted men—"flirting one minute and pulling rank the next," making it hard on the other nurses. For example, when Harman made her rounds, the men asked why *she* didn't sit on their beds as the other nurse did. "I didn't want to sound like a party pooper. Or a Miss Goody Two-shoes," wrote Harman. "Some of these patients would be leaving soon. It was good to see them distracted from thoughts of returning to the front. 'I think you guys deserve the best professional care you can get,' was all I could come up with." When the nurse in question reported that a patient had called her a "slut," the chief nurse demanded that the patient be court-martialled as an example that the nurses should be respected. Harman felt that the nurse in question did not "represent the Army Nurse Corps . . . some of us think that respect has to be earned. It can't just be pinned on our shoulders."[47] When several patients testified that the defendant had not made the ugly remark, the patient was exonerated.

But most nurses remember the men as gentlemen.

Louine Connor remembered the shipboard doctor/nurse relationship as a good one and said, "That's why I don't like the MASH type where all that went on. None of that stuff went on, it couldn't have."[48]

"Every one was a gentleman," said Constance "Connie" Sansone. "I will never say anything [bad] about the Army personnel. Not one got out of line. I dated many of them . . . they never got out of line." Even the generals treated the women with respect. On one occasion Sansone was dressing a wound when a general walked up to her. She couldn't salute because both of her hands were busy. She apologized and the general responded, 'Carry on nurse' . . . He stood right there and talked to me,"[49] she said.

Most men just wanted the attention of an American woman.

A chief nurse in Italy said that she often felt as if she were running a dating service. "Word often gets around that there are American women in the vicinity and we begin to receive some guests who are not patients—young officers just out of the fighting who want to talk to a nurse just for a few hours."[50]

A similar account was written for the *American Journal of Nursing* by Ann C. Deeds, who reported that one of her biggest thrills was walking down a street in Australia and having a young Marine stop her to ask, "Are you an American nurse? Could I just talk to you? It has been eighteen months since I've seen an American girl."[51]

Navy Flight Nurse Jane "Candy" Kendeigh, the first nurse on Okinawa, reported that the boys on Okinawa "are the same as they are anywhere—they all whistle!"[52]

And while today's military men are accustomed to seeing women in uniforms and fatigues, it was still a new experience in World War II, and the women were very aware of their appearance.

Modesty and vanity, glamour and make-up are things of the past. Don't think of course for a moment that we've left glamour behind; we have our own standards, that's all. The 1944 Normandy glamour girl is brown as a berry, wears no make-up except lipstick, and shows only trousers and shirts, leggings and boots in their summer wardrobe this year. Head-gear this year is a tin helmet, worn at only one angle.[53]

Actually, the women were encouraged to maintain an attractive appearance, even when wearing fatigues in the jungles of the South Pacific. It not only cheered the men, it helped dismiss the negative stereotypes and aided in recruitment.

Flight Chief Nurse Elizabeth Pukas said, "I expect my nurses to be as if they just came out of Elizabeth Arden's salon, with her hairdo, with her makeup, with her uniform absolutely immaculate. . . . She is to be immaculately clean, and as beautiful and as presentable as she has been trained in flight nursing school to be."[54]

In the Aleutian Islands, the nurses wore their white uniforms when working in the wards and their dress blues whenever practical because, according to their chief nurse, Judy Wilson, "it's good for the boys."[55]

Chief nurse of the 110th Evacuation Hospital Georgie Moss said of the patients, "Their eyes sparkle when they see an American girl with freshly combed hair, wearing lipstick and nail polish."[56]

When men live for months without the domestic influence of women, they often revert to their boyish ways and give no thought to modesty or privacy, like showering out in the open. And while the arrival of women changed some things, like enclosing showers, men were still men.

Inez Combites and Helen Pon wondered why there was so much air traffic over their sun-bathing area—then learned that the men were spying on them. Flight nurse Josephine Malito remembered:

[W]e had an outdoor shower, and the shower was a large drum, and it had holes in it . . . . And it was the shower that everybody used. So this one time I was in there taking a shower and went to rinse the water, and I see a face up there. Well . . . I screamed, and of course everybody came running. It was one of the fellows who hadn't seen a white woman for so long. So from then on we wore bathing suits in the shower.[57]

Ruth Claff remembered a latrine carved out of a corner of a bombed-out building with a door that had to be held up for privacy. The front of the building was wide open, she said, and there were "very friendly soldiers across the street." She compared the accommodations to a goldfish bowl—"with mirrors!"[58]

After their ship was caught in the crossfire between the Germans and the Allies near Gibraltar, Louine Connor said that the nurses were gun-shy, so it wasn't surprising that they were scared each time they saw American gun turrets pointed in their direction—until they learned that the gunners were looking at them through their telescopic sites.

But of all the relationships formed during wartime, perhaps the most fondly remembered was that of friend and cohort, and their mutual respect was never stronger than in the Philippines. Dorothea Daley said, "I went to see a doctor who was only my age, but he looked like a broken old man. He was quivering and shaking his head, saying, 'I can't believe it. I can't believe it's possible.' Then we knew that Bataan was falling. Everybody was like that, because we had believed all along that someday help would come. The patients didn't know we were leaving. Doctors and chaplains, who were staying, started to give us home addresses and asked us to tell their folks they were all right in case we got home. They gave us little personal trinkets to take along."[59]

In her dissertation on flight nurses, Judith Barger wrote, "Social support was a key element in dealing with the demands of war. This support came from squadron members, family, patients, and other people with whom the flight nurses came in contact. An esprit de corps developed among the flight nurses, and between the flight nurses and others with whom they worked, that fostered morale, devotion, and respect."[60]

Eugenie Rutkowski agreed. "The Troop Carrier flight crews were a remarkable group of people. Their assignments were not easy. The C-47 had no fire power. If trouble appeared they were clay pigeons and had to either outmaneuver or outfox the enemy." Even when she taught at the flight nurse training school at Randolph Field, Rutkowski said that she felt a closeness and camaraderie with the men. "Some military brass seem to use the expression 'our people' or 'my guys' when talking about personnel. I like that."[61]

In *The Army Nurse*, Judith Bellafaire wrote that when the 48th Surgical Hospital was located between targets for German bombers—an ammunition dump and an airfield—the danger only served to make the 48th a tighter and more cohesive unit.

Army Nurse Helen Summers remembered the same thing happening on Bataan.

Our common danger out there created a strong sense of unity among us. We were each working for the other and all doing our supreme best. There was no griping. The simple courage and fortitude of our people was unbelievable. I understand the word "brotherhood" as I never understood it before. An experience like that matures a person and brings out real values, but it doesn't embitter. The little things of life that used to be so important have all receded. They can never be so important again. I find myself now more tolerant, better able to understand people and much more willing to do so.[62]

NOTES

1. Ruth Claff, *Lady with the Flashlight*, Unpublished memoirs, 1947, p. 2.
2. Priv. 1st Class Michael Geoghegan, "Salute to G.I. Jane," *American Journal of Nursing*, April 1945, p. 297.
3. Quoted in "Opportunity—Now!" *American Journal of Nursing*, February 1943, p. 129.
4. "Nights I couldn't sleep she'd sit 'n' talk to me. She was, well yeah, you could call that nurse an angel . . ." *The Army Nurse*, January 1945, p. 3.
5. Quoted in "Justice for Army and Navy Nurses," *American Journal of Nursing*, August 1943, p. 703.
6. S/S Private Walter Cook, Letter to President Roosevelt, *American Journal of Nursing*, February 1944, p. 100.
7. Quoted in Mary Jose, "Hi, Angels!" *American Journal of Nursing*, April 1945, p. 268.
8. Juanita Hamilton Webster Questionnaire.
9. "Somewhere in the Pacific," *American Journal of Nursing*, December 1942, p. 1433.
10. Lt. Alice Goudreau, R.N., USN, "Nursing at an Advanced Naval Base Hospital," *American Journal of Nursing*, November 1945, p. 885.
11. Louine Lunt Connor Peck, United States Army Nurse Corps Oral History Program, Interviewed by Col. Clara Adams-Ender, A.N., Major Wynona Bice-Stephens, A.N., ed., North East Harbor, Maine, August 31, 1986, pp. 28-29.
12. Alice Lofgren Andrus, Interview with author, November 20, 1993.
13. Brig. Gen. (Ret.) Lillian Dunlap, ANC, Interview with author, December 20, 1991.
14. Henry Noyes, "Anzio is Coming of Age for Army's Nurses," Series: Warriors of Mercy, Chapter 24, *The Mercury* (Fort Sam Houston: U.S. Army of Public Affairs, April 1994), no p. #.
15. Goudreau, p. 886.
16. Rachel Gilbert Francis, Note to author, September, 1993.
17. Quoted in Claff, p. 39.
18. Claff, p. 43.
19. Quoted in Vincoe M. Paxton, R.N., "With Field Hospital Nurses in Germany," *American Journal of Nursing*, February 1945, p. 133.
20. Quoted in Judith A. Bellafaire, *The Army Nurse Corps: A Commemoration of World War II Service* (Washington, D.C.: U.S. Army Center of Military History, no date), Pub. 72-14, p. 25.
21. Lt. Sarah O'Toole, R.N., USNR, "In the Southwest Pacific: They Pioneered on Tinian," *American Journal of Nursing*, December 1945, p. 1015.
22. Dunlap interview.
23. Peck oral history, pp. 52, 62.
24. Lt. Col. (Ret.) Ruth Frances Shadewaldt, ANC, Taped interview with sister, July 1992.
25. Claff, p. 3.
26. Juanita Hamilton Webster, Unpublished memoirs, no date, p. 10.

27. Claff, pp. 2, 21.

28. Quoted in Judith Barger, B.S.N., M.S.N., "Coping with War: An Oral History of United States Army Flight Nurses Who Flew with the Army Air Forces in World War II," Dissertation, The University of Texas at Austin, December 1986, p. 95.

29. Dunlap Interview.

30. Janina Smiertka Davenport Questionnaire.

31. Robert Love Tayloe, *Combat Nurse: A Journal of World War II* (Santa Barbara: Fithian Press, 1988), p. 13.

32. Quoted in "How to Beat the Heat—Get Assigned to the Aleutians!" *The Army Nurse*, August 1945, p. 4.

33. Claff, pp. 13, 37.

34. 1st Lt. Matilda E. Dykstra, ANC, "Army Life in India," *American Journal of Nursing*, March 1944, p. 290.

35. 1st Lt. Rosemary Forsythe, ANC, "En Route to the Philippines—January 1945," *The Army Nurse*, June 1945, p. 7.

36. Quoted in Paula Allen, "Generally Speaking," *San Antonio Express-News*, October 2, 1994, p. 5.

37. Quoted in Webster, Unpublished memoirs, p. 14.

38. Webster, Unpublished memoirs, p. 14.

39. Claff, pp. 5, 6, 15, 32.

40. Page Cooper, *Navy Nurse* (New York: McGraw-Hill, p. 1946), p. 116.

41. Andrus interview.

42. Quoted in Barger, "Coping with War," p. 125.

43. Bellafaire, p. 26.

44. Lt. Jg. Mary H. Staats, USNR, "Navy Nurses in the Solomons," *American Journal of Nursing*, July 1945, p. 534.

45. Quoted in Claff, p. 42.

46. Claff, pp. 17, 19, 20, 42.

47. Elizabeth Harman Masterson, "The Court Martial," Unpublished essay, 1988, pp. 1-3.

48. Peck oral history, p. 51.

49. Constance Sansone, Telephone Interview with author, July 6, 1992.

50. Maj. Gen. Norman T. Kirk (Surgeon General), "Girls in the Foxholes," *The American Magazine*, May 1944, p. 97.

51. Quoted in 1st Lt. Ann C. Deeds, ANC, "There Goes an American Nurse," *American Journal of Nursing*, September 1944, p. 848.

52. Quoted in Lt. Gill DeWitt, USN, *The First Navy Flight Nurse on a Pacific Battlefield* (Fredericksburg, TX: The Admiral Nimitz Foundation, 1983), no p. #.

53. "Excerpts from a M.D.D.'s Letter," *The Army Nurse*, November 1944, p. 13.

54. Quoted in Barger, "Coping with War," p. 108.

55. Quoted in Cooper, p. 108.

56. Quoted in Mary Jose, "Night Shift in an Army Hospital," *American Journal of Nursing*, June 1945, p. 433.

57. Quoted in Barger, "Coping with War," p. 92.

58. Claff, p. 39.

59. Quoted in Col. Julia O. Flikke, *Nurses in Action* (New York: Lippincott, 1943), p. 181.

60. Barger, "Coping with War," p. 131.

61. Eugenie Rutkowski Wilkinson, Letter to daughter, no date, no p. #.

62. Quoted in Janet M. Geister, R.N., "She Came Back from Bataan," *Trained Nurse and Hospital Review*, October 1942, p. 252.

Chapter 12

Leaving a Legacy

> Aside from the gallantry and heroism displayed by nurses in
> World War II, their contribution to patient care had a
> tremendous influence on the recovery of patients fresh from the
> front lines, but it also had a marked influence on civilian
> nursing as it is practiced today.
> —Lena Dixon Dietz and Aurelia R. Lehozky
> *History and Modern Nursing*

Although the exact cost in lives and money cannot be assessed, World War II
"took the lives of more persons than any other war in history"[1]—an estimated
55 million civilian and military. More than 50 countries were involved in a
conflict that changed lives and territorial boundaries around the world.

Jobs created by war industries caused people in the United States to move
away from home and family, while the devastation and persecution in Europe
and Asia left millions homeless and starving. Women discovered that they
could built a tank or airplane as well as a man; the Alaska Highway and an oil
pipeline were built through the joint efforts of Canada and the United States;
and the world's scientists both aided humanity with penicillin and threatened it
with the atomic bomb. In man's attempt to avoid another war, 50 nations
formed the United Nations on October 24, 1945.

The U.S. military also changed. Wartime medical procedures were studied
and/or adopted—such as the MASH unit, "R&R" for military personnel, and
"the team concept and patient-centered care."[2] All military branches were
integrated via the executive order of July 26, 1948, and female doctors were
admitted to the Army Medical Corps.

Uncle Sam finally established permanent Army and Navy Nursing Corps
in April 1947, and gave members permanent officer status with the same pay

and benefits as male officers. The Navy organized their first strong peacetime Naval Reserve and a Regular Nurse Corps up to three times greater than that on duty on December 3, 1941. (By August 1955, male nurses were given commission status in the Army. The Navy followed in November 1964.)

In addition, the introduction of the U.S. Cadet Corps and the GI Bill helped create major changes in nursing education: improved curricula, the admission of minorities, an increased number of nursing schools with better facilities, more students, and better instructors.

And because nurses had taken on so much responsibility during the war, they were now seen—along with doctors—as leaders in medical teams. Because this new role included more supervisory, administrative, and teaching functions, nurses now needed more education. In her book *History and Trends of Professional Nursing*, Deborah MacLurg Jensen wrote, "There would need to be more graduate nurses or she would have to get someone to help her at the lower level."[3]   This need was answered with the licensing of practical (vocational) nurses beginning in 1947.

All of these changes meant a departure from hands-on nursing, a direction not all nurses believed was the right one to take. Author D'Ann Campbell posed the problem in her book *Women at War with America*:

Nursing enjoyed a great humanitarian tradition and clearly attracted so many women because of its goal of helping sick people. On the other hand, the remarkable advances in medical science and technology and in the organizing, financing, and delivery of patient care had wrought radical transformations since the days of Nightingale and Barton. Nursing was poised to become a technological field that required extensive training, far more than was usually available. Should nurses be technicians or humanitarians?

Even before the war was over, there were some doctors who complained that some of the nurses "were losing their nurturant bedside manner," and some patients who complained that their medical care was "too impersonal." The problem, wrote Campbell, seemed to be between the "better trained, more scientific 'professionalizers' and the older 'traditionalizers.' The latter were more willing to hold hands and empty bedpans and resented the superior skills and attitudes of the new women."[4]

But there was no turning back for the women who'd served overseas— especially those who had served in field and evacuation hospitals—because they had "become accustomed to taking the initiative, making quick decisions, and adopting innovative solutions to a broad range of medical-related problems." They had also learned supervisory and organizational skills that had increased their professional status and increased their self-esteem. Author Judith Bellafaire put it quite simply in her pamphlet *The Army Nurse Corps*: "World War II had forever changed the face of military nursing."[5]

Because of what these women had proven during the war, new avenues began to open for nurses—in public health nursing, psychiatric nursing, and industrial nursing; administration, education, rehabilitation, and research. Employment with the World Health Organization, part of the United Nations, gave nurses the chance to travel and act as advisors in the many facets of nursing that affected nursing methods around the world.

But what of the women who brought about these tremendous changes? How did they feel about their service and how did they embrace their future?

When the American Red Cross sent out 31,000 questionnaires to Army nurses asking if they planned to return to their prewar employment, 69 percent responded that they planned to continue nursing, but only one in six wanted to return to her prewar job. After what they had accomplished and the responsibility they had earned, why return to jobs that made them perform like mindless robots?

Many of the women missed the servicemen and wanted to follow through with the work they'd started during the war. After all, who could better relate to the men than the women who'd shared similar experiences? Most of the women who remained with the Army Nurse Corps were sent to general hospitals where they treated men still returning from battlefields, and many of the women who were forced out of the service found satisfaction in Veterans Hospitals.

But before they made their postwar career choices, the women had to settle their affairs with Uncle Sam.

SEPARATION AND REASSIGNMENT

When you've traveled a bit with the Army you begin to realize the problem posed by numbers. Why, even to move one general hospital takes two trains for the people and about three more for the equipment. There are over 600 in a general hospital—medical officers, administrative officers, nurses, enlisted men. And the trains must be on hand, and rations must be arranged for, and billets for overnight unless you can step directly from train to boat, and trucks to carry you if it is not walking distance. And the ship, with space and accommodation and supplies, must be there too. Now multiply that by several hundred hospitals, and remember that they can't all be on the same railroad track at the same hour, and that all ships can't pull up to the same dock at the same time, and you begin to see the problem.[6]

Because there was still a war in the Pacific, the Army faced a monumental task: How to provide the best care to those in the Pacific and still be fair to those who'd earned enough points to go home? As Charles M. Wiltse wrote in his book *Medical Service in the Mediterranean and Minor Theaters*, "For [members of] the Medical Department, essentiality was the primary factor."[7] The process was, indeed, quite complicated. In their book *Medical Service in the European Theater of Operations*, Graham A. Cosmas and Albert E. Cowdrey wrote that the process meant shuffling people around within "a system that was as complex as a Bach fugue but far less harmonious." And the breakup of units caused a lowering of morale: "the reassignment process tore veteran units to pieces and destroyed, all too often, the morale it was meant to sustain."

The sooner-than-expected victory over Japan caused even more problems with the deployment process. According to Cosmas and Cowdrey, "The vast medical establishment built for the war must now, in large part, be collapsed like a tent and disposed of."[8]

The Army and Navy used similar criteria and points systems to classify military personnel. Using the Adjusted Service Rating Score (ASRS), personnel earned points for each month overseas, for each child under 18, and for combat decorations and battle participation awards. After the individual's essentiality was added into the equation, the person was placed into one of three categories: (1) those who would stay and help with demobilization, (2) those who would be sent to the Pacific, and (3) those who would be deactivated and sent back to the States.

The process of classifying Army nurses began in April 1945. The women were sent questionnaires that asked for their nursing experience and their choice of future service. This information was combined with earned points and the Army's other criteria (age, marital status, dependents), an efficiency rating (determined by the chief nurse), and the results of a recent physical to determine the nurse's eligibility to return home.

Nurses who'd served in the harsh conditions of the Pacific or Asian theaters were rotated home as quickly as replacements could be found, especially those who'd been prisoners in the Philippines.

An expected 25,000 Army nurses were to be relieved from duty by January 1946; 15,000 more six months later. Those who wished to remain in the Corps had to wait until the legislature decided upon the size of the peacetime army. Many were forced to leave the Corps and "freely expressed their unhappiness"[9] at being made to do so.

Under the Navy's system, 800 Navy nurses were scheduled for release to the Inactive Reserve by the middle of September 1945; 7,000 were scheduled for release by the following September. By November 1945, the points needed for release from the Naval Reserve were reduced from 35 to 32. By November 1, 1945, all married nurses—regular or reserve—were released no matter how many points they'd earned.

When sent to one of the many staging areas in Europe, nurses found themselves among a sea of humanity waiting to go home: battle casualties, displaced persons, newly freed American POWs, and other American military personnel. Upon arrival, nurses were given chest x-rays, dental examinations, new glasses, and current immunizations. Their equipment was checked and supplemented; their records were updated; and they took classes to prepare them for their new assignments.

While some camps were existing structures that often needed major overhauls, some were new ones built by the U.S. engineers. And Uncle Sam did what he could to make the camps as comfortable as possible. The one in Carlysle, France, had a fully stocked PX, beauty parlor, and full laundry facilities. It also provided a dayroom and game room, Coke bar, Ping-Pong tables, bridge tables, volleyball courts, and movies three times a day. There was even a Rainbow Room for parties and dances. Nurses were given 16-hour and three-day passes to Paris and seven-day trips to Great Britain and the Riviera.

But because nurses are always happiest when nursing, the redeployment process was maddening for them. In an article for the *American Journal of Nursing*, four nurses wrote, "The weeks of idleness . . . are leaving their mark upon the morale of the nurses." The *Journal* responded that "specific protests of nurses who believe they are being delayed too long are sent to the War Department."[10]

As the number of hospitals in Europe dwindled—from more than 250,000 beds on VE Day to 19,955 beds in January 1946—the patient load changed. Most combat troops were gone by the fall of 1945, and their replacements were often less-trained "green troops" who brought disease with them. According to authors Cosmas and Cowdrey, "Crowding, rapid turnover, and cold weather resulted in epidemic outbreaks of respiratory complaints and childhood diseases—chiefly measles, German measles, scarlet fever, mumps, and meningitis." Many ailments were spread by these new recruits on the crowded troopships bound for Europe.

The inexperience and boredom of the newcomers also contributed to injuries different than those seen before VE Day. For example, there were gunshot wounds inflicted by recruits who were poorly trained in the use of firearms and by collectors with souvenir weapons. There were also altercations between the different groups in the camps.

When they finally received their assignments, most personnel "settled down to enjoy the amenities of the Continent." Doctors and nurses studied at universities and enjoyed Swiss winter sports and Riviera beaches. Cosmas and Cowdrey wrote, "Men and women who had come to make war stayed to learn and to enjoy."[11] And there were other pleasing assignments. Aboard the USS *Consolation*, Alice Lofgren enjoyed visits to Guantanamo, Trinidad, and Puerto Rico and said, "We all had many carefree happy experiences."[12]

Elizabeth Harman—a member of the 164th General Hospital and among the nurses preparing to go to the Pacific—gave a colorful description of her experience.

We went by train to Marseilles to a huge staging area of what seemed like thousands of nurses. (Probably just hundreds—I never believed in the shortage of nurses after that.) In getting there, our 80 "female personnel" were jammed into two wooden "third class carriages." At night, we strapped the smaller girls in the overhead racks. The rest of us drew lots for sleeping on the wooden bench seats, and the losers bunked down on the floor. But the GIs had it worse: cattle cars.

At the staging area we spent our time standing in chow lines, and in classes on tropical diseases. I didn't like the sound of any of them, but it was a great summer. We "learned" "Marseilles" by heart and each of us had two weeks on the Riviera.

After our unit had been alerted, we heard the news of the first atom bomb. But we boarded a Navy vessel anyway—scheduled to take us directly thru the Panama Canal to the Pacific. The loud speakers were blaring "Sentimental Journey" as we boarded and it was. As we pulled out of the harbor, the speaker announced, "The destination of this ship is—Newport News, Virginia." We were lucky to get home after only one year overseas. Others served 2-3 years there.[13]

Upon returning to the States, Navy nurses were given the choice of remaining a member of the Navy Reserve or becoming a part of the Inactive Reserve. And because the nurses had given such "outstanding service during the war,"[14] many were offered a chance to join the Regular Navy Nurse Corps who wouldn't have been eligible otherwise—members of the Reserve whose active duty service had started before their 38th birthday. (The regular age qualification for joining the Corps was 22 to 28.) Alice Lofgren was among those who could have stayed in the Navy and who would have if they'd let her remain at sea. "But when 'they' insisted I would have to be transferred to shore duty, I was eligible to leave the Navy on 'points' and was soon a civilian again."[15]

The first stop for Army nurses were reception stations where they were issued leaves. Upon return from their leaves, they reported to reassignment or redistribution stations and were given new assignments. Although the nurse could request a certain assignment, there was no guarantee that she would receive it. For example, many of them requested overseas duty but were denied because of the War Department's policy of keeping personnel in the States for six months between overseas assignments. In her article "Our Nurses and Redistribution Stations," Army nurse Dorothy Lopnow wrote, "The first reaction of the average nurse, is that she wishes to go back overseas immediately, not realizing how much she needs a change and relaxation . . . Assignments are usually made to general or regional hospitals where the wounded return from overseas. They [the wounded] can thus receive care from nurses who have had similar experiences."

Lopnow also reported that the nurses who had served in the South Pacific or China-Burma-India theaters had the hardest time adjusting because "the difficult conditions under which they lived are so drastically different from that to which they have been accustomed."[16]

THE WOMEN WHO SERVED

Leave-taking was not a gala occasion. It meant breaking up daily associations of more than three years duration. Air Corps, Navy, and infantry friends in the vicinity came to say good-by.[17]

For many men and women, the end of the war not only meant saying good-bye to friends and lovers, but saying good-bye to a feeling of usefulness and of knowing that you did your best at a job worth doing. Even learning to live without wartime tension and military regimentation left many feeling depressed and useless.

But leaving friends was probably the hardest adjustment, and even those nurses anxious to go home spoke of the camaraderie as their happiest wartime memory. As one Army nurse said when reunited with two friends in 1957, "When you live so closely together for two years, you become almost like sisters. It's pretty hard to break up a relationship like this."[18]

Commanding Officer of the 118th General Hospital Colonel James Bordley III said, "You can go home feeling that you have played a significant part in the war. Our unit has been recognized for its outstanding job. I wish I could be jocular in this farewell but I can't. All I can say is—get a good rest and don't forget us."[19]

Different agencies did what they could to help the women readjust. Pamphlets such as *W for Welcome, Serve Those Who Served,* and *After Military Service, What?* were distributed in separation centers, American Red Cross hospitality and information centers, and state and district nurses' associations; the latter were given to nurses while they were still overseas. Many nurses went through redistribution/separation stations:

The mission of a Redistribution Station is to obtain maximum utilization of Army personnel who have returned to the United States from overseas stations for reassignment. This is accomplished through occupational and physical classification, mental and physical reconditioning, orientation, and indoctrination for the purpose of assigning individuals to appropriate positions to further the war effort, in accordance with their civilian and overseas combat experience. An attempt is made to carry on this important work in an atmosphere of comfort and complete relaxation by having the station as unmilitary as possible, except for courtesy and necessary discipline.[20]

At three such centers in Santa Barbara, California, one of the orientation classes, "Home Front," was to acquaint the returnee to the current nature of life in the United States. Another, "Sound Off," gave the women an opportunity to discuss their overseas experiences—both good and bad. Their stories were consolidated and used to improve conditions for troops going overseas. After her time in Santa Barbara, one nurse wrote, "We arrived there in an unsettled and confused state after traveling here and there, with nothing definite to look forward to—but you just seemed to settle all that. Thanks a million."[21]

But adjusting to civilian life was hard for many of these women. Even some of those who had been so sure about entering the Army or Navy weren't nearly as confident about what to do afterward. Writing candidly about her life in *Warrior in White*, Lucy Wilson said she tried private duty nursing but "the difference from the rules and regulations of the military and the lack of tension, I suppose, in civilian life . . . the time to dwell on the horrors of the past, the loneliness, the decisions to make for myself—all this was confusing and frustrating."[22]

Ruth Claff wrote of similar feelings in her memoirs, *Lady with the Flashlight*. "We were quiet and depressed," she said. "We began to realize that we couldn't be led around by the nose for years and then face the prospect of starting over again on our own without a little panic. Doctors especially were pretty worried, a lot of them [in] the air corps just couldn't seem to face the sudden stop of excitement—and flight pay. Most of them didn't know anything but combat flying, and that was practically useless as a peacetime profession!"

When Claff got back home, her plans were to take "a long and luxurious vacation," but "in two weeks I had the screaming meemies, so I went to Philadelphia and signed up for a course in psychiatry, mostly to find out what made ME tick, and eventually I worked the whole damned war out of my system—I think." But she added that some veterans had a harder time than others. "I still hear from a lot of the nurses who are clinging desperately together in one way or another—unadjusted even at this date [1947], but I'm all right."[23]

When her interview for the U.S. Army Nurse Corps Oral History Program began, Louine Connor couldn't remember "any real happy times"[24] during the war and said that she "had spent some trying time, trying to forget, because she had some very painful memories from that time and she didn't want to bring them up." By the end of the interview, however, her feelings had changed, and she said that speaking of the past had been "a blessing. I couldn't even talk about it and now [have] no need to suppress it. . . . My husband, who fought with the 1st Marines . . . said, do not grieve, do not mourn about those who were killed . . . let their lives live on. It is how you carry on your life, the rest of it, that is the important thing." She then remembered her "overall" military experience "as being a fond and good one."

Marriage (often to men they'd met during war) and college (through the new GI Bill) were the answers for many returning nurses.

Connor had married before the war, was separated during the war, and was divorced after the war. "There was nothing there," she said. "I had locked him out." The war, she said, "cost me my husband."[25] After attending Columbia University, Connor served as director of a nursing school.

Lucy Wilson married the man she'd become engaged to right before her escape from Bataan. After the war, she joined the Army Nurse Corps Reserve and remained a member until 1950.

Helen Pon spent the last months of the war at Camp Patrick, Virginia, where she met her husband. After being discharged in December 1945, and going into the reserves, she earned her degree in biological sciences from Indiana University and went to work for Wausau Insurance as an occupational health consultant. After retiring from Wausau and the Army, she became a volunteer for the Army Medical Museum at Fort Sam Houston in Texas.

Alice Lofgren left the Navy Nurse Corps in August 1946. After she earned her B.S. degree in Public Health Nursing from the University of Michigan, she worked as a Public Health Nurse in Oregon and Utah.

Since it wasn't until 1945 that Navy nurses could marry *and* remain in the service, Janina Smiertka ended her military service when she married Gordon Davenport in 1943. She earned her B.S. at Arizona State University, worked at Good Samaritan Hospital, and volunteered at a children's camp. After her divorce in 1966, she went back to school, spent summers studying at various universities, and traveled extensively. At 68, she was the oldest student in her class when she graduated from the University of Massachusetts in 1982.

Dora Cline was another Navy nurse who chose to marry and leave the Corps. She met her future husband when both were stationed in New Zealand.

They married in 1944. After the war, she worked as a private nurse, in nursing homes, and in physical therapy.

Genevieve Van de Drink also left the Navy to get married. "I traded my Officer's bars for a wedding ring in 1943, and became a Navy wife. We have had 49 years of marital bliss."[26] Van de Drink appeared on Sally Jessy Raphael's "50th Anniversary of Pearl Harbor" telecast.

Agnes Jensen married and followed her military husband on several overseas tours and even did civilian nursing in Osaka Army Hospital during the Korean War. She later worked with Red Cross bloodmobiles.

Helena Ilic married after the war and worked for Pan American Airlines and the City of San Antonio.

Edith Atwell met her husband at Fort William McKinley. She left the Army Nurse Corps and married in September 1946. After the war she nursed in offices and hospitals.

After her discharge in November 1945, Eugenie Rutkowski returned to school to study music. She also worked for the Veterans Administration and married a Marine.

Although they'd come from the same small town in Sycamore, Illinois, Marian Hooker didn't meet her husband until they both were stationed in Milne Bay, New Guinea. They married in 1947.

Elizabeth Harman married a member of the Army Combat Engineers in 1949. After her discharge from the Army Nurse Corps in spring 1946, she worked in a children's hospital, as a staff nurse for Duval County Health Department, and as a visiting-school nurse for the Department of Public Health.

An Army nurse with the 153rd Station Hospital, Juanita Hamilton was one of the first nurses in New Guinea. She also served in Australia. After the war, she worked in hospitals in Texas and Louisiana. Her happiest memory was her wartime marriage to Douglas Webster, with whom she lived until his death in 1981. A perfect example of the evolved nurse, Hamilton has been a nurse anesthetist, anesthesia instructor, director of the Department of Anesthesia at Baylor University, clinical instructor in a LPN School, public health nurse, hospital administrator, and nurse surveyor for the Joint Commission on Accreditation for Hospitals.

After her discharge from the Army Nurse Corps in 1946, Connie Sansone returned to her hometown of Dallas, Texas, where she worked in a veterans hospital, private clinics, and a major department store. While at the store, Sanger Harris, Sansone was awarded the Good Samaritan Award and the American National Red Cross Certificate of Recognition for Extraordinary Personal Action for saving a life by using cardiopulmonary resuscitation.

Marion Blissett served in the Navy Nurse Corps from 1942 to 1945. Married in 1946, she spent her postwar years as a school nurse. Before her death in 1989, she worked in a hospital as a Gray Lady volunteer.

Many nurses remained with the military after the war. Army Nurse Ruth Shadewaldt earned her B.S.N. from Denver University and attended the

Nursing Administration School at Fort Sam Houston in Texas. She served in Germany and Puerto Rico, and in stateside hospitals in Chicago, Hot Springs, and Denver. She was also an instructor at Letterman Army Hospital in San Francisco. She retired in February 1967, with the rank of lieutenant colonel.

Marion Kern served with the 20th General Hospital in the China-Burma-India Theater and married after the war. She served in the Army from 1942 through 1946 and again from 1953 through 1972, retiring with the rank of colonel.

After her service in World War II, Marian Tierney retired then returned to the Army Nurse Corps and served until her final retirement with the rank of colonel in 1974. Tierney spent a year in Vietnam where, as chief of Army nursing for the Army Vietnam Command, she supervised 400 nurses in up to 18 hospitals. Known for her personal touch, Tierney met each of those 400 nurses and even visited the hospital wards herself and considered the patients "her young men."[27] Wounded in a plane crash in Vietnam, Tierney treated the other passengers even though she suffered from broken ribs and a sprained ankle. She died in December 1999, and was buried at Fort Sam Houston National Cemetery with full military honors.

Madeline Ullom was among the nurses held prisoner in the Philippines until February 1945. She earned her B.S. from Incarnate Word College in 1948, and her M.S. in Nursing Education from Catholic University in 1951. Before retiring as Lieutenant Colonel Ullom in 1964, she served at many Army hospitals around the world.

Hattie Brantley, also a prisoner in the Philippines, remained with the Army Nurse Corps and retired as a lieutenant colonel in 1969.

Lorraine Ripps married Karl W. Kircher, Sr. in England after the war. One of the first Army Air Force nurses, she nursed at Brooke Army Medical Center and retired from the service in 1975. "The military was her life,"[28] said her son after her death in April 1994.

Inez Combites remained with the Army of Occupation until 1948. She later married and worked in a doctor's office in Los Angeles and at the Muskogee Veterans Hospital.

Selma Moody retired from the Army Nurse Corps Reserves in 1963, as a colonel. She met her husband in the Philippines, but they didn't marry until after the war. She earned her M.A. during her service years and helped establish a collegiate school of nursing.

Lillian Dunlap remained in the Army Nurse Corps almost by accident. After the war, Dunlap's discharge was delayed because she was a patient at Brooke General Hospital (now Brooke Army Medical Center) at Fort Sam Houston. After recuperating, she was offered a job at Brooke and eventually became a brigadier general and chief of the Army Nurse Corps. She retired on September 1, 1975.

Marie Helen Glennon earned her Ph.D. from the University of Erlangen, Germany and remained in the Air Force until 1950 and in the Reserves until 1956. Her marriage to Dr. Roger Charlier was the inspiration for the Cary Grant movie *I Was A Male War Bride*. Glennon died in 1956.

Rachel Gilbert married in 1946, and served in the Air Force Nurse Corps until 1948. She also went to school on the GI Bill and worked as a civilian nurse in an army hospital during the Korean War.

Most women joined the Army or Navy Nurse Corps to do their patriotic duty—not for praise or to change women's societal roles—and most saw their patriotic duty as the right thing to do. Quite naturally, however, many of the women felt some bitterness at the lack of recognition for what they did during the war. Louine Connor said, "We didn't expect to be thanked, we never were. . . . We knew we weren't going to be. . . . But later it was hard to take." The first time they were honored, said Connor, was at the DAR convention in April 1986, and even then they were among numerous other groups and *not* singled out for recognition.

Even during the war, Connor said that it sometimes seemed that the patients took the nurses for granted. "They were so relieved by being there and we became somewhat of a comfort to them. They took more than they could possibly give because they felt so secure. They said that because of the women, they weren't in danger and that seemed to make them relax."[29]

In a 1991 article for the *Austin American-Statesman,* "Women's War 'Whited Out' of History Books," Scott W. Wright wrote, "[M]ost women who helped with the war effort received little in return after the war ended. The veterans of Foreign Wars, for example, prohibited women from joining or receiving benefits until the 1970s."[30]

Thanked or not, how did the military nurses of World War II view their experiences? "Just knowing I was serving my country"[31] made Army Nurse Mary L. Barbero happy. After her discharge in 1946, Barbero worked as an operating room nurse supervisor and head nurse for the Veterans Administration.

Earlyn Black Harding, one of the Army nurses taken captive in the Philippines, said of her experience, "It made me a stronger person."[32]

One of the nurses June Willenz interviewed, identified only as "Alice," said that her time in the Army was "a high point of her life." According to Willenz, "Alice is even more certain that her military service did well by her. She feels she learned a great self-discipline that has been useful to her in all her later pursuits. Besides, she came in contact with people she never would have before. And she was one of the lucky ones who got overseas."[33]

Learning of her mother's wartime experiences offered Elizabeth L. Dick "a glimpse of the source of courage and strength she saw in her mother as she was growing up."[34] Her mother, Ruth L. Kinzeler Solot, died in April 1994, in Cleveland, Ohio. Solot spent three years in the Pacific then served as head nurse at a veterans hospital in Pittsburgh. Although she'd met her future husband during the war—he'd served under her as a corporal—they didn't meet again and marry until after the war.

"I've made a footprint," said Martha E. McCrary of Mayfield Heights, Ohio. At the age of 89, McCrary still had plans of publishing a record of her war years "when I have time." But since she doesn't think, "God's going to let me live forever,"[35] her Army Nurse uniform has been cleaned and pressed and is pinned with instructions for her burial. During the war, McCrary was in charge of 2,500 Army nurses in Normandy and one of the first American women to see Paris after its liberation.

Janina Smiertka said that joining the Navy Nurse Corps was "the best thing I ever did. It was another world which widened your horizons . . . exploring the large cities, museums, libraries, zoos, concerts, etc." She added, "The Navy was a different world. We all worked together and formed friends that we have to this day."[36]

Ruth Claff, ANC, said, "Never, never, never would I think of milk, lettuce or ice cream as anything but a luxury again. For months I ate every meal as if it were the last one I'd get, and that eventually and inevitably began to show on my hips."[37]

Ann Bernatitus said, "My feelings are that I have never been anybody special or that I did anything special. You were in the Navy and you had a job to do and you did it, that is all."[38] Bernatitus retired from active duty in 1959.

Eugenie Rutkowski said that she learned two very important lessons from her war years: (1) The military cares for its own and goes to great expense and effort to do so, and (2) she can handle herself under severe stress.

African-American Nurses

There were some nurses who experienced the war differently than most—women of color: the women of African-American descent and the women of Japanese descent, called Nisei.

Just like their white counterparts, these women wanted to serve their country and experience adventure, yet the still-segregated military refused to utilize them to their fullest capacity even when the need for nurses was at its most critical. In fact, it wasn't until his hand was forced by the National Association of Colored Graduate Nurses (NACGN) and other groups that Surgeon General James C. Magee even accepted the women at all, and even then he set a quota of 56. Although this quota was raised several times, by the end of the war there still were only 479 African-American nurses in the Army Nurse Corps and four in the Navy Nurse Corps. (Note: These numbers vary from 48 to 56 and from 479 to 512.) They trained and nursed in segregated quarters at Fort Bragg, North Carolina; Fort Huachuca, Arizona; and Camp Livingston, Louisiana.

Army hospital wards were integrated before October 1940, when the Surgeon General proposed that hospital wards be segregated, that all-black hospitals be established in the United States, and that all-black hospitals be staffed by only black personnel. (It turned out that only two all-black hospitals were ever established and that segregated wards were discontinued before war's end.) Therefore, early war years found the women treating only black patients. In later years, however, the black nurses were assigned to "at least" 15 hospitals in the United States where they treated patients of both races. In the 1963, U.S. Surgeon General's report, *Personnel in World War II*,

"According to the report of one of these hospitals, 'no case was found where a white patient objected to a colored nurse taking care of him'."[39]

Athough many of these women were anxious to go overseas, most of them remained in the States. Those who made it to foreign shores were the women of the following units:

168th Station Hospital—England
268th Station Hospital—Southwest Pacific and the Philippines
383d, 335th Station Hospitals—Burma
25th Station Hospital—West Africa

Susan Elizabeth Freeman was one of the original 56 nurses. Her promotion to first lieutenant was the first promotion at Camp Livingston for a nurse—black or white. While serving in Liberia as chief nurse of the first unit of black nurses to go overseas—the 25th Station Hospital—Freeman was made a knight official of the Liberian Humane Order of Africa Redemption for leading her nurses "in the face of difficult circumstances" and for showing "fidelity to duty, a sense of responsibility, and understanding of their positions as officers that is well above the average."[40] Freeman retired for medical reasons from the Army Nurse Corps with the rank of captain in July 1945.

The women of the 25th were sent home in late 1943, with "poor health" and "low morale" given as reasons. According to Judith Bellafaire, they felt "superfluous" because the work they performed was routine and could have been performed by corpsmen. Some of these women returned to the States and some were sent to Tagap, Burma, where they treated black soldiers working on the Ledo Road.

The women of the 168th in England had similar feelings. Although nurses of all colors worked in POW camps, these women worked under white officers who complained that they were "less efficient and required more supervision than a comparable number of white nurses."[41] When a black officer conducted an inspection, he found that the black nurses "feel that they are a separate group, set apart for a particular type of service, and have little hope for advancement or any variation in the type of service they are performing."[42] Authors Cosmas and Cowdrey wrote that the black medics in the European Theater felt the same way, and it *is* known that the women were deliberately excluded from a formal reception given for their new base commander.

When she flew with an Australian pilot to pick up patients, Prudence Burns said she had an enjoyable flight. While on the ground, however, she was sent to a room by herself to eat her lunch and wait until the plane was loaded and ready to leave. On another occasion, she tried to help a wounded white man who needed a blood transfusion, but since the blood of whites and African-Americans (labeled "A") was kept separate, Burns apologetically told the man that the "A" blood was all that was available. He chose to accept it. Always optimistic and cheerful, Burns said that she was used to segregation and accepted it.

Married while stationed in the Philippines, Burns was one of the first black Army nurses. She helped recruit the other members of the 268th Station Hospital and served in the Philippines, Australia, and New Guinea. After her discharge in 1945, she traveled with her Army husband and worked as a civilian nurse at military medical facilities around the world. She also served as an educator and member of the Battle Creek research team that developed the PAS and streptomycin treatment for TB patients.

Even though Elinor Powell Albert said that segregation was "constantly a shock to me" and that she was angry most of the time, she still found her overall military experience "interesting, maddening, frustrating, and even fun." Nadine Davis Lane said, "I was ecstatic most of the time I served."[43]

Della Raney Jackson was the first black nurse commissioned in the Army as a lieutenant. After the war, she served in Japan before retiring as a major and being honored by the Tuskegee Airmen for personifying the "Tuskegee Spirit."

Margaret E. Bailey was the first black nurse to become lieutenant colonel and spent 27 years in the Army, most of them in Europe. When she retired in 1971, she was awarded the Legion of Merit, the Army's second highest noncombat award. The following year she became a consultant to the Surgeon General of the Army.

Phyllis Mae Daley became the first black member of the Navy Nurse Corps on March 9, 1945.

Japanese-American Nurses

When war began, women of Japanese ancestry, Nisei, weren't allowed in the military because it was felt that their presence would "antagonize"[44] the patients. Again, however, the shortage of nurses—and the National Council for War Service (NNCWS)—forced the Surgeon General's hand. As part of their effort to "assure equal opportunities for minority groups,"[45] the NNCWS worked to release some of the women from relocation camps and get them into nursing schools. To be considered, they had to fill out special questionnaires and have their loyalty affirmed by the Provost Marshal General's Department. By 1945, 300 to 800 young Nisei women were available for military service. The four who were commissioned were restricted to service inside the continental United States.

LEAVING A LEGACY

What is the legacy of the World War II military nurse?

One is the example they set for future nurses, both military and civilian. Their untiring dedication, persistence, ingenuity, eager acceptance of responsibility, and cheerfulness in the face of very rough times proved that nurses were more than just helpmates for doctors or emptiers of bedpans. Because of the work the WWII nurse performed, today's nurses have a wide avenue of occupations from which to choose, including nurse anesthetists, nurse practitioners, nurse midwives, and even primary-care providers. But they owe these new avenues to the work performed by their predecessors without whom, "the emergence of the women's liberation movement almost two decades later would have been inconceivable."[46]

But if you ask one of these women, chances are good that she will tell you that her most important legacy is the number of daughters and sons who were born and raised by men who survived the war because of the nurse who kept them alive. As Retired Brigadier General Lillian Dunlap said, "The nursing care that we were able to do under those conditions I consider quality care. By today's standards it might not be because we didn't have all of the fancy equipment, but our patients survived and that's what it was all about."[47]

NOTES

1. Theodore Ropp, "World War II," *World Book Encyclopedia* (Chicago: World Book-Childcraft Int'l., 1982), p. 410.

2. Lena Dixon Dietz and Aurelia R. Lehozky, *History and Modern Nursing,* 2nd ed. (Philadelphia: F. A. Davis, 1967), p. 160.

3. Deborah MacLurg Jensen, R.N., B.S., M.A., *History and Trends of Professional Nursing*, 4th ed., (St. Louis: C. V. Mosby, 1959), p. 305.

4. D'Ann Campbell, *Women at War with America: Private Lives in a Patriotic Era* (Cambridge: Harvard University Press, 1984), pp. 50, 52.

5. Judith A. Bellafaire, *The Army Nurse Corps: A Commemoration of World War II Service* (Washington, D.C.: U.S. Army Center of Military History, no date), Pub. 72-14, p. 31.

6. "When . . . Are You Coming Home, Nurse?" *The Army Nurse*, August 1945, p. 2.

7. Charles M. Wiltse, *Medical Service in the Mediterranean and Minor Theaters*, Series: U.S. Army in World War II, The Technical Services, The Medical Department, (Washington, D.C.: Office of the Chief of Military History, Department of the Army, 1965), pp. 521, 522.

8. Graham A. Cosmas and Albert E. Cowdrey, *Medical Service in the European Theater of Operations*, Series: U.S. Army in World War II, Technical Services (Washington, D.C.: U.S. Army Center of Military History, 1992), pp. 600, 601.

9. Mary M. Roberts, R.N., *American Nursing: History and Interpretation* (New York: Macmillan, 1955), p. 351.

10. Four Army Nurses, "Waiting Is Disheartening," *American Journal of Nursing*, December 1945, p. 1062.

11. Cosmas and Cowdrey, p. 612.

12. Alice Lofgren Andrus, "Navy Experiences," Unpublished essay, November 1993, p. 7.

13. Elizabeth Harman Masterson Questionnaire.

14. "Navy Nurse Reserves May Become Regulars," *American Journal of Nursing*, November 1945, p. 962.

15. Alice Lofgren Andrus Questionnaire.

16. 1st Lt. Dorothy E. Lopnow, ANC, "Our Nurses and Redistribution Stations," *The Army Nurse*, March 1945, p. 3.

17. Mary Jose, "Army Nurses Return from the Pacific," *American Journal of Nursing*, October 1945, p. 810.

18. Quoted in "Relive Years Spent Overseas," *Syracuse Herald-Journal*, August 17, 1957, p. 8.

19. Quoted in Jose, "Army Nurses Return from the Pacific," p. 810.

20. Lopnow, p. 3.

21. Quoted in Lopnow, p. 3.

22. Lucy Wilson Jopling, *Warrior in White* (San Antonio: Watercress Press, 1990), p. 96.

23. Ruth Claff, *Lady with the Flashlight*, Unpublished memoirs, 1947, pp. 49, 50.

24. Louine Lunt Connor Peck Questionnaire.

25. Louine Lunt Connor Peck, United States Army Nurse Corps Oral History Program, Interviewed by Col. Clara Adams-Ender, A.N., and Maj. Wynona Bice-Stephens, A.N., ed., North East Harbor, Maine, August 31, 1986, pp. 34, 71-72, 74, 75.

26. Genevieve Van de Drink Stepanek Questionnaire.

27. Quoted in Cindy Tumiel, "Tierney, 78, Was Army Nurse," *San Antonio Express-News*, December 14, 1999, p. 8B.

28. Quoted in "Kircher Lived for the Military," *San Antonio Express-News*, April 10, 1994, p. 4B.

29. Peck oral history, pp. 28, 65-66.

30. Scott W. Wright, "Women's War 'Whited Out' of History Books," *Austin American-Statesman*, December 5, 1991, p. A:12.

31. Mary Barbero Questionnaire.

32. Quoted in Wright, "Women's War 'Whited Out' of History Books, p. A:12.

33. June A. Willenz, *Women Veterans: America's Forgotten Heroines* (New York: Continuum, 1983), p. 88.

34. "Ruth Solot, 84, WWII Army Nurse," *Plain Dealer*, April 29, 1994, no pg. #.

35. Quoted in Grant Segall, "'You Go to Topside!': Life's Been Eventful for Colonel Mac, 89," *Plain Dealer*, November 21, 1993, pp. 4B, 1B.

36. Janina Smiertka Davenport Questionnaire.

37. Claff, p. 45.

38. Quoted in Melissa A. Rosenbaum, "A Navy Nurse Remembers," *U.S. Navy Medicine*, Vol. 72, June 1981, p. 25.

39. Col. John Boyd Coates, Jr., ed. *Personnel in World War II* (Washington, D.C.: Office of the Surgeon General, U.S. Army Medical Department, 1963), p. 322.

40. Quoted in Mary Elizabeth Carnegie, *The Path We Tread: Blacks in Nursing, 1854-1990* (New York: National League for Nursing Press, 1991), p. 203.

41. Cosmas and Cowdrey, p. 123.

42. Quoted in Cosmas and Cowdrey, p. 123.

43. Quoted in Barbara Tomblin, *G.I. Nightingales: The Army Nurse Corps in World War II* (Lexington: The University Press of Kentucky, 1996), pp. 194, 195.

44. Coates, p. 153.

45. Elmira B. Wickenden, R.N., "The National Nursing Council Reports," *American Journal of Nursing*, September 1943, p. 808.

46. Willenz, p. 106.

47. Brig. Gen. (Ret.) Lillian Dunlap, ANC, Interview with author, December 20, 1991.

APPENDICES

Appendix A

Nurses Who Responded to Author's Questionnaire

Name Used During War	Branch	Where Served	Name Used Now
Atwell, Edith	ANC	Pacific	Edith Smith
Barbero, Mary L.	ANC	CBI	Same
Blissett, Marion	NNC	Pacific	Marion Stafford
Claff, Ruth W.	ANC	Pacific	Same
Cline, Dora	NNC	Pacific	Dora Fechtmann
Combites, Inez	ANC	Mediterranean	Inez Hood
Connor, Louine	ANC	USS *Acadia*	Louine Peck
Dunlap, Lillian	ANC	Pacific	Same
Gilbert, Rachel	AAF	Europe	Rachel Francis
Glennon, Marie	AAF	Europe	Marie Charlier
Hamilton, Juanita	ANC	Pacific	Juanita Webster
Harman, Elizabeth	ANC	Europe	Elizabeth Masterson
Hooker, Marian	ANC	Pacific	Marian Stran
Jensen, Agnes	AAF	Mediterranean	Agnes Mangerich
Kern, Marion	ANC	CBI	Marion Kennedy
Lofgren, Alice	NNC	USS *Consolation*	Alice Andrus
Moody, Selma	AAF	Pacific	Selma Brawner
Pon, Helen	ANC	North Africa	Helen Pon Onyett
Rutkowski, Eugenie	AAF	Mediterranean	Eugenie Wilkinson
Sansone, Constance	ANC	Pacific	Same
Shadewaldt, Ruth	ANC	Pacific	Deceased
Smiertka, Janina	NNC	Stateside	Janina Davenport
Tierney, Marian A.	ANC	Europe	Deceased
Ullom, Madeline M.	ANC	Pacific	Same
Van de Drink, Genevieve	NNC	Pacific	Genevieve Stepanek

Appendix B

Pledge of the Army Nurse

As an Army nurse, I accept the responsibilities of an officer in the Army Nurse Corps.

I shall give faithful care to the men who fight for the freedom of this Country and to the women who stand behind them.

I shall bring to the American soldier wherever he may be the best of my knowledge and professional skill.

I shall approach him cheerfully at all times under any conditions I may find.

I shall endeavor to maintain the highest nursing standards possible in the performance of my duties.

I shall appear fearless in the presence of danger and quiet the fears of others to the best of my ability.

My only criticism shall be constructive. The reputation and good name of the Army Nurse Corps and of the nursing profession shall be uppermost in my thoughts, second only to the care of my patients.

I shall endeavor to be a credit to my Country and to the uniform I wear.

—Provided by Ethel Lane

Appendix C

Prayer of an Army Nurse

Hear my prayer in silence before Thee
As I ask for courage each day.
Grant that I be worthy of the sacred pledge of my profession,
And the lives of those entrusted to my care.
Help me to offer hope and cheer in the hearts of men and my country.
For their faith inspires me to give the world and nursing my best.
Instill in me the understanding and compassion of those who led the way.
For I am thankful to You for giving me this life to live.

—Provided by Ethel Lane

Appendix D

"Eternal Father, Strong to Save" (Navy Hymn)

1)   Eternal Father, strong to save,
Whose arm hath bound the restless wave,
Who bidd'st the mighty ocean deep
Its own appointed limits keep,
O hear us when we cry to thee
For those in peril on the sea!

(8)   O God, protect the women who,
In service, faith in Thee renew;
O guide devoted hands of skill
And bless their work within they will;
Inspire their lives that they may be
Examples fair on land and sea.

—Provided by Jan K. Herman, Historian
Bureau of Medicine and Surgery,
Department of the Navy

Appendix E

Pledge of the Flight Nurse

I will summon every resource to prevent the triumph of death over life.

I will stand guard over the medicines and equipment entrusted to my care and ensure their proper use.

I will be untiring in the performance of my duties, and I will remember that upon my disposition and spirit will in large measure depend the morale of my patients.

I will be faithful to my training and to the wisdom handed down to me by those who have gone before me.

I have taken a nurse's oath reverent in man's mind because of the spirit and work of its creator, Florence Nightingale.

She, I remember, was called the lady with the lamp. It is now my privilege to lift this lamp of hope and faith and courage in my profession to heights now known by her in her time.

Together with the help of flight surgeons and surgical technicians I can set the very skies ablaze with life and promise for the sick, injured, and wounded who are my sacred charges.

This I will do.

I will not falter.

In war or in peace.

—Victor Robinson, *White Caps: American Nursing in the World Wars*
Philadelphia: J. B. Lippincott Co., 1946

Appendix F

Pledge of the Cadet Nurse

I am solemnly aware of the obligations I assume toward my country and toward my chosen profession.

I will follow faithfully the teachings of my instructors and the guidance of the physicians with whom I work.

I will hold my body strong, my mind alert, and my heart steadfast.

I will be kind, tolerant, and understanding.

Above all, I will dedicate myself now and forever to the triumph of life over death.

As a Cadet Nurse, I pledge to my country my service in essential nursing for the duration of the war.

—Victor Robinson, *White Caps: American Nursing in the World Wars*
Philadelphia: J. B. Lippincott Co., 1946

Appendix G

The Evacuation Process

We have brought our surgical talents closer to the soldier than
ever before. In the last war we brought the wounded to the
hospital; in this war we are bringing the hospitals to the
wounded.

—Quoted in "Care of the Wounded Overseas"
American Journal of Nursing, January 1944, p. 20

But the first link in this chain was the wounded soldier himself. He carried
first aid dressing and a package of 12 sulfa tablets in a spillproof metal box
that could be opened with one hand. Instructions were on the back of the box
but were also explained to each unit by its medical officer, and periodic checks
were made to make sure each man had them. The sulfa tablets were taken
orally by the soldier as soon as he was wounded and sometimes meant the
difference between life and death because they prevented infection.

Next in the chain were the medics or company aidmen. These were
enlisted men who faced the danger of frontline combat but carried only a first-
aid kit—no weapons: "The aid man has been the unsung hero of this war. He
is required to do everything the line soldier of his outfit must do except fight.
. . . yet his is the most important link in the whole chain of evacuation of the
wounded because it is he who sees the wounded man first."[1] Although the
ordinary soldier was known to administer first aid to himself quite efficiently
when necessary, medics "reported that wounded men preferred them to treat
even minor wounds, perhaps in the belief that the 'professional' would do a
better job."[2] Aidmen tagged the patient and indicated on the tag what
treatment was given, where the patient was found, and the patient's name and
next of kin. They carried morphine, splints, bandages, and sulfa drugs and
were trained to dress wounds, control bleeding, treat shock and exhaustion,
and inject drugs. Litter bearers, who also moved with the troops, put the

patient on a stretcher and carried him away from the front line to a battalion aid station.

Battalion aid stations moved with the troops and were usually 300 to 800 yards behind the front. Here the wounded soldier received "limited emergency surgery,"[3] usually just plasma, morphine, or splints. His wounds were immobilized "to minimize the shock of further transportation," and he was sent via litter, ambulance, or jeep to the division collecting station or clearing station (there weren't always collecting stations). If his wound was not severe, he was patched up and sent back to the front.

Each battalion or regiment had its own aidmen and doctors, and all were part of a division. Each division had a medical battalion with three collecting companies and a clearing company. The collecting company consisted of ambulance and litter-bearer units whose doctors classified the patient's injury type (head, chest, etc.), and made a complete record of the injury and treatment received. If still more treatment was needed, the patient was taken to a clearing station—"the most forward hospital serving the division and therefore the most accessible from the front lines, where disease might claim as many victims as bullets."[4] At this stage, "more serious cases passed on farther to the rear to a 'station' hospital, and if long-term recovery was indicated, by air or ship to the United States."[5]

From the clearing company's station, the patient usually went to a nearby platoon or field hospital for forward surgery. The field hospital operated as either a single 400-bed hospital or as three 100-bed hospitals. When operating as three units, auxillary surgical teams were added. Although often crude in appearance—often in a tent with a dirt floor—the field hospital was as efficient as Stateside hospitals.

Author Judith A. Bellafaire said that the evaluations made at field hospitals "were of critical importance. The severity of a patient's condition and the need for special treatment determined when, how, and where the patient was to be sent. Improper evacuation might result in the death of a patient from lack of immediate care."[6]

When separated into three sections, the field hospitals leapfrogged each other: "The usual procedure was to have one platoon in operation, the other packed and ready to 'leapfrog' forward as the line of battle advanced."[7] Vincoe M. Paxton wrote, "If a patient's condition does not permit immediate evacuation, he is held until he can safely be moved back. When the need for each hospitalization unit ends, the unit is held in reserve, available for further commitment."[8]

If, after being seen in a field hospital, a patient still could not return to battle, he was sent to an evacuation hospital. These hospitals—located 12 to 100 miles from the front—were both very mobile and semimobile, could bed up to 400 patients, and usually staffed 40 nurses. It was the first time since leaving home that soldiers enjoyed "the luxury of warm baths, clean pajamas, and soft bathrobes."[9] Evacuation hospitals "were prepared to give definitive treatment to all casualties. They were staffed and equipped, that is, to do whatever might be necessary for the recovery of the patient." They also grouped patients in preparation for transport. If a patient's expected recovery time was a few weeks, he was sent to a convalescent hospital in the area. If recovery time was longer, he was sent by ambulance, plane, or ship to a station hospital or to a general hospital several hundred miles from the front lines.

In the general hospital, the patient might "have another, more leisurely, operation." These hospitals had room for 1,000 to 2,000 beds and staffed about 120 nurses. The station hospitals were smaller general hospitals with "fewer specialists and less complete equipment" and housed 25 to 900 beds (avg. 500). The length of time a patient was kept in a general hospital was determined by "the theater evacuation policy and by the judgment of the medical officers on his case." The average was 90 days, but it varied from 30 to 120 days. "It is the availability of beds and of trained personnel in relation to the incidence of battle wounds, injuries, and disease that determines the policy."[10] And while general hospitals were considered "fixed" installations, Col. Florence Blanchfield reported that some moved "almost as frequently as the field and evacuation hospitals."[11]

When the patient returned stateside, he was delivered to a debarkation hospital. These sent reports of their patient load to the Medical Regulating Office, which then decided to which general hospital each man should be sent—the one nearest his home when possible. The decision was also affected by the available bed space and the patient's particular medical problem; each of the 60 Army general hospitals had a specialty—amputations, plastic surgery, burns, and so forth.

As hospitals in the theaters adapted to their needs, so did hospitals in the Zone of Interior. Originally, there were only station hospitals and general hospitals. Station hospitals provided emergency and general care to their own military personnel and then sent patients needing longer or more specialized care to general hospitals located throughout the country. By 1944, however, general hospitals were filling with returning GIs, and there weren't enough specialized medical personnel. The regional hospital was created to take patients from all station hospitals within about 75 miles. They were staffed with special personnel and operated like general hospitals.

All along the lines of evacuation, patients were categorized and as many as possible were sent back to the front lines. In some cases, men skipped one or more of these stops, and sometimes not all types of these hospitals were utilized. This was determined by the severity of the injury and what transportation options were available due to the theater, combat conditions, location, terrain, available personnel, and so forth.

It was these very different locations in which men fought that not only brought different medical problems, but also affected the chain of medical evacuation. Men wounded in the European Theater were usually evacuated to a station or general hospital in Great Britain quite quickly, but the Pacific Theater's tactical situation and terrain made evacuation extremely difficult, and many times men stayed in beachhead surgical hospitals longer than was preferred. According to Author Charles M. Wiltse, "There is nothing rigid about the field medical service. Improvisation and adaptation were the rule in

World War II as they are today. There is a job to be done, and quickly, with whatever means are at hand. The job . . . is to get a man to surgery with the least possible delay consistent with keeping him alive."[12]

NOTES

1. Vincoe M. Paxton, R.N. and Stuart D. Rizika, M.D., "Soldiers of the Medical Detachment," *American Journal of Nursing*, September 1945, p. 694.

2. Lee Kennett, *G.I:. The American Soldier in World War II* (New York: Charles Scribners, 1987), p. 177.

3. Charles B. MacDonald, "The U. S. Soldier," *Fighting Men of the Second World War* (Marshall Cavendish USA Ltd., 1973), p. 7.

4. Charles M. Wiltse, *Medical Service in the Mediterranean and Minor Theaters*, U.S. Army in World War II, The Technical Services, The Medical Department (Washington, D.C.: Office of the Chief of Military History Department of the Army, 1965), pp. 3, 4.

5. MacDonald, p. 7.

6. Judith A. Bellafaire, *The Army Nurse Corps: A Commemoration of World War II Service* (Washington, D.C.: U.S. Army Center of Military History, no date), Pub. 72-14, p. 12.

7. Wiltse, p. 3.

8. Vincoe M. Paxton, R.N., "With Field Hospital Nurses in Germany," *American Journal of Nursing*, February 1945, p. 131.

9. Philip A. Kalisch and Beatrice J. Kalisch, *Advance of American Nursing* (Boston: Little, Brown, 1978), p. 457.

10. Wiltse, pp. 5, 6.

11. Col. Florence A. Blanchfield, "Report from the ETO and the MTO," *American Journal of Nursing*, June 1945, p. 427.

12. Wiltse, p. 3.

Bibliography

"28 Yank Nurses Happily Landed in Philippines." *The Army Nurse*, December 1944, p. 5.

"50th Anniversary of the Cadet Nurse Corps" Video, *Nursing Approaches*. Sigma Theta Tau, Samuel Merritt College, Studio Three Productions, 1993.

"1943—A Stern and Terrible Year!" *American Journal of Nursing,* January 1943, p. 1.

Aaron, Lt. Col. Margaret. "With Army Nurses in Britain." *American Journal of Nursing*, October 1943, pp. 954-955.

Abrahamson, James L. *The American Home Front.* Washington, D.C.: National Defense University Press, 1983.

"Accrediting of Schools of Nursing." *American Journal of Nursing*, February 1942, p. 192.

"Adventure in 1943." *American Journal of Nursing*, April 1943, p. 394.

"Air Evacuation . . . Returning Wounded Fly under Care of Army Flight Nurses." *The Army Nurse*, March 1945, p. 9.

"All Army Nurses to Be in Olive Drabs." *American Journal of Nursing*, June 1944, p. 600.

Allen, Paula. "Generally Speaking." *San Antonio Express-News*, October 2, 1994, pp. 4-5.

Allen, Thomas B. "Pearl Harbor: A Return to the Day of Infamy." *National Geographic*, 1991, pp. 50-77.

"American Hospital in Australia." *American Journal of Nursing*, June 1943, p. 599.

American Legion, John D. Mathis. "Memorial Day Service: Commemorating Veterans of All Wars," Post No. 2, Americus, Georgia, May 27, 1990.

"American Nurses with the Armed Forces." *American Journal of Nursing*, May 1942, p. 572.

"American Nurses at Guinea Bases Happiest of All." *New Orleans Times-Picayune*, November 24, 1942, no p. #.

"American Nurses Prisoners in Japan." *American Journal of Nursing*, April 1942, pp. 446, 448.

American Red Cross Release (June 1944). *American Journal of Nursing*, August 1944, p. 728.

"American Soldiers Carry Sulfanilamide." *American Journal of Nursing*, April 1942, p. 376

"American-Born Nurses of Japanese Ancestry Serve in the ANC." *American Journal of Nursing*, May 1943, p. 506.

Anderson, Charles R. *Papua*, Series: The U.S. Army Campaigns of World War II. Washington D.C.: U.S. Army Center of Military History, 1992.

Anderson, Col. Robert S., MC, USA, editor-in-chief. *Army Medical Specialist Corps.* Office of the Surgeon General, U.S. Army, Washington, D.C., 1968.

Andrus, Alice Lofgren. Interview with author, November 20, 1993.

———.   Letter to author, September 30, 1993.

———.   Letter to parents, May 30, 1945.

———.   "A Moment in History," Unpublished essay, March 1993.

———.   "Navy Experiences," Unpublished essay, November 1993, pp. 1-7.

———.   Questionnaire.

———.   "Random Navy Memories," Unpublished personal essay, November 1993, pp. 1-3.

"Another Nurse Wins the Soldiers' Medal." *American Journal of Nursing*, September 1943, p. 859.

"The ARC Blood Donor Service." *American Journal of Nursing*, March 1943, pp. 264-266.

"The Army Air Forces Needs Nurses." *American Journal of Nursing,* June 1943, p. 599.

"Army and Navy Hospital Facilities." *American Journal of Nursing*, March 1944, p. 246.

"Army and Navy Nurses Are Ready for Bad Weather." *American Journal of Nursing*, February 1944, p. 179.

"Army and Navy Nurses Return to the Philippines and Guam." *American Journal of Nursing*, April 1945, p. 317.

"Army and Navy Nurses Safe." *American Journal of Nursing*, January 1944, p. 74.

"Army and Navy Nurses Tell Us." *American Journal of Nursing,* February 1943, pp. 221-222.

———.   *American Journal of Nursing*, March 1943, p. 307.

———.   *American Journal of Nursing*, June 1943, p. 600.

———.   *American Journal of Nursing*, July 1943, p. 686.

———.   *American Journal of Nursing*, April 1944, p. 403.

———.   *American Journal of Nursing*, May 1944, p. 498.

———.   *American Journal of Nursing*, July 1944, p. 700.

———.   *American Journal of Nursing*, December 1944, pp. 1180-1181.

———.   *American Journal of Nursing*, January 1945, pp. 64-65.

———.   *American Journal of Nursing*, May 1945, pp. 408-409.

———.   *American Journal of Nursing*, June 1945, p. 489.

"Army and Navy Nurses Voted among America's Best-Dressed Women." *The Army Nurse*, May 1945, p. 16.

"Army Develops Artificial Plastic Eye." *American Journal of Nursing,* April 1945, p. 289.

"Army Flight Nurses in China." *American Journal of Nursing*, January 1945, p. 64.

"Army Hospital Trains." *American Journal of Nursing*, June 1943, pp. 565-566.

"Army Issues Regulations Covering Wearing of Nurses' Uniform." *American Journal of Nursing*, March 1943, p. 954.

"Army Needs Nurses for Emergency." *American Journal of Nursing,* November 1944, p. 1084.

"Army Neuropsychiatric Nursing Schools." *The Army Nurse*, January 1945, p. 12.

"Army Nurse Awarded Soldier's Medal." *American Journal of Nursing*, March 1944, p. 295.

"The Army Nurse Corps Celebrates 44th Anniversary." *The Army Nurse*, February 1945, p. 2.

"Army Nurse Tells of Experience with Overseas Surgery." *The Army Nurse*, February 1945, p. 3.

"The Army Nurse in War Exhibit." *American Journal of Nursing*, June 1945, pp. 434-435.

"Army Nurse Wears Purple Heart and Bronze Star." *American Journal of Nursing*, July 1944, p. 699.

"Army Nurse Week." *American Journal of Nursing*, September 1944, pp. 819-820.

"Army Nurse Wins Air Medal." *American Journal of Nursing*, May 1943, pp. 443-444.

"An Army Nurse Writes an Editorial." *American Journal of Nursing*, January 1945, p. 1.

"Army Nurses in the Air." *American Journal of Nursing*, August 1942, p. 954.

"Army Nurses on the Air." *American Journal of Nursing*, August 1942, pp. 955, 957.

"Army Nurses at American Hospital in Paris." *American Journal of Nursing*, February 1945, p. 150.

"Army Nurses Can Take It." *American Journal of Nursing*, August 1943, p. 775.

"Army Nurses' 'Commando Course' in England." *American Journal of Nursing*, September 1943, p. 860.

"Army Nurses in the ETO." *American Journal of Nursing*, May 1945, pp. 386-387.

"Army Nurses' Gift to Auckland." *American Journal of Nursing*, April 1943, p. 350.

"Army Nurses on Hospital Trains." *American Journal of Nursing*, November 1943, p. 1044.

"Army Nurses in Ireland and Iceland." *American Journal of Nursing*, November 1942, p. 1314.

"Army Nurses in Ireland and India, New Caledonia and Africa." *American Journal of Nursing*, February 1943, p. 211.

"Army Nurses Killed in USS Comfort Attack." *American Journal of Nursing*, October 1945, p. 871.

"Army Nurses Needed in the Army Air Forces." *American Journal of Nursing*, March 1943, p. 306.

"Army Nurses' New Slack Suit." *American Journal of Nursing*, November 1943, pp. 1042-1043.

"Army Nurses from the Philippines Now in Australia." *American Journal of Nursing*, July 1942, p. 820.

"Army Nurses Play Important Role in Evacuation by Train and Plane." *American Journal of Nursing*, November 1944, p. 1087.

"Army Nurses' Rank Bill." *American Journal of Nursing*, June 1944, p. 594.

"Army Nurses in Southern France." *American Journal of Nursing*, October 1944, p. 996.

"Army Nurses Tell Us." *American Journal of Nursing*, November 1943, p. 1044.

————. *American Journal of Nursing*, March 1945, pp. 241-242.

"Army Nurses Training Program Expanded." *American Journal of Nursing*, July 1943, p. 685.

"Army War Show Aids Recruitment." *American Journal of Nursing*, August 1942, p. 957.

"Army's New Release Policy." *American Journal of Nursing*, October 1945, p. 852.

Associated Press. *World War II: A 50th Anniversary.* New York: Henry Holt and Co., 1989.

Avery, Capt. Dorcas C., ANC. "Army Nurses in India." *American Journal of Nursing,* August 1943, p. 769.

Aynes, Major Edith A., R.N., ANC. "The Hospital Ship *Acadia.*" *American Journal of Nursing,* February 1944, pp. 98-100.

Bacon, 1st Lt. Deborah, ANC. "Across the Rhine—by Air." *The Army Nurse,* July 1945, pp. 3-4.

Bailey, Jennifer L. *Philippine Islands.* Series: The U.S. Army Campaigns of World War II. Washington D.C.: U.S. Army Center of Military History, 1992.

"Bands for Army Nurses' Caps." *American Journal of Nursing,* August 1944, p. 810.

Banfield, Gertrude S., R.N. "American Nurses—We Are at War!" *American Journal of Nursing,* April 1942, pp. 354-358.

———.   "This War—The Business of Every One of Us." *American Journal of Nursing,* October 1942, pp. 1126-1127.

Banks, Lt. Lillian M., NC, USN. "Christmas, Christmas, Everywhere!" *American Journal of Nursing,* December 1944, p. 1112.

Barbero, Mary. Questionnaire.

Barger, Judith, BSN, MSN. "Coping with War: An Oral History of United States Army Flight Nurses Who Flew with the Army Air Forces in World War II." Dissertation, University of Texas at Austin, December 1986.

———.   Ph.D. "Preparing for War: Lessons Learned from U.S. Army Flight Nurses of World War II." *Aviation, Space, and Environmental Medicine,* August 1991, pp. 772-775.

Barker, 2nd Lt. Andres L., ANC. "Christmas Overseas." *American Journal of Nursing,* December 1943, p. 1062.

"Basic Training Center at Fort Devens." *American Journal of Nursing,* October 1943, p. 954.

Beard, Mary. Letter to Marion Blissett, July 27, 1941.

Beattie, Edith M., R.N. "Nurse Draft Legislation and the ANA—A Summary." *American Journal of Nursing,* July 1945, pp. 546-548.

Bellafaire, Judith A. *The Army Nurse Corps: A Commemoration of World War II Service.* Washington, D.C.: U.S. Army Center of Military History, Pub. 72-14, no date.

"A Birthday Present from Uncle Sam." *American Journal of Nursing,* March 1943, p. 237.

Bishop, Louis Faugeres Jr., M.D. "Soldier's Heart." *American Journal of Nursing,* April 1942, pp. 377-380.

Blanchfield, Col. Florence A. "Calling All Nurses." *American Journal of Nursing,* February 1945, pp. 91-93.

———.   "The Needs of the Army Nurse." *American Journal of Nursing,* November 1943, pp. 991-992.

———.   "Report From the ETO and the MTO." *American Journal of Nursing,* June 1945, pp. 427-430.

Blassingame, Wyatt. *Combat Nurses of World War II.* New York: Landmark Books, Random House, 1967.

Bleier, Lt. Anna M., ANC. "From Many Fronts." *American Journal of Nursing,* December 1944, p. 1177.

Blissett, Lt. Col. William G.   "Biographical Sketch: Marion Blissett Stafford," unpublished, October 20, 1990.

Blumenson, Martin. *Liberation*. Series: World War II. Alexandria: Time-Life Books, 1978.

Boddy, Manchester. *War Guide*, Los Angeles: *Daily News*, no date.

Bolotin, Susan, ed. *Pearl Harbor: December 7, 1941–December 7, 1991*. Life Collector's Edition, Fall 1991.

"The Bolton Bill." *American Journal of Nursing*, July 1943, p. 678.

Bolton, Frances Payne. "Home from ETOUSA." *American Journal of Nursing*, January 1945, pp. 5-9.

———. "Nursing Answers." *American Journal of Nursing*, February 1942, pp. 138-140.

"Both Negro and White Nurses Care for Prisoners." *American Journal of Nursing*, March 1945, p. 234.

Box, Terry. "They Also Served." *The Dallas Morning News*. December 5, 1991, A: 1, 28.

Brantley, Lt. Col. Hattie R. (Ret.) Lecture: "The Women POWs," *Quiet Shadows: Women in the Pacific War—A Symposium*. Southwest Texas State University, March 27, 1993.

Brawner, Selma Moody. Questionnaire.

Briggs, W. P. "Men Nurses in the U.S. Navy." *American Journal of Nursing*, January 1943, pp. 39-42.

Brown, Daniel M., R.N. "Men Nurses and the U.S. Navy." *American Journal of Nursing*, May 1942, pp. 499-501.

Brown, Lt. Jg. Mary Jane, R.N., NC, USNR. "Psychiatric Nursing in Naval Base Hospitals." *American Journal of Nursing*, December 1944, pp. 1135-1137.

Bullough, Bonnie. "Lasting Impact of World War II on Nursing." *American Journal of Nursing*, January 1976, pp. 118-120.

Bullough, Bonnie and Vern L. Bullough. *Emergence of Modern Nursing*. New York: Macmillan, 1964.

Burns-Burrell, Prudence L. Lecture: "The Black Nurse Experience," *Quiet Shadows: Women in the Pacific War—A Symposium*. Southwest Texas State University, March 27, 1993.

Callahan, Lt. Margaret, ANC. "Christmas, Christmas, Everywhere!" *American Journal of Nursing*, December 1944, p. 1114.

Callori, 2nd Lt. Marie A., ANCR. "A Year in the Army." *Pacific Coast Journal of Nursing*, September 1941, pp. 533-534.

Campbell, D'Ann. *Women at War with America: Private Lives in a Patriotic Era*. Cambridge: Harvard University Press, 1984.

Cardinal, Catherine, ENS, NC, USN. "Navy Nursing—Original Womens Lib." *The Pulse Beat*. May 1973, p. 4.

"Care of the Wounded Overseas." *American Journal of Nursing*, January 1944, p. 20.

Carnegie, Mary Elizabeth, DPA, R.N., FAAN. *The Path We Tread: Blacks in Nursing, 1854-1990*, 2nd ed. New York: National League for Nursing Press, 1991.

"Chain of Medical Support—WWII." Chart, U.S. Army Medical Department Museum, San Antonio, TX.

"Chaplain Praises CBI Nurses." *The Army Nurse*, December 1944, p. 4.

Charlier, Capt. Marie Helen Glennon, ANC. Questionnaire.

Charlier, Dr. Roger H. Letter to author dated December 30, 1993.

———. Notes on author's letter dated January 8, 1994.

"Chic and Practical." *Trained Nurse and Hospital Review*, November 1943, p. 367.

"Christmas Overseas." *American Journal of Nursing*, December 1943, pp. 1062-1066.

"Christmas Overseas." *American Journal of Nursing*, December 1945, p. 1063.

"Civilian Nurses See that Army Nurses Have Fun and Comfort." *American Journal of Nursing*, July 1943, p. 686.

Claff, Ruth. *Lady with the Flashlight,* Unpublished memoirs, 1947.

Clarke, Lt. Alice R., ANC. "An Army Nurse Returns to the Philippines." *American Journal of Nursing*, March 1945, pp. 177-178.

———. "Interesting Personalities of the Army Nurse Corps in the Philippines." *The Army Nurse*, May 1945, p. 5.

———. "Thirty-Seven Months as Prisoners of War." *American Journal of Nursing*, May 1945, pp. 342-345.

———. "'Thirty-Seven Months as Prisoners of War' as Told by Liberated Army Nurses to Lieutenant Alice R. Clarke, Army Nurse Corps." *The Army Nurse*, March 1945, pp. 10-12.

———. "The Use of Penicillin in the SWPA." *American Journal of Nursing*, November 1945, pp. 938-940.

Clay, Lt. Geneva, ANC. "Christmas, Christmas, Everywhere!" *American Journal of Nursing*, December 1944, pp. 1114-1115.

Clayton, Frederick. "An Evacuation Unit Serves under Fire." *American Journal of Nursing*, May 1944, pp. 453-455.

———. "Front-Line Surgical Nurses." *American Journal of Nursing*, March 1944, pp. 234-235.

Coates, Col. John Boyd, Jr., ed. *Personnel in World War II.* Washington D.C.: Office of the Surgeon General, U.S. Army Medical Department, 1963.

Colaw, Capt. Becky. "An Operation Called Overlord." *Airman*, June 1994, pp. 24-26.

Collier, Richard. *The War in the Desert.* Series: World War II. Alexandria: Time-Life Books, 1977.

"Colonel Blanchfield Returns from a Two-Month Tour of the ETO." *The Army Nurse,* May 1945, p. 6.

"Colonel Forrest in Southwest Pacific." *American Journal of Nursing*, December 1944, pp. 1178-1179.

Comer, Lt. Winona G., ANC. "Somewhere in the British Isles." *American Journal of Nursing*, October 1944, p. 989.

"Commendation Ribbons for Navy Nurses." *American Journal of Nursing*, March 1944, pp. 294-295.

"Commissioned." Newspaper photo of Constance Sansone sent by Constance Sansone. No source, date, p. #.

Cook, S/S Private Walter. Letter to President Roosevelt (no title). *American Journal of Nursing*, February 1944, p. 100.

Cooper, Page. *Navy Nurse.* New York: McGraw-Hill, 1946.

Cosmas, Graham A. and Albert E. Cowdrey. *Medical Service in the European Theater of Operations.* Series: U.S. Army in World War II, Technical Services, Washington D.C.: U.S. Army Center of Military History, 1992.

Cosner, Shaaron. *War Nurses.* New York: Walker & Co., 1988.

Craig, May. "Report from Germany." *The Army Nurse*, August 1945, p. 6.

"Criteria of Essentiality for Nurses." *American Journal of Nursing,* November 1943, p. 977.

"Critical Months Ahead." *American Journal of Nursing,* July 1943, p. 626-630.

Crowder, Randolph. "A Brief History of Air Evacuation through World War II," partial requirements of AFS 611A, December 7, 1978.

"Current and Recent Federal Legislation." *American Journal of Nursing*, August 1944, p. 791.

Curtis, 1st Lt. Dorothy E., R.N. "Nurse, There's Typhus in Camp." *American Journal of Nursing*, September 1945, pp. 714-715.

Curto, LCDR Christine, NC, USN. "Nurse Pioneers and the Hospital Ship *Relief*." *Navy Medicine*, May-June 1992, pp. 20-25.

Danner, Dorothy Still. "Reminiscences of a Nurse POW." *Navy Medicine*, May-June 1992, pp. 36-40.

Dauser, Capt. Sue S., NC, USN. Preface, *Navy Nurse*, by Page Cooper. New York: McGraw-Hill, 1946, pp. ix-x.

Davenport, Janina Smiertka. Letter to author received December 1993.

———. Letter to author dated March 7, 1994.

———. Letter to author dated March 19, 1994.

———. Questionnaire.

Davis, Dorothy, R.N. "I Nursed at Santo Tomas, Manila." *American Journal of Nursing*, January 1944, pp. 29-30.

"D-Day Found Nurses Prepared." *American Journal of Nursing*, August 1944, p. 728.

"D-Day Plus 4." *Trained Nurse and Hospital Review*, December 1944, p. 450.

Deeds, 1st Lt. Ann C., ANC. "There Goes an American Nurse." *American Journal of Nursing*, September 1944, pp. 847-848.

"Demobilization of Army Nurses." *American Journal of Nursing*, December 1945, p. 1065.

DePauw, Linda Grant. *Founding Mothers: Women in America in the Revolutionary Era*. Boston: Houghton Mifflin, 1975.

———. *Remember the Ladies: Women in America (1750-1815)*. New York: Viking, 1976.

Desmarais, Ensign Mary Virginia, R.N., USNR. "Navy Nursing on D-Day Plus 4." *American Journal of Nursing*, January 1945, p. 12.

Devlin, Jennifer. "America's Black Women Patriots." *The Register*, Washington, D.C.: Women in Military Service for America Memorial Foundation, Spring 1994, p. 4.

DeWitt, Lt. Gill, USN. *The First Navy Flight Nurse on a Pacific Battlefield*, Fredericksburg,TX: Admiral Nimitz Foundation, 1983 (no p. #).

Dial, Donald E., M.D. "Treatment of War Injuries." *American Journal of Nursing*, November 1942, pp. 1229-1235.

"Did You Not Know?" *American Journal of Nursing*, December 1944, p. 1109.

Dietz, Lena Dixon and Aurelia R. Lehozky. *History and Modern Nursing*, 2nd ed. Philadelphia: F. A. Davis, 1967.

"Discipline." *The Army Nurse*, November 1944, p. 12.

Dixon, Lt. (jg) Dorothy and Marjorie Cheney, NC, USN. "Christmas, Christmas, Everywhere!" *American Journal of Nursing*, December 1944, p. 1114.

Dixon, Kenneth. "A Job Well Done." *The Army Nurse*, March 1944, pp. 2-3.

Dolan, Josephine A., MS, R.N. *Goodnow's History of Nursing*, 10th ed. Philadelphia: W. B. Saunders, 1958.

———. *History of Nursing*, 12th ed. Philadelphia: W. B. Saunders, 1968.

"Don't Miss These New Pamphlets." *American Journal of Nursing*, September 1942, p. 1075.

"Don't Miss This Opportunity." *American Journal of Nursing*, September 1943, p. 855.

Dooley, Capt. Helen A., ANC. "Very Little Time to Think." *American Journal of Nursing*, March 1945, p. 235.

Dowd-Smart, Lt. Rita, ANC. Computer printout of family history provided to author by Robinson, Linda.

Downen, 1st Lt. Mary Lillian, ANC. "Easter in the Aleutians." *American Journal of Nursing*, March 1945, p. 235.

Draper, Captain Claudia M., ANC. "From Normandy." *American Journal of Nursing*, October 1944, p. 989.

Dubbs, Marion Clark. "Bivouac in the Kentucky Hills." *The Story of Air Evacuation, 1942-1989*, compiled by the World War II Flight Nurses Association. Dallas: Taylor Publishing Co., 1989.

Dunbar, Lt. Comdr. Ruth B., R.N., USN. "Return to the Philippines." *American Journal of Nursing*, December 1945, pp. 1015-1018.

Dunbar, Virginia M., R.N. "England—1942." *American Journal of Nursing*, October 1942, pp. 1142-1143.

———. "My Visit to England." *American Journal of Nursing*, September 1942, pp. 1032-1033.

Dunlap, Brig. Gen. Lillian, ANC, (Ret). Interview with author, December 20, 1991.

———. Lecture: "The Army Nurse Story," *Quiet Shadows: Women in the Pacific War—A Symposium*. Southwest Texas State University, March 27, 1993.

Durgin, Rear Admiral Calvin T., USN. "The Invasion of Southern France." *Battle Stations! Your Navy in Action*, New York: Wm. H. Wise, 1946.

Durward, Lt. Evelyn, ANC. "'Home' in the Aleutians." *American Journal of Nursing*, April 1944, p. 398.

Dwyer, Sheila M., R.N. "Nursing Care of War Injuries." *American Journal of Nursing*, November 1942, pp. 1236-1240.

Dykstra, 1st Lt. Matilda E., ANC. "Army Life in India." *American Journal of Nursing*, March 1944, p. 290.

Encyclopedia of World War II. Thomas Parrish, ed. New York: Simon & Schuster, 1978.

"Enrollment Made Easier." *American Journal of Nursing*, February 1942, p. 208.

E.R., R.N. "With the Army in Australia." *American Journal of Nursing*, July 1942, p. 814.

"The Evacuation Hospital in France." *The Army Nurse*, March 1945, p. 8.

Evans, Jessie Fant. "Release from Los Banos." *American Journal of Nursing*, June 1945, pp. 462-463.

E. W. "Schools for Negro Nurses." *American Journal of Nursing*, December 1943, p. 1129.

"Excerpts from a M.D.D.'s Letter." *The Army Nurse*, November 1944, p. 13.

"Facts about the Army Nurse Corps." *The Army Nurse*, January 1945, pp. 4-6.

"Fashion Show in England Displays ETO Uniforms," Photo caption. *The Army Nurse*, August 1945, p. 5.

Fechtmann, Dora Cline. Letter to author, no date.

———. Questionnaire.

Fellmeth, 1st Lt. Floramund, R.N. "Army Nurses in Australia and Iceland." *American Journal of Nursing*, June 1942, p. 689.

Fessler, Diane Burke. *No Time for Fear: Voices of American Military Nurses in World War II*. East Lansing: Michigan State University Press, 1996.

The Fighting Men of Texas. Volume I. A History of the Second World War, a Memorial, a Remembrance, an Appreciation. Dallas: Historical Publishing Company, 1948.

———. Volume II. A History of the Second World War, a Memorial, a Remembrance, an Appreciation. Dallas: Historical Publishing Company, 1948.

———. Volume III. A History of the Second World War, a Memorial, a Remembrance, an Appreciation. Dallas: Historical Publishing Company, 1948.

———. Volume IV. A History of the Second World War, a Memorial, a Remembrance, an Appreciation. Dallas: Historical Publishing Company, 1948.

————. Volume V. A History of the Second World War, a Memorial, a Remembrance, an Appreciation. Dallas: Historical Publishing Company, 1948.

"Film Strips for Recruitment Programs." *American Journal of Nursing,* January 1942, p. 92.

"First Nurse Killed in France." *Trained Nurse and Hospital Review*, November 1944, p. 449.

Fitch, Vice-Admiral Aubrey W., USN. "The Battle of the Coral Sea." *Battle Stations! Your Navy in Action.* New York: Wm. H., 1946.

Fletcher, Vice-Admiral Frank J., USN. "The Battle of Midway." *Battle Stations! Your Navy in Action.* New York: Wm. H. Wise, 1946.

Flick, David. "A Nurse's Patience." *The Dallas Morning News*, November 12, 1993, A: 1, 8.

Flikke, Col. Julia O. *Nurses in Action.* New York: Lippincott, 1943.

"Flying Nurses." *American Journal of Nursing*, November 1943, p. 1043.

"Flying Nurses Aid U.S. African Campaign." *Life*, April 19, 1943, pp. 41-42.

"For Army and Navy Nurses in New York." *American Journal of Nursing*, June 1943, pp. 599-600.

"For Your Information Headquarters, Island Command, Saipan." *The Army Nurse*, January 1945, p. 12.

"Former Internees Pay Tribute to Navy Nurse Internees." *American Journal of Nursing*, October 1945, p. 856.

Forrest, Lt. Col. Nola G. "Army Nurses at Leyte." *American Journal of Nursing*, January 1945, p. 44.

————. "Report from the Philippines." *The Army Nurse*, December 1944, p. 13.

Forsythe, 1st Lt. Rosemary, ANC. "En Route to the Philippines—January 1945." *The Army Nurse,* June 1945, p. 7.

Four Army Nurses. "Waiting Is Disheartening." *American Journal of Nursing*, December 1945, p. 1062.

"Frances Slanger Killed in France." *The Army Nurse*, December 1944, p. 8.

Francis, Rachel Gilbert. "The Gardelegen Barn," Unpublished essay, October 22, 1993, p. 1.

————. "A Gift of Wooden Shoes." *New Hampshire Sunday News*, December 22, 1991, no p. #.

————. Letter to author, August 25, 1993.

————. Questionnaire.

Frank, Sr. Charles Marie, CCVI, R.N., MSNE. *Foundations of Nursing.* Philadelphia: W. B. Saunders, 1959.

Franklin, 1st Lt. Ann, R.N. "An Army Nurse at Dachau. 1. Assignment to Dachau." *American Journal of Nursing*, November 1945, pp. 901-902.

————. "An Army Nurse at Dachau. 2. We Care for Typhus Fever Patients." *American Journal of Nursing*, November 1945, pp. 902-903.

Frid, Rhoda E. "Training on Bivouac," *American Journal of Nursing,* August 1943, pp. 734-736.

"From an Army Nurse in India." *American Journal of Nursing*, January 1943, p. 93.

"From New Caledonia." *American Journal of Nursing*, August 1942, p. 946.

Frye, 2nd Lt. Maren A., ANC. "From the Home Front." *The Army Nurse*, September 1944, pp. 3-4.

Furer, Rear Adm. Julius Augustus, USN, Ret. *Administration of the Navy Department in World War II.* Washington, D.C.: U.S. Government Printing Office, 1959.

Geister, Janet M., R.N. "She Came Back from Bataan." *Trained Nurse and Hospital Review*, October 1942, pp. 252-254.

————. "They Need You So!" *Trained Nurse and Hospital Review*, December 1944, pp. 432-433.

"Gen. Clark Honors Wagoner Nurse for Heroism at Anzio." Newspaper clipping sent by Inez Hood Combites. No source, date, p. #.

"General Eisenhower Pays a Fine Tribute to Nurses." *The Army Nurse,* September 1944, p. 5.

Geoghegan, Priv. 1st Class Michael. "Salute to G.I. Jane." *American Journal of Nursing,* April 1945, p. 297.

Ghio, Sgt. Bob. "The Ladies of Assam." *YANK*, September 13, 1943, no p. #.

Glines, Edna Lee. *Heads in the Sand.* Los Angeles: Authors Unlimited, 1990.

Goolrick, William K. and Ogden Tanner. *The Battle of the Bulge*, Series: World War II. Alexandria: Time-Life Books, 1979.

Goudreau, Lt. Alice Aurora, R.N., USN. "Nursing at an Advance Naval Base Hospital." *American Journal of Nursing*, November 1945, pp. 884-886.

Granberg, Corp. W. J. "Where Blows the Williwaw." *American Journal of Nursing*, July 1945, pp. 535-537.

Green, Katy. "Not All Veterans Are Men, Women Too, Served Country." *Wagoner Tribune*, November 11, 1986, p. 3.

Gress, 1st Lt. Agnes D. "The 14th Evac on the Ledo Road." *American Journal of Nursing*, September 1945, pp. 704-706.

————. "With the Army Nurse Corps along the Ledo Road." *The Army Nurse*, February 1945, pp. 11-12.

Griffin, Gerald Joseph and H. Joanne King Griffin. *Jensen's History and Trends of Professional Nursing*, 5th ed. St. Louis: C. V. Mosby, 1965.

Griffith, Lt. J., NC, USNR. "Nurse Corps History Shared." *The Pulse Beat*, May 1973, pp. 7-8.

Griggs, Lt. (jg) Marie H., NC, USNR. "Christmas, Christmas, Everywhere!" *American Journal of Nursing*, December 1944, p. 1112.

Grope, Major Edna B., ANC. "Both Negro and White Nurses Care for Prisoners." *American Journal of Nursing*, March 1945, p. 234.

Gruhzit-Hoyt, Olga. *They Also Served: American Women in World War II.* New York: Birch Lane, 1995.

"Guidance Pamphlets for Nurse Veterans." *American Journal of Nursing*, November 1945, p. 963.

Gurney, Major Cindy, ANC. Point Paper, U.S. Center of Military History, January 7, 1987.

Halladay, Capt. Hazel, ANC. "1st Service Command School for Psychiatric Nursing." *The Army Nurse*, January 1945, p. 12.

Hamilton, 2nd Lt. Elizabeth R., ANC. "Christmas Overseas." *American Journal of Nursing*, December 1943, p. 1065.

Hanwell, Lt. (jg) P., NC, USNR. "Christmas, Christmas, Everywhere!" *American Journal of Nursing*, December 1944, p. 1115.

Harman, 1st Lt. Mary Ann, ANC. "Housecleaning in a Station Hospital." *American Journal of Nursing*, June 1944, pp. 594-595.

Hartley, Lt. (jg) Reba K., (NC) USNR. "A Nurse Looks at the Navy." *American Journal of Nursing*, April 1945, p. 294.

Hayes, Lt. Jg. Teresa M., R.N., USNR. "It Was Hot on the Island." *American Journal of Nursing*, November 1944, pp. 1058-1059.

Heaney, Lt. Alice ANC. "Christmas, Christmas, Everywhere!" *American Journal of Nursing*, December 1944, p. 1114.

"Helmets Have Many Uses for Army Nurses in France." *The Army Nurse*, January 1945, p. 12.

Hentsch, Yvonne. "The Treaty of Geneva." *American Journal of Nursing*, January 1944, pp. 34-36.

Herbert, Bob. "Nurses' Growing Role Holds Costs Down." *The Herald*, December 18, 1993, 7A.

Herman, Jan Kenneth. "Navy Medicine at Pearl Harbor. *Navy Medicine*, November-December 1991, pp. 12-19.

———. "Trial by Fire." *Navy Medicine*, November-December 1991, pp. 14-15.

"The Heroic Nurses of Bataan and Corregidor." *American Journal of Nursing*, August 1942, pp. 896-898.

"Heroism in Iceland." *American Journal of Nursing*, December 1943, p. 1143.

Hewitt, Admiral H. K., USN. "The Invasion of North Africa." *Battle Stations! Your Navy in Action*. New York: Wm. H. Wise, 1946.

Hicks, Dorothy, R.N., ANC. "On Maneuvers." *American Journal of Nursing*, January 1942, p. 87.

Hogan, David W. *India-Burma*, Series: The U.S. Army Campaigns of World War II. Washington, D.C.: U.S. Army Center of Military History, 1992.

Hohf, 2nd Lt. Josephine, R.N., ANC. "Somewhere in Australia." *American Journal of Nursing*, January 1945, pp. 42-43.

Hollister, 2nd Lt. Louise M., ANC. "From the Pacific: Army Nurses Write Us." *American Journal of Nursing*, November 1943, p. 1026.

Holm, Maj. Gen. Jeanne (USAF, Ret). *Women in the Military: An Unfinished Revolution.* Navato, CA: Presidio Press, 1983 ed.

"Honolulu, December 7, 1941." *American Journal of Nursing*, March 1942, pp. 317-318.

Hood, Inez Combites. Questionnaire.

Hornback, 2nd Lt. Margaret, ANC. "Christmas Overseas." *American Journal of Nursing*, December 1943, p. 1066.

"Hospital Ship Named For Frances Slanger." *The Army Nurse*, March 1945, p. 3.

"How to Beat the Heat—Get Assigned to the Aleutians!" *The Army Nurse*, August 1945, p. 4.

"How Our Wounded Are Cared For." *American Journal of Nursing,* February 1945, p. 136.

"How We Prepared for Defense in '41." *American Journal of Nursing,* January 1942, pp.1-4.

Hufcut, 1st Lt. Dorothy L., ANC. "Pioneers in New Caledonia." *American Journal of Nursing*, June 1943, p. 591.

Humphrey, 2nd Lt. Yvonne E., R.N., ANC. "On Shipboard with German Prisoners." *American Journal of Nursing*, September 1943, pp. 821-822.

Hyman, 1st Lt. Sidney, M.A.C. "The Medical Story of Anzio." Medical Section Headquarters, Fifth Army, September 25, 1944.

"I Haven't Seen My Best Friend in 50 Years." *Sally Jessy Raphael.* December 6, 1991, Show #1206-91, Transcript #849.

"Iceland Occupation Vivid in Her Memory." Newspaper clipping sent by Wm. G. Blissett; unidentified by paper name or date.

"I'd Take Combat Duty Again." *American Journal of Nursing*, July 1944, p. 676.

"In Honor of the Nurses of Bataan and Corregidor." *American Journal of Nursing*, March 1944, p. 294.

"In Their Own Words, In the Register . . ." *The Register*. Washington, D.C.: Women in Military Service for America Memorial Foundation, Summer 1994.

"Increased Responsibilities for Army Nurses." *The Army Nurse,* April 1945, p. 6.

"Indispensable!" *American Journal of Nursing,* February 1942, pp. 136-137.

"Indoctrination Course for Navy Nurses." *American Journal of Nursing,* December 1943, p. 1144.

"An Ingenious Army Nurse!" *American Journal of Nursing,* January 1945, p. 24.

Ireland, Pfc. Millard, Inf. "More People Like You." *The Army Nurse,* December 1944, p. 2.

"Isn't It Amazing!" *The Army Nurse,* August 1945, p. 5.

Jackson, Kathi. "50 Years Ago—World War II and the Navy Nurse." *Navy Medicine,* Bureau of Medicine and Surgery, Department of the Navy, July-August, 1995, pp. 18-22.

Jackson, Leona, R.N. "I Was on Guam." *American Journal of Nursing,* November 1942, pp. 1244-1246.

Jamieson, Elizabeth M. and Mary F. Sewall. *Trends in Nursing History: Their Relationship to World Events,* 4th ed. Philadelphia: W. B. Saunders, 1954.

"January 6, 1945." *American Journal of Nursing,* February 1945, pp. 85-86.

Jarman, 2nd Lt. Juanita (Royce), ANC. "From the Pacific: Army Nurses Write Us." *American Journal of Nursing,* November 1943, p. 1026.

Jensen, Deborah MacLurg, R.N., BS, MA. *History and Trends of Professional Nursing,* 4th ed. St. Louis: C. V. Mosby, 1959.

J. E. S., R.N. "Men Nurses in the Army." *American Journal of Nursing,* April 1945, p. 313.

Johnson, Lt. Golda L., ANC. "From New Guinea," *American Journal of Nursing,* November 1944, p. 1103.

Jones, Mildred, R.N. Recruitment Letter. *American Journal of Nursing,* February 1942, back cover.

Jopling, Lucy Wilson, R.N. Lecture: "The Army Nurse Story." *Quiet Shadows: Women in the Pacific War—A Symposium.* Southwest Texas State University, March 27, 1993.

————. *Warrior in White,* San Antonio: Watercress Press, 1990.

Jose, Mary. "Army Nurses Return from the Pacific." *American Journal of Nursing,* October 1945, p. 810.

————. "Hi, Angels!" *American Journal of Nursing,* April 1945, pp. 267-270.

————. "Night Shift in an Army Hospital." *American Journal of Nursing,* June 1945, pp. 430-433.

"Justice for Army and Navy Nurses." *American Journal of Nursing,* August 1943, p. 703.

Kalisch, Philip A. and Beatrice J. Kalisch. *Advance of American Nursing.* Boston: Little, Brown, 1978.

Kane, Joseph Nathan. *Famous First Facts,* 3rd ed. New York: H. W. Wilson, 1964.

Kemp, Lt. T. B. "A Report from London." *The Army Nurse,* August 1945, p. 8.

Kennedy, Col. Marion Kern (Ret.). Telephone Interview with author, June 22, 1992.

Kennett, Lee. *G.I.: The American Soldier in World War II.* New York: Charles Scribners, 1987.

Kerber, Linda K. *Women of the Republic: Intellect and Ideology in Revolutionary America.* Chapel Hill: University of North Carolina, 1980.

Kinkaid, Admiral Thomas C., USN and Admiral Marc A. Mitscher, USN. "The Battle for Leyte Gulf." *Battle Stations! Your Navy in Action,* New York: Wm. H. Wise, 1946.

Kinzeler, 1st Lt. Ruth, ANC. "An Overseas Venture in Kindergarten Aid." *American Journal of Nursing,* December 1944, pp. 1138-1139.

"Kircher Lived for the Military." *San Antonio Express-News*, April 10, 1994, p. 4B.

Kirk, Vice Adm. Alan G., USN. "The Invasion of Normandy." *Battle Stations! Your Navy in Action*. New York: Wm. H. Wise, 1946.

Kirk, Maj. Gen. Norman T. (Surgeon General). "Girls in the Foxholes." *The American Magazine*, May 1944, pp. 17, 94-95, 97, 100.

Kirkpatrick, Charles E. *Defense of the Americas*. Series: The U.S. Army Campaigns of World War II. Washington D.C.: U.S. Army Center of Military History, 1991.

LaFrage, Capt. Susan W., ANC. "Christmas, Christmas, Everywhere!" *American Journal of Nursing*, December 1944, p. 1112.

Laird, Thelma F., R.N. "RHIP and the Navy Nurse." *American Journal of Nursing*. December 1944, pp. 1123-1124.

Lally, Lt. (jg) Grace B., NC, USN. "What Nurses Do." *American Journal of Nursing*, August 1943, p. 724.

Lance, Mary. "Nurses Unwrapped Special Christmas for Soldiers." *San Antonio Light*, December 19, 1991: G3.

"The Last Word—Flying Nurses." *Trained Nurse and Hospital Review*, November 1943, pp. 360-361.

Lawrence, 2nd Lt. Bessie, ANC. "What to Take Overseas." *American Journal of Nursing*, March 1944, p. 289.

Lee, Ulysses. *The Employment of Negro Troops*, Series: U.S. Army in World War II Special Studies. Washington, D.C.: Office of the Chief of Military History, U.S. Army, 1966.

"Letters from Readers." *American Journal of Nursing*, April 1942, pp. 425-426.

"The Liberation of Our Army Nurses from the Santo Tomas Prison Camp." *The Army Nurse*, April 1945, pp. 3-4.

"Lieutenant Fox Awarded the Purple Heart." *American Journal of Nursing*, January 1943, pp. 101-102.

"Lieutenant Wood Receives Citation." *American Journal of Nursing*, March 1944, p. 295.

"*Life* Visits U.S. Army Nurses in New Caledonia." *Life*, October 5, 1942, pp. 126-133.

Lincoln, Nan. "Captains Courageous." *Bar Harbor Times* "Selects," February 21, 1991, B1-2.

Lindstrom, Captain Iva F., ANC. "From the USS *Blanche Sigman*." *American Journal of Nursing*, May 1945, p. 405.

Link, Mae Mills and Hubert A. Coleman. *Medical Support of the Army Air Forces in World War II*. Washington, D.C.: Office of the Surgeon General, USAF, 1955.

Lopnow, 1st Lt. Dorothy E., ANC. "Our Nurses and Redistribution Stations." *The Army Nurse*, March 1945, p. 3.

"Lt. Mary Ann Sullivan Wins Legion of Merit." *American Journal of Nursing*, December 1943, p. 1143.

MacDonald, Charles B. "The U.S. Soldier." *Fighting Men of the Second World War*. New York: Marshall Cavendish USA Ltd: 1973, pp. 4-7.

MacGregor, Morris J., Jr. *Integration of the Armed Forces, 1940-1965*, Series: Defense Studies. Washington, D.C.: Superintendent of Documents, U.S. Government Printing Office, 1980.

Madere, Jeanette. "An Open Letter." *American Journal of Nursing*, March 1944, p. 268.

Mahar, Major Edna L., ANC. "Christmas Overseas." *American Journal of Nursing*, December 1943, pp. 1063-1064.

Main, Ensign Dorothy Lucille, R.N., USN. "Sailors and Marines Come Back." *American Journal of Nursing,* April 1944, pp. 355-357.

Mangerich, Agnes Jensen. Questionnaire.

"Manual for State Nursing Councils." *American Journal of Nursing,* February 1943, p. 215.

Marley, Faye. "Red Cross Clubs All Over the World." *American Journal of Nursing,* December 1943, pp. 1080-1082.

"Married Nurses in the Army." *American Journal of Nursing,* March 1943, p. 306.

"Married Nurses for Army Nurse Corps." *American Journal of Nursing,* December 1942, p. 1451.

"Married Nurses Retained in the Army." *American Journal of Nursing,* November 1942, p. 1322.

Martin, Brig. Gen. J. I. Martin, Fifth Army. Memo dated September 25, 1944, re: "The Medical Story of Anzio."

Masterson, Elizabeth Harman. "The China Doll," unpublished composition, 1988.

―――. "The Court Martial," unpublished composition, 1988.

―――. Questionnaire.

―――. "Rain on a Tent in Normandy," unpublished composition, 1988.

Maxwell, Captain Pauline, ANC. "The Journal Abroad." *American Journal of Nursing,* March 1945, p. 235.

McLaughlin, Elizabeth, R.N., ANC. "Adventure in 1943." *American Journal of Nursing,* April 1943, p. 394.

"Medical Care in the Armed Forces." *American Journal of Nursing,* March 1944, p. 267.

"Medical Care in the Southwest Pacific." *American Journal of Nursing,* August 1943, p. 736.

Mella, Lt. Marguerite Regina, ANC. "From the Home Front." *The Army Nurse,* December 1944, p. 5.

"Men Nurses and the Armed Services." *American Journal of Nursing,* December 1943, pp. 1066-1069.

"Men Nurses in the Army." *American Journal of Nursing,* April 1945, p. 313.

"Men Nurses and the U.S. Navy." *American Journal of Nursing,*" November 1942, p. 1282.

Methot, Fred. "I Am the Nurse." *American Journal of Nursing,* June 1944, back cover.

M. H. H., Capt. "This Is Our Privilege." *American Journal of Nursing,* March 1945, p. 235.

"Military Awards and Honors." *American Journal of Nursing,* May 1945, pp. 407-408.

"Military Honors to Nurses." *American Journal of Nursing,* October 1945, pp. 852-856.

"Military Nursing Course." *Trained Nurse and Hospital Review,* December 1944, p. 450.

Miller, Robert. "One Baylor 'Unit' Has Lots of Memories Stashed 'Over There.'" *The Dallas Morning News,* no date or p. #.

Mitchum, Jennifer. "Navy Medicine May-June 1942." *Navy Medicine,* May-June 1992, pp. 31-35.

Mixsell, 2nd Lt. Mary, ANC. "We Improvise and Economize." *American Journal of Nursing,* March 1944, p. 290.

M. M., Capt., ANC. "From Normandy." *American Journal of Nursing,* September 1944, p. 914.

Moline, Capt. Anna Lisa, ANC. "U.S. Army Nurses in Russia." *American Journal of Nursing,* November 1945, pp. 904-906.

"More Army Nurses Win Honors." *American Journal of Nursing,* August 1943, p. 774.

"More Awards to Army Nurses." *American Journal of Nursing,* December 1944, pp. 1179-1180.

Mosley, Leonard. *Battle of Britain*. Series: World War II. Alexandria: Time-Life Books, 1977.

Murphy, Clara Morrey and Dottie Lonergan Jouvenat, Harold Carter, John Matrise, Catherine Laver, Charles Bybee, Leona Benson, Anne Wilson, Barb Clay, Jane Faulkner, and Vito Tursi. "History of 802nd MAES." *The Story of Air Evacuation, 1942-1989*, compiled by the World War II Flight Nurses Association. Dallas: Taylor Publishing Co., 1989.

Mushrush, Vincoe C., R.N., ANC. "What 'Mopping Up' Operations Mean." *American Journal of Nursing*, March 1944, pp. 228-230.

"Naval Reserve Nurses Released." *American Journal of Nursing*, November 1945, p. 962.

"Navy Flight Nurses." *American Journal of Nursing*, June 1945, p. 487.

"Navy Flight Nurses in the Pacific Area." *American Journal of Nursing*, April 1945, p. 318.

"Navy Flight Nurses Serve the Pacific Bases." *American Journal of Nursing*, October 1945, p. 795.

"Navy Nurse Receives Bronze Star." *American Journal of Nursing*, December 1944, p. 1180.

"Navy Nurse Reserves May Become Regulars." *American Journal of Nursing*, November 1945, p. 962.

"Navy Nurses." *American Journal of Nursing*, February 1945, p. 90.

"Navy Nurses Granted Citation." *American Journal of Nursing*, February 1943, p. 220.

"Navy Nurses Keep Fit." *American Journal of Nursing*, September 1943, p. 817.

"Navy Point System." *American Journal of Nursing*, October 1945, p. 852.

"Needed Now." *American Journal of Nursing*, November 1943, pp. 971-972.

"Negro Nurse Commissioned in Navy." *American Journal of Nursing*, April 1945, p. 316.

"Negro Nurses and the NNC." *American Journal of Nursing*, March 1945, p. 240.

"Negro Nurses and the War." *American Journal of Nursing*, April 1943, p. 396.

"New Army Hospital Ship." *American Journal of Nursing*, June 1943, p. 599.

"New Gauze Roller." *American Journal of Nursing*, January 1945, p. 12.

"New Styles for Army Nurses." *American Journal of Nursing*, July 1942, p. 820.

"New Training Course for Army Nurses." *American Journal of Nursing*, March 1943, p. 306.

"New Uniform Trousers Developed for Tropical and Cold Climates." *The Army Nurse*, December 1944, p. 4.

"A New Wardrobe for the ANC." *American Journal of Nursing*, March 1943, pp. 240-241.

Newell, Lt. Col. Clayton R. *Central Pacific*, Series: The U.S. Army Campaigns of World War II. Washington D.C.: U.S. Army Center of Military History, 1992.

Newhouser, Capt. L. R., MC, USN. "U.S. Navy Hospital Ship *Consolation*: General Information for Patients Enroute from Wakayama, Japan to Okinawa," no date.

"NIB Recruitment Posters." *American Journal of Nursing,* May 1943, p. 497.

"Nights I Couldn't Sleep She'd Sit 'N' Talk to Me. She Was, Well Yeah, You Could Call That Nurse an Angel . . ." *The Army Nurse*, January 1945, p. 3.

"No Complaints from New Guinea." *American Journal of Nursing*, April 1943, p. 400.

Norman, Elizabeth M. *We Band of Angels: The Untold Story of American Nurses Trapped on Bataan by the Japanese*. New York: Random House, 1999.

North, John Paul, MD. "The 20th General Hospital—I.S. Ravdin, Commanding General." *Surgery*, Vol. 56, No. 4, October 1964, pp. 614-623.

Noyes, Henry. "Anzio End-Around Turns into Grim Stalemate." Series: Warriors of Mercy, Chapter 23. *The Mercury*. Fort Sam Houston: U.S. Army of Public Affairs, March 1994, no p. #.

——. "Anzio Is Coming of Age for Army's Nurses." Series: Warriors of Mercy, Chapter 24. *The Mercury*. Fort Sam Houston: U.S. Army of Public Affairs, April 1994, no p. #.

——. "Easy Landing Gives Way to Bloody Struggle, Stalemate." Series: Warriors of Mercy, Chapter 23. *The Mercury*. Fort Sam Houston: U.S. Army of Public Affairs, March 1994, no. p. #.

——. "Evacuation from Anzio Never Gets Routine." Series: Warriors of Mercy, Chapter 24. *The Mercury*. Fort Sam Houston: U.S. Army of Public Affairs, April 1994, no. p. #.

——. "Hell's Half Acre: Anzio Hospital Center Becomes Magnet for Stray Bombs, Artillery Shells." Series: Warriors of Mercy, Chapter 23. *The Mercury*. Fort Sam Houston: U.S. Army of Public Affairs, March 1994, no p. #.

"Nurse 'Over There' Sends Red Cross Questionnaire." *Trained Nurse and Hospital Review*, October 1944, p. 282.

"Nurse Prisoners." *Trained Nurse and Hospital Review*, November 1944, p. 449.

"Nurse's Log Pictures 12 Days in Lifeboat." Newspaper clipping sent by Wm. G. Blissett; unidentified by paper name or date.

"Nurses with American Hospital in Britain Join U.S. and Canadian Army Corps." *American Journal of Nursing*, October 1942, pp. 1202-1203.

"Nurses with the Armed Forces." *American Journal of Nursing*, December 1942, pp. 1452-1453.

"Nurses, to the Colors!" *American Journal of Nursing*, August 1942, pp. 851-852.

"Nurses Entitled to Protection as Non-combatants." *American Journal of Nursing*, October 1942, p. 1202.

"Nurses Make with the Quick Time." *Fort Sill Army News*, December 24, 1942, p. 4.

"Nurses in War." *R.N.*, February 1970, pp. 48-57.

"Nursing Care of the Amputee in the General Hospital." *The Army Nurse*, November 1944, pp. 7-8.

"Nursing in a Debarkation Ward." *American Journal of Nursing*, February 1945, pp. 134-136.

"Nursing—In the Marketplace?" *American Journal of Nursing*, January 1944, p. 1.

"Nursing School Programs Accelerated and Expanded." *American Journal of Nursing*, March 1943, pp. 304-305.

Office of the Surgeon General. "Men Nurses in the Army." *American Journal of Nursing*, April 1945, p. 313.

O'Harran, Kristi. "Don't Need Doctor for Anesthesia." *The Herald*, May 3, 1994, 2B.

"Okay and Ready for Duty." *American Journal of Nursing*, May 1942, pp. 528-529.

"Olive Drabs for Army Nurses." *American Journal of Nursing*, January 1944, p. 75.

"On Going into the Army." *American Journal of Nursing*, December 1942, pp. 1351-1356.

"On Leave from Africa." *American Journal of Nursing*, June 1943, p. 559.

"On Reassignment." *The Army Nurse*, October 1944, p. 3.

Onyett, Col. Helen Pon (Ret.). Interview with author, December 19, 1991.

"Opportunities for Men Nurses in the Maritime Service." *American Journal of Nursing*, January 1943, p. 108.

"Opportunity—Now!" *American Journal of Nursing*, February 1943, p. 129.

O'Toole, Lt. Sarah, R.N., USNR. "I'm in the Navy Now." *American Journal of Nursing*, December 1943, p. 1077.

———. "In the Southwest Pacific: They Pioneered on Tinian." *American Journal of Nursing*, December 1945, pp. 1013-1015.

"Our Okinawa Nurses Settle Down to Their Last Big Job of Combat Duty on Japan's Doorstep Defenses." *The Army Nurse*, August 1945, p. 7.

Paine, Lt. Esther W., ANC. "From Australia." *American Journal of Nursing*, October 1944, p. 989.

Parran, Thomas, M.D. "Professional Nurses Needed in Postwar Years. *American Journal of Nursing*, February 1945, p. 133.

Parrish, Thomas, ed. *The Simon & Schuster Encyclopedia of World War II*. New York: Simon & Schuster, 1978.

Parsons, Margaret, R.N., Ph.D. "The Profession in a Class by Itself." *Nursing Outlook*, Vol. 34, No. 6, November/December 1986, pp. 270-275.

Paxton, Vincoe M., R.N. "ANC Reinforcements Land in France," *American Journal of Nursing*, January 1945, pp. 13-16.

———. "With Field Hospital Nurses in Germany." *American Journal of Nursing*, February 1945, pp. 131-133.

Paxton, Vincoe M., R.N. and Stuart D. Rizika, M.D. "Soldiers of the Medical Detachment." *American Journal of Nursing*, September 1945, pp. 693-696.

Peck, Louine Lunt Connor. Letter to author, August 17, 1993.

———. Oral history. United States Army Nurse Corps Oral History Program, Interviewed by Col. Clara Adams-Ender, AN., North East Harbor, Maine, August 31, 1986; Major Wynona Bice-Stephens, A.N., ed.

———. Questionnaire.

Perry, Lt. Jg. Carol M., USN, NC. "At Home in the South Pacific." *American Journal of Nursing*, October 1944, pp. 988-989.

Peterson, Susan C. and Beverly Jensen. "The Red Cross Call to Serve: The Western Response from North Dakota Nurses." *Western History Quarterly* XXI, pp. 321-340.

Photo caption. *American Journal of Nursing*, July 1944, p. 701.

———. *American Journal of Nursing*, October 1945, p. 855.

———. *The Army Nurse*, October 1944, p. 15.

———. Photo caption. Newspaper photos of Jean Osborn and Inez Combites sent by Inez Hood Combites. No source, date, p. #.

Piemonte, Col. Robert V. and Major Cindy Gurney, eds. *Highlights in the History of the Army Nurse Corps*. Washington, D.C.: U.S. Army Center of Military History, 1987.

Piercy, Ruth Arundel, R.N. "To Those Nurses in Service." *American Journal of Nursing*, January 1943, p. 125.

———. "To Whom It May Concern." *American Journal of Nursing,* February 1944, p. 97.

Pisano, Marina. "Gender Battles." *San Antonio Express-News,* November 22, 1994, 11-12B.

Pitt, Barrie. *The Battle of the Atlantic*. Series: World War II. Alexandria: Time-Life Books, 1977.

"Policy Governing the Duty Assignment of Flight Nurses." AAF Letter 35-164, dated December 6, 1944. *The Army Nurse*, January 1945, p. 7.

Poole, Raidie, R.N. "Army Course in Operating Room Technic." *American Journal of Nursing*, April 1945, pp. 270-271.

Proctor, Ph. M. 1/C Clarence L., R.N. "Men Nurses in the Coast Guard." *American Journal of Nursing*, June 1943, p. 591.

"A Proud Profession." *American Journal of Nursing,* June 1944, pp. 525-526.

"Radio and Magazine Publicity." *American Journal of Nursing,* February 1943, p. 214.

"Radio Programs." *American Journal of Nursing,* March 1943, p. 301.

"Radio Publicity Brings Results." *American Journal of Nursing,* March 1943, p. 301.

Rankin, Col. Robert H., USMC. *Uniforms of the Sea Services: A Pictorial History,"* Annapolis: United States Naval Institute, 1962.

Ratledge, Abbie C. *Angels in Khaki.* San Antonio: Naylor Co., 1975.

Raymer, Lt. Sara M., ANC. "Christmas, Christmas, Everywhere!" *American Journal of Nursing,* December 1944, p. 1114.

"The Reasons Why It Takes Nurses." *American Journal of Nursing,* December 1943, pp. 1128-1129.

"Reassignment in the ANC." *American Journal of Nursing,* December 1945, p. 1065.

"Reception for Navy Nurses in England." *American Journal of Nursing,* April 1944, p. 402.

"Recruiting College Women." *American Journal of Nursing,* March 1943, p. 301.

"Recruitment Kits for High Schools." *American Journal of Nursing,* March 1943, p. 301.

"Red Cross Club for Nurses in London." *American Journal of Nursing,* November 1942, p. 1323.

"Redeployment." *American Journal of Nursing,* October 1945, pp. 808-809.

"Redeployment of Nurses in the ETO." *American Journal of Nursing,* July 1945, pp. 507-512.

"Relive Years Spent Overseas." *Syracuse Herald-Journal,* Aug. 17, 1957, p. 8.

"A Report from the French Front." *The Army Nurse,* March 1945, p. 16.

"A Report from the USS *Comfort."* *The Army Nurse,* July 1945, p. 10.

"Results of Informal Survey Show Seersucker Preferred." *The Army Nurse,* April 1945, p. 8.

Reynolds, Lt. (jg) Georgia Reynolds, NC, USN. "On a Navy Hospital Ship." *American Journal of Nursing,* March 1945, pp. 234-235.

Rhyne, Lt. (jg) Mildred M. and Mary T. DeLoach, NC, USNR. "Christmas, Christmas, Everywhere!" *American Journal of Nursing,* December 1944, p. 1113.

Rice, 1st Lt. Dorothy M., R.N., ANC. "Flight to Kirawagi." *American Journal of Nursing,* January 1945, pp. 10-11.

Richardson, Lt. Henrietta, R.N., ANC. "Flight Nursing: II. Skyway Nursing." *American Journal of Nursing,* February 1944, pp. 102-103.

Riley, Glenda. *Inventing the American Woman: A Perspective on Women's History 1607-1877,* Vol. I. Arlington Heights, IL: Harlan Davidson, 1986.

Roberts, Mary M., R.N. *American Nursing: History and Interpretation.* New York: Macmillan, 1955.

Robinson, Linda. Letter to author about Lt. Rita Dowd-Smart, ANC, September 23, 1993.

Robinson, Victor, M.D. *White Caps: The Story of Nursing.* Philadelphia: Lippincott, 1946.

Rodgers, 2nd Lt. Kate, ANC. "Christmas Overseas." *American Journal of Nursing,* December 1943, p. 1065.

Roland, Edith Blissett. Letter dated March 11, 1991.

Romanus, Charles F. and Riley Sunderland. *Time Runs Out in CBI.* Series: United States Army in World War II. Washington, D.C.: Office of the Chief of Military History, Department of the Army, 1959.

Ropp, Theodore. "World War II." *World Book Encyclopedia.* Chicago: World Book-Childcraft Int'l., 1982.

Rosenbaum, Melissa A. "A Navy Nurse Remembers." *US Navy Medicine*, Vol. 72, June 1981, pp. 22-25.

"Rotation, Not Release, for Army Nurses." *American Journal of Nursing*, July 1945, p. 575.

Roush, H. A. "Men Nurses." *American Journal of Nursing*, May 1943, p. 496.

"Ruth Solot, 84, WWII Army Nurse." *Plain Dealer*, April 29, 1994, no p. #.

Salisbury, Harrison. Foreward. *World War II: A 50th Anniversary*. Writers and Photographers of the Associated Press. New York: Henry Holt, 1989.

"San Francisco's Zonta International Sponsors Rest Home for Navy Nurses." *American Journal of Nursing*, December 1944, p. 1179.

Sanner, Margaret C., R.N., MA. *Trends and Professional Adjustments in Nursing*. Philadelphia: W. B. Saunders, 1962.

Sansone, Constance. American National Red Cross Certificate of Recognition, July 12, 1979.

————. Commission certificate, October 16, 1944.

————. Enlistment certificate, Feb. 15, 1941.

————. Good Samaritan Award, Nov. 7, 1979.

————. Separation Qualification Record, Army of the United States, Jan. 30, 1946.

————. Telephone Interview with author, July 6, 1992.

Scheips, Lt. (jg) Edna Marie, USNR. "Navy Nurse Officers' Club." *American Journal of Nursing*, September 1943, p. 816.

Schmidt, Lt. Gen. Harry, USMC. "The Battle for Iwo Jima." *Battle Stations! Your Navy in Action*, New York: Wm. H. Wise, 1946.

Schmidt, 2nd Lt. Katharine, ANC. "Down Under." *American Journal of Nursing*, December 1943, p. 1130.

Schneider, Catheren M., R.N., ANC. "The Displaced Person as a Patient." *American Journal of Nursing*, September 1945, pp. 690-692.

"School for Navy Flight Nurses." *American Journal of Nursing*, January 1945, p. 64.

Schwartz, 1st Lt. Doris, R.N., ANC. "Nursing Aboard a Hospital Ship." *American Journal of Nursing*, December 1945, pp. 996-998.

Schwitalla, Alphonse M., SJ. *The U.S. Cadet Nurse Corps,* Bulletin #225, 1943. Reprinted from *Hospital Progress*, Official Journal of the Catholic Hospital Association of U.S. and Canada, October 1943.

Scott, Col. Raymond, MC, United States Army. "Eleventh Evacuation Hospital in Sicily." *American Journal of Nursing*, October 1943, pp. 925-926.

"See Here, Lieutenant Margrave!" *American Journal of Nursing*, February 1943, pp. 189-190.

Segall, Grant. "'You Go to Topside!': Life's Been Eventful for Colonel Mac, 89." *Plain Dealer*, November 21, 1993, p. 1B, 4B.

"Service Nurses' Legislation: A Step Forward for Permanent Rank." *R.N.* March 1947, pp. 30-32, 66, 68.

Shadewaldt, Lt. Col. Ruth Frances, ANC (Ret.) Letter to Agnes Summers, Aug. 25, 1945.

————. Questionnaire.

————. Taped interview with sister, July 1992.

Shaw, Lt. (jg) Catherine, NNC. "We Traveled by Transport." *American Journal of Nursing*, November 1943, pp. 1022-1024.

"She's First Lieutenant Now." Newspaper clipping sent by Constance Sansone. No source, date, p. #.

Short, Lt. Col. Augusta, ANC. "The Educational Program of the Army Nurse Corps." *Military Surgeon*, June 1949, pp. 442-445.

Silvera, John D. *The Negro in World War II*. The American Negro: History and Literature Series. New York: Arno Press and *New York Times*, 1969.

Sinclair, Bernice J., R.N., "My Preview of Army Nursing." *American Journal of Nursing*, January 1942, pp. 17-18.

Slanger, Frances Y., Sec. Lt. "Basic Training, ANC." *American Journal of Nursing*, December 1943, p. 1128.

Slinkman, John. "Looking into the Army and Navy Future." *R.N.*, April 1946, pp. 32-34, 100, 102, 104.

"Smart for Summer." Newspaper photo sent by Constance Sansone. No source, date, p. #.

Smith, Bonnie G. *Changing Lives: Women in European History Since 1700*. Lexington, MA: D.C. Heath, 1989.

Smith, Clarence McKittrick. *The Medical Department: Hospitalization and Evacuation, Zone of Interior*, Series: United States Army in World War II: The Technical Services. Washington, D.C.: Office of the Chief of Military History, Department of the Army, 1956.

Smith, Edith Atwell. Questionnaire.

Smith, Lt. Gen. Holland M., USMC. "The Battle for the Marianas." *Battle Stations! Your Navy in Action*. New York: Wm. H. Wise, 1946.

Smith, Major General Julian C. USMC. "The Battle for Tarawa." *Battle Stations! Your Navy in Action*. New York: Wm. H. Wise, 1946.

Smith, Pattie S. "Nurses and the USO." *American Journal of Nursing*, May 1943, pp. 462-463.

"Somewhere in the Pacific." *American Journal of Nursing*, December 1942, p. 1433.

Speck, Jane Maggard. "Captured on Guam." *Trained Nurse and Hospital Review*, December 1942, pp. 414-416.

Sprague, Capt. Howard B. (MC), USN. "Evacuating the Wounded from Tarawa." *American Journal of Nursing*, June 1944, 554.

"Spring Recruitment Campaign." *American Journal of Nursing*, April 1943, p. 396.

Spruance, Admiral Raymond A., USN. "The Battle of the Philippine Sea." *Battle Stations! Your Navy in Action*. New York: Wm. H. Wise, 1946.

St. Peter, Lt. Jg. Olivine B., R.N., USNR. "In the Southwest Pacific: The Marianas." *American Journal of Nursing*, December 1945, pp. 1012-1013.

Staats, Lt. Jg. Mary H., USNR. "Navy Nurses in the Solomons." *American Journal of Nursing*, July 1945, p. 534.

Stanton, Shelby. *US Army Uniforms of World War II*. Harrisburg: Stackpole Books, 1991.

"A State of War Exists." *American Journal of Nursing*, January 1942, p. 1.

"Status of Men Nurses in the Army and Navy." *American Journal of Nursing*, May 1944, pp. 518-519.

Steele, Major Coralee I., ANC. "With an Army Nurse at the Paris Study Center." *American Journal of Nursing*, October 1945, p. 849.

Stepanek, Genevieve Van de Drink. Questionnaire.

Stewart, Isabel Maitland, R.N., A.M. *Education of Nurses*. New York: Macmillan, 1947.

Stewart, Isabel Maitland, R.N., A.M. and Anne L. Austin. *A History of Nursing from Ancient to Modern Times: A World View*, 5th ed. New York: G. P. Putnam, 1962.

Stickles, Lt. (jg) Norma V., NC, USNR. "Christmas, Christmas, Everywhere!" *American Journal of Nursing*, December 1944, p. 1115.

Stiehm, Judith Hicks. *Arms and the Enlisted Woman*. Philadelphia: Temple University, 1989.

"Still Free to Choose." *American Journal of Nursing,* February 1942, p. 179.

Stimson, Maj. Julia C. "Our Hour." *American Journal of Nursing,* February 1942, p. 140.

"Stop That Rumor!" Army Nurse Corps Fact Sheet (January 15, 1945) reprinted in *American Journal of Nursing,* March 1945, p. 231.

Storch, Lt. Amelia, ANC. "Christmas, Christmas, Everywhere!" *American Journal of Nursing,* December 1944, p. 1115.

Stran, Marian Hooker. Questionnaire.

Stroup, Capt. Leora B., R.N., ANC. "Aero-Medical Nursing and Therapeutics." *American Journal of Nursing,* June 1944, pp. 575-577.

Stuart, Frank S. "Invasion by Angels." *The Rotarian,* August 1944, pp. 14-16.

"Student Recruitment." *American Journal of Nursing,* May 1943, p. 497.

Sullivan, 2nd Lt. Mary Ann, ANC. "Christmas Overseas." *American Journal of Nursing,* December 1943, p. 1065.

"Supplies in Wartime." *American Journal of Nursing,* March 1944, p. 210.

"Survey of Government and Civilian Nursing Services." *American Journal of Nursing,* January 1942, pp. 90-91.

Sutherland, Dorothy. "Nurses Also Cry!" *The Army Nurse,* May 1945, pp. 4-5.

Swinden, Sgt. Tech. H. and Sgt. Tech. J. Guerra. "From Men Nurses with the 'Overseas' Forces." *American Journal of Nursing,* September 1942, p. 1071.

Tayloe, Roberta Love. *Combat Nurse: A Journal of World War II.* Santa Barbara: Fithian Press, 1988.

Taylor, Howard P., M.D. "The 36th Evacuation Hospital in World War II—An Oral History." Unpublished Personal Oral History.

"Team Work." *The Trained Nurse and Hospital Review,* December 1944, p. 450.

"Tell Me about Procurement and Assignment." *American Journal of Nursing,* March 1944, pp. 251-254.

"They Brought Us Back." *The Trained Nurse and Hospital Review,* December 1944, p. 450.

"Third Service Command Basic Training Anniversary." *The Army Nurse,* October 1944, pp. 3-5.

Thomason, First Lt. Hazel W., ANC. "The Journal Abroad." *American Journal of Nursing,* March 1945, p. 235.

Thuma, Capt. Marion, E., R.N. "'Anchors Aweigh', ANC." *American Journal of Nursing,* September 1944, pp. 830-831.

———. "Task Forces, ANC." *American Journal of Nursing,* January 1944, pp. 15-18.

Tierney, Col. Marian (Ret.). Questionnaire.

"The Time Is Now." *American Journal of Nursing,* August 1942, pp. 924-925.

"Time Out for Music." Photo caption. *The Raleigh,* no date, no p. #.

Todd, Capt. Genevieve, ANC. "Memories We Shall Cherish." *American Journal of Nursing,* April 1945, p. 314.

Tomblin, Barbara. *G. I. Nightingales: The Army Nurse Corps in World War II.* Lexington: The University Press of Kentucky, 1996.

Towse, Cmdr. Mary D., R.N., NNC. "Naval Hospital in San Diego." *American Journal of Nursing,* March 1943, pp. 268-269.

Tracy, Margaret A., R.N. "Speeding Up Production of Nurses." *American Journal of Nursing,* February 1942, pp. 193-195.

"Transitions in Nursing as a Result of the War." *The Army Nurse,* February 1945, pp. 8-9.

"Travel Light if You're Going Overseas." *American Journal of Nursing*, August 1943, p. 709.

Treen, Joe, Don Sider, Joseph Harmes, Kent Demaret, and Janice Fuhrman. "Bloody Sunday." *People*, December 9, 1991, pp. 40-45.

Tumiel, Cindy. "Tierney, 78, was Army Nurse." *San Antonio Express-News*, December 14, 1999, p. 8B.

Turner, William P. *1912 to 1941: World War I, the Depression and the New Deal*, Series: The Essentials of United States History. Piscataway, NJ: Research and Education Association, 1990.

"Two Undaunted Nurses." *American Journal of Nursing*, March 1942, p. 324.

Tynan, Helen Ilic. Lecture: "The Army Nurse Story." *Quiet Shadows: Women in the Pacific War—A Symposium*. Southwest Texas State University, March 27, 1993.

"Typical Army Nurse." *The Army Nurse*, April 1945, p. 6.

Ullom, Lt. Col. (Ret.) Madeline. Questionnaire.

Umbach, Edna D. ANC. "Army Nurses in Australia and Iceland." *American Journal of Nursing*, June 1942, p. 689.

———. "Christmas Overseas." *American Journal of Nursing*, December 1943, pp. 1064-1065.

UNRRA Press Release No. 145. "Relapsing Fever and Cholera." *American Journal of Nursing*, November 1945, p. 903.

U.S. Army Center of Military History. Historical Division, Washington, D.C., 1990. *Anzio Beachhead: 22 January–25 May 1944*.

———. "History—ANC," File #314.7, Washington, D.C., no date.

———. *Logistics in World War II: Final Report of the Army Service Forces*. Director of the Service, Supply, and Procurement Division War Department General Staff, Washington, D.C.: 1993.

U.S. Department of Defense, 50th Anniversary of World War II Commemoration Committee, "African Americans in World War II Fact Sheet." Washington, D.C.

———. "Women in World War II Fact Sheet." Washington, D.C.

U.S. Medical Department. *Medical Supply in World War II*. Washington, D.C.: Office of the Surgeon General, Department of the Army, 1968.

U.S. Navy Department. *"Consolation."* Dictionary of American Naval Fighting Ships, Vol. II, 1963. Reprint with corrections, 1969. Washington, D.C.: Office of the Chief of Naval Operations, Naval History Division.

———. "History of Men Nurses in the Navy Nurse Corps." Bureau of Medicine, March 1, 1966.

———. "Nurse Corps History." Information Sheet, Bureau of Medicine and Surgery, no date.

———. "Outline History of the Navy Nurse Corps." Draft provided by Bureau of Medicine and Surgery, 1989.

———. *White Task Force*. NAVMED 939, Bureau of Medicine, 1945, no p. #.

Vandegrift, General Alexander A., USMC. "Victory at Guadalcanal." *Battle Stations! Your Navy in Action*. New York: Wm. H. Wise, 1946.

"Victory—Europe and the ANC." *The Army Nurse*, July 1945, p. 4.

Voorhees, Col. Tracy S., JAGD. "Commendation of Nurses." *The Army Nurse*, February 1945, p. 3.

Wainwright, 2nd Lt. Lucy, ANC. "Christmas Overseas." *American Journal of Nursing*, December 1943, pp. 1062-1063.

Wallace, Robert. *The Italian Campaign*. Series: World War II. Alexandria: Time-Life Books, 1978.

"The War." *This Fabulous Century 1940-1950*, Vol. V. New York: Time-Life Books, 1969.

"War Advertising Council and OWI in Nursing Campaigns." *American Journal of Nursing*, July 1945, pp. 543-544.

War Department. *Dictionary of United States Army Terms*, War Department Technical Manual TM 20-205, January 18, 1944. Washington, D.C.: U.S. Government Printing Office, 1944.

"The War Manpower Commission." *American Journal of Nursing*, October 1943, pp. 885-887.

"Wartime Confusions and a Draft." *American Journal of Nursing*, March 1945, pp. 169-170.

"WAVES, WAACS, SPARS, and Nurses." *American Journal of Nursing*, February 1943, pp. 134-137.

"Wearing of the Service Uniform." *The Army Nurse*, January 1945, p. 11.

Weatherford, Doris. *American Women and World War II*. New York: Facts on File, 1990.

Webster, Juanita Hamilton. Questionnaire.

———. Unpublished memoirs, no date.

Webster-Case, Stephanie. Letter to author, no date.

Wellman, Lt. Thora, NC, USNR. "Christmas, Christmas, Everywhere!" *American Journal of Nursing*, December 1944, p. 1112.

Wells, 2nd Lt. Frances, ANC. "North Africa." *American Journal of Nursing*, December 1943, p. 1130.

Wells, Paul G., R.N. "Men Nurses in Military Service." *American Journal of Nursing*, November 1943, p. 1038.

West, Iris J., LTC, AN, Army Nurse Corps Historian, Department of the Army, The Center for Military History, Washington, D.C., Letter to author regarding Anzio, May 4, 1994.

West, Tommy. "History of Caring." *San Antonio Express-News Magazine*, August 15, 1993: pp. 8-9, 17.

"What about the White Uniform?" *The Army Nurse*, December 1944, p. 5.

Wheal, Elizabeth-Anne and Stephen Pope and James Taylor. *Encyclopedia of the Second World War*. Secaucus, NJ: Castle Books, Div. of Book Sales, 1989.

"When Are You Coming Home, Nurse?" *The Army Nurse*, August 1945, p. 2.

"Where We Stand and What We Can Do." *American Journal of Nursing*, February 1945, pp. 88-89.

White, Ruth Y. "Army Nurses—in the Air." *American Journal of Nursing*, April 1943, pp. 342-344.

———. "At Anzio Beachhead." *American Journal of Nursing*, April 1944, pp. 370-371.

White, Ruth Young. "Red Cross Clubs in Australia." *American Journal of Nursing*, August 1944, p. 751.

———. "The *Solace* Plies the Tasman and Coral Seas." *American Journal of Nursing*, June 1944, pp. 552-554.

Whitehead, Spc. Travis M. "Retired Nurse Recalls Army Days with Fondness." *News Leader*, April 19, 1991, p. 10.

"Who Will Teach Them?" *American Journal of Nursing*, April 1942, p. 401-402.

Wickenden, Elmira B., R.N. "The National Nursing Council Reports." *American Journal of Nursing*, September 1943, pp. 807-809.

Wilkinson, Eugenie Rutkowski. Letter to daughter, no date.

———. Questionnaire.

Willenz, June A. *Women Veterans: America's Forgotten Heroines.* New York: Continuum, 1983.

Wiltse, Charles M. *Medical Service in the Mediterranean and Minor Theaters.* U.S. Army in World War II, The Technical Services, The Medical Department. Washington, D.C.: Office of the Chief of Military History Department of the Army, 1965.

Wisniewski, Richard A, ed. *Pearl Harbor and the USS Arizona Memorial: A Pictorial History.* Honolulu: Pacific Basis Enterprises, 1977.

Woerdman, Sec. Lt. Maria S., ANC. "Somewhere—," *American Journal of Nursing,* December 1943, p. 1130.

"Women's Clubs Provides Scholarships." *American Journal of Nursing,* February 1943, p. 215.

"A Word to the Wise." *The Army Nurse,* March 1944, pp. 3-4.

World War II: Asia and the Pacific. Map. Washington D.C.: National Geographic Society, December 1991.

World War II: Europe and North Africa. Map. Washington D.C.: National Geographic Society, December 1991.

"World War II Casualties: Ainsworth, Ellen G., 2/Lt. ANC, N732 770." Provided by Center for Military History, Washington, D.C.

"World War II Casualties: Farquhar, LaVerne, 2/Lt., ANC, N734 732." Provided by Center for Military History, Washington, D.C.

World War II Flight Nurses Association. *The Story of Air Evacuation 1942-1989.* Dallas: Taylor Publishing Company, 1989.

Wright, 1st Lt. Chester S., Jr. "True American Soldiers." *American Journal of Nursing,* February 1945, p. 149.

Wright, Scott W. "Nurse Remembers Attack's Deadly Effect." *Austin American-Statesman,* December 5, 1991, A:13.

———. "Women's War 'Whited Out' of History Books." *Austin American-Statesman,* December 5, 1991, A:1, 12.

York, Capt. Wilma, ANC. "Sink or Float?" *American Journal of Nursing,* October 1945, p. 850.

"You Are a Gift." *Trained Nurse and Hospital Review,* October 1944, p. 282.

"You Should Serve." *American Journal of Nursing,* August 1942, p. 852.

"Your Classification." *American Journal of Nursing,* September 1944, pp. 819-820.

"Your Part in Recruitment." *American Journal of Nursing,* January 1942, p. 5.

Zich, Arthur. *Rising Sun.* Series: World War II. Alexandria: Time-Life Books, 1977.

Zurney, Mary Brady. "Jeannie of the Medicine Show," Unpublished essay, no date.

Zwisler, Irene L. R.N. "Buckingham Palace Tea." *American Journal of Nursing,* March 1944, pp. 256-257.

Index